linguistics and the
new english teacher

linguistics and the

an introduction to linguistics approaches in language instruction

COLLIER-MACMILLAN LIMITED, LONDON

new english teacher –

Burt Liebert
Department of Education
University of California, Davis

THE MACMILLAN COMPANY, NEW YORK

THE MACMILLAN COMPANY
866 Third Avenue, New York, New York 10022

COLLIER-MACMILLAN CANADA, LTD., TORONTO, ONTARIO

Library of Congress catalog card number: 78-120342

First Printing

To Margie, Mark,
Nina, Scott, and Judy

acknowledgments

The author wishes to thank those who have contributed their time and talents toward the completion of this volume. Among those contributors are Caroline Bailey, Charlene De Graaf, Jerry Fishman, Fred Seibel, Kenneth Shrable, J. Burton Vache, Jr., and George Yonge. I particularly wish to acknowledge the efforts of Walter Loban for his careful reading and numerous commentaries. Finally, I want to thank my wife, Margie, who gave me the idea for Figure 4-3, and who has been both my severest critic and my greatest source of encouragement.

contents

section three: *alternatives*

section one

---

the background

introduction to section one

It has long been a tradition in academic circles that the teacher of language stands at the top of the educational hierarchy. From the days when grammar headed the venerable *trivium* of grammar, rhetoric, and dialectic to the present, in which English is the most universally required subject in American public schools and colleges, language teaching has enjoyed a prestige unsurpassed by any other subject.

Nevertheless, the teaching of English, as it is currently practiced in thousands of classrooms throughout the United States, has recently come under attack. The value of much of our language curriculum has been questioned by highly responsible individuals. Some classroom teachers have originated the criticism or have been the first to admit that the keys to the academic kingdom do not lie in the District Course of Study or the latest textbook adoption. Other teachers have reacted by counter challenging the critics to produce a better system of teaching language arts. Others have ignored the whole problem as one might ignore a child's temper tantrum, believing that it will soon blow over.

English teachers are currently faced with two disquieting factors. First, there is the evidence. Almost any English program beyond the primary grades reveals a disturbing lack of sequence. In contrast to mathematics, for example, the typical English curriculum rambles all over the field and gets nowhere. In mathematics one begins by learning simple addition, increasing the complexity until subtraction can be attempted, then multiplication, and finally division. Only then are fractions, decimals, and percentages introduced. So the sequence progresses, through algebra, geometry, and calculus. Granted, recent developments in mathematics have resulted in a certain amount of shifting of subject matter and of the introduction of concepts at different grade levels, but a math student still progresses from elementary to increasingly complex processes.

3

This is true of our language arts program only at the primary grade level. A beginning student learns to make letters, to read and write words, to combine words into thoughts, and to go from first- to second- to third-grade reading level. After this, things become muddled.

Huckleberry Finn might be encountered by students at any level from upper elementary to graduate courses at a university. True, the level of understanding with which the same work is read at different grade levels—or by different students at the same grade level—will vary enormously. But the English teacher would be hard-pressed to demonstrate that growth in literary skills is the result of a sequence of experiences that took place in the classroom rather than the natural result of having lived, thought, and used language to communicate with others. The math teacher, however, could easily demonstrate the need for learning the multiplication table before attempting long division.

Composition skills are another example. Each year we painfully squeeze from our charges paragraphs and pages about everything from their thoughts on how much allowance a teen-ager should be given to mankind's greatest challenge in the space age. And week after week, year after year, these "compositions" are returned with the usual polyglot of red marks giving advice on everything from how to write well-constructed paragraphs to the use of *lie* and *lay*. Real improvement in depth of thinking and style of expression from week to week and year to year is so minuscule that one may again speculate whether it is the result of anything that happened in the classroom or of simply having survived in a language-centered civilization for a greater period of time.

But the confusion that exists in the other language arts is dwarfed in the teaching of grammar. A student may be "taught" subject-verb agreement in the sixth, seventh, eighth, ninth, tenth, eleventh, and twelfth grades. And each time it may seem to him and to his teacher that he is learning it for the first time.

Examine a typical "series" of published English grammars. Without looking at the grade-level designation on the cover, it is almost impossible to determine which one was intended to be used first. Sometimes the writers do not even bother to change the wording of the lessons encountered from one year to the next. I remember a time when textbook shortages forced me to use a twelfth-grade text in a tenth-grade class, and then to use the tenth-grade text with the same students the following year. No noticeable difficulty resulted.

This repetitious course of study stems largely from the teaching of "functional" grammar. Instead of looking at the over-all structure of English, we break language education into a series of lessons designed to eliminate writing "errors." It is as if we taught auto mechanics without looking at the operation of the internal combustion engine, teaching only how to repair certain types of mechanical breakdowns.

The second factor that leads us to re-examine our practices is the difficulty we frequently have in justifying some of our textbooks' pronouncements about language. I recently witnessed the painful scene of a high school teacher trying to convince a class that the word *argument* is a noun (because it is a *thing*). Most of the class insisted that it is a verb.

"But is *argument* an action word?" asked the teacher.

"It is when I have one," came the honest reply.

At this point the frustrated teacher simply informed the class that the word *argument* is a noun—a thing—AN ARGUMENT. The "better" of the unconvinced and uncomprehending students filed this data in their notebooks, along with other assorted bits of useless information. The less academic students acted with more intelligence. They promptly forgot the whole distasteful incident.

The sad fact is that this situation need never have occurred. There are many things the teacher might have said. She could have placed the word *argument* on the chalk board along with a number of other words—*dog, cat, house, idea, brontosaurus,* and *concept*. Added to the list might be *ride, argue, sit, do,* and *conceive*. She could have asked the students to sort the words into three groups: those that have a plural form, those that have a past tense form, and those that have both forms. Thus *one argument—two arguments* could be matched with *cat—cats, dog—dogs, house—houses, idea—ideas, brontosaurus—brontosauruses,* and *concept—concepts,* as opposed to *argue—argued, sit—sat, do—did,* and *conceive—conceived*. Some words would fit both lists: *ride—rides; ride—rode*. If names for categories were needed, she could have labeled words that have plural forms *nouns* and those that have past-tense forms *verbs,* noting that some words could be used as both.

But the teacher was relying on a traditional approach to grammar that has many weaknesses, not the least of which is that it is indefensible. You can debate all day whether *argument* is an action word, but can you debate whether a speaker of English can say *one argument, two arguments*?

During that painful classroom observation my sympathies were with the students, and I could not help agreeing that a good argument does contain plenty of action. But I also sympathized with the teacher, for I could remember being backed into the same type of corner when I was teaching. The first time it happened was a turning point in my professional life. I had been teaching high school students rules for comma usage, and was doing an exercise from our grammar text.

Put a comma between two independent clauses connected by a coordinating conjunction. That was the rule. Most of the class did the exercise well, and, I thought, things were going quite smoothly.

Then it happened. One of my students brought up his literature anthology and showed me a compound sentence with no comma. The author was John Steinbeck.

I had a ready answer, glib and trite: "Steinbeck was a master. He knew the rules and knew when to break them. He left out the comma to speed up the action, to give his story pace. When you are a Steinbeck you can break the rules, too."

I was saved—or so I thought. But that wasn't the end. The next day the same student showed me several dozen compound sentences from the same anthology. The sentences without commas outnumbered those in which commas were used.

Other students in the class entered the game. We started looking up compound sentences in other books. The results were indisputable. Professional writers in every field from great literature to mail order catalogues broke the comma rule more often than they followed it.

What kind of rule was this, then, that was broken more often than not? Could we conclude that John Steinbeck and Ernest Hemingway, Patrick Henry and Abraham Lincoln were incompetent in the use of language? Charles Fries gave us a clue when he likened English teachers to doctors of the recent past: In 1628 it was demonstrated that the letting of blood was useless in curing an illness, yet doctors continued to bleed patients for years afterward, simply on the basis of tradition.[1] Are we teaching grammar today on the same level?

In this volume we shall explore a number of areas. First we examine the traditional approach to the teaching of English, tracing its development from early speculation about the nature of language to a full-blown public school subject. Next we introduce linguistic analysis and discuss its possible uses in the classroom. But we hope to go beyond comparing traditional with modern methods of teaching grammar. Both the traditional and the newer approaches must be examined for their value to the public school student.

To do this we must deal with the question of value *per se*. What are the real needs of the modern student, and what kind of educated public will society need in the days to come? Which of these needs can be served in a school language arts program?

This book is not, therefore, exclusively about language. It is really about teaching. And it deals with whatever subject matter is relevant to a worthwhile English program. Finally, it is a book about English teachers, because the success of any course of study rests on the competence and dedication of the thousands of teachers who must translate abstract knowledge into a concrete program involving specific content, appropriate methods, and the interchange of ideas on which learning ultimately depends.

---

[1] Charles Carpenter Fries, *The Structure of English* (New York: Harcourt, Brace and World, Inc., 1952), p. 1.

1

genesis to exodus
a tradition develops

THE GREEKS

That the history of teaching grammar can be traced back to the speculations of the early Greeks should come as no surprise, for it is a common pattern in the history of Western culture. That the earliest works on grammar came not from grammarians but from philosophers who speculated upon a number of subjects—among them the nature of language— is somewhat less well known. That Plato, Aristotle, Varro, and Quintilian were the progenitors of the modern English teacher has been firmly established by scholars of classical philology. But the significance of the philosophical origin of grammar has not been fully explored nor understood by the classroom teacher. These early chapters are not intended to be a comprehensive history of the subject; other writers have already done a competent job in this area. Rather, they present a brief look at selected works for the purpose of throwing some light on why the teaching of language is undergoing a revolution today.

Although there is some evidence of grammatical writing from an earlier time, one of the earliest extant works on grammar is the *Cratylus* of Plato. In this essay a major grammatical argument of the classical era is brought into focus. Hermogenes and Cratylus have been arguing about the nature of language. Cratylus claims that language is a *natural* process, that is, the assigning of names for specific objects comes about naturally, as the result of some connection between the word itself and the object it represents. Hermogenes argues that language is *conventional*, that words

7

are abstract symbols of things but bear no resemblance to them. This reflected the debate between the "naturalists" and the "conventionalists," which stimulated the Greek desire to examine language and to speculate about its nature. In *Cratylus* much of the dialogue is carried on by Socrates, who is brought in to settle the dispute. Plato has Socrates champion both sides of the argument with equal vigor. On one hand he argues, with very dubious accuracy, that not every man is capable of giving names to things (making up language), but only the highly skilled.[1] Furthermore, the work of the giver of names must be treated by skilled users. Therefore, with this much directed thinking involved in the composition of language, the assignment of specific words to specific objects cannot be merely a random process; it must be the result of the careful fitting together of the appropriate combination of sounds for each object named.

On the other hand, Socrates also argues that just as some artisans are more skilled than others, so are some of the people who create language. Therefore, some names are more accurately descriptive than others, and he who depends on names to learn about the nature of their referents is risking receiving misinformation.[2] Thus Socrates is portrayed by Plato as taking a middle ground in this popular *nature* versus *convention* controversy.

Although this debate seems pointless today, it is historically interesting, mainly because a remnant of the controversy can still be seen. As Robins pointed out:

descendants of the 'naturalist' school still argue for the dependence of linguistic changes on cultural changes and for the reflection in grammatical distinctions of real distinctions, outside language and grammar, either in the world at large or in the processes of the human mind.[3]

Robins further explained and supported the view of the conventionalist school, which denies a resemblance between symbol (word) and referent (object), except in scattered cases of onomatopoeia (words such as *crack*, *splash*, and *buzz*). They claim language can only be examined in relation to itself, not to the world that language represents.

Exactly how Plato himself felt about the controversy is not clear, although he has Socrates present a fairly good case for looking at both sides with caution. How the real Socrates felt on this matter is not clear either, for Socrates did not leave us his thoughts in written form. We know him chiefly from commentaries such as the

---

[1] Plato, *Cratylus* in *The Dialogues of Plato*, B. Jowett, trans. (Oxford: The Clarendon Press, 1953), Vol. III, fourth ed., Section 387d–391.

[2] *Ibid.*, Section 429.

[3] Robert Henry Robins, *Ancient and Medieval Grammatical Theory in Europe* (London: G. Bell and Sons, Ltd., 1951), p. 10.

dialogues of Plato. We do know, however, that in *The Clouds* Aristophanes poked fun at Socrates for trying to divide the Greek word for *chicken* into two forms so there would be a feminine form for *hen* as well as a masculine form for *rooster*.[4]

The method by which Plato seeks his conclusions is interesting. It is all done through a *reasoning* process. Namers of names are presumed to be skilled in their art. (Today this would be considered inaccurate, as language comes from many segments of the community.) Therefore names must be appropriate for the objects named. Analysis is not based upon observation of language itself. In fact, when asked by Hermogenes to do so, Socrates is unable to give an example of any specific word that shows a natural relation to its referent.[5] But it does not occur to any member of the cast of characters that this lack of evidence should cause them to doubt the potency of the argument. This was an age of reasoning, not an age of scientific observation.

Much of the rest of the *Cratylus* is taken up with an examination of many words of the Greek language. However, the relationships discussed are always those of various words *to each other*, rather than to nonlinguistic phenomena. For example, Socrates mentioned that the Greek word for *hero* resembles the word *Eros*, the Greek word for Cupid, god of love.[6] He explained this by saying that most of the heroes of mythology were the children of a *love* of a god for a mortal or a mortal for a god. Thus, much of the *Cratylus* can be described as a rather inaccurate treatise on etymology.

It is Plato's reasoning, philosophical approach, lacking in careful study of the language, that sets the tone for the development of grammatical thought. Further examples can be seen in the same work in his discussion of the phonetic (sound) system of the language. Here he argues that just as a painter cannot paint a picture without using pigments similar to those found in his subject, so words cannot be composed of elements that are not similar to elements in their referents.[7]

A number of other concepts of language that are standard fare in modern grammatical study can also be found in Plato. His discussion of phonology includes the breaking of sounds into consonant and vowel. He does not clearly distinguish between a sound, which is a spoken unit of language, and a letter, which is not always its exact written counterpart.[8] He reports that letters build into syllables, which in turn build into nouns and verbs.[9] This may be the earliest isolation of the terms

---

[4] Aristophanes, *The Clouds*, line 666.
[5] Plato, *Cratylus*, Section 391.
[6] *Ibid.*, Section 398c.
[7] *Ibid.*, Section 434.
[8] *Ibid.*, Section 434.
[9] *Ibid.*, Section 399b, 425.

noun and *verb*. Plato goes on to state that it is the combining of noun and verb that produces language (a forerunner of the subject-predicate concept).

In giving the reasons for his "in-between" position in the nature-convention controversy, Plato stated that even though words should be natural, we must recognize that custom and convention play a part in language formation.[10] The interesting point is his use of the term *should be*. Plato reveals an attitude here that has characterized much grammatical teaching to the present day. It is simply that language *should be* anything at all. The Greeks wanted to see all human functions, including language, built upon reason and logic. Plato speaks disparagingly of the "corruption" of some of the "original" words for the sake of euphony, and dismisses words he cannot explain as being of "foreign origin."[11]

The exact meaning of *Cratylus* is somewhat obscure, and some commentators have suggested that much of this dialogue may even be a satire on the grammatical thinking of the day.[12] Nevertheless, it remains a revelation of some of the speculation out of which our thinking on the question of grammar grew.

When Plato made the statement that language should be natural, he was supporting what came to be known among Greek philosophers as the *analogist* theory. This was the theory that language should be *analogous* to logic, that it should be consistent in construction and free from illogical usages, such as inconsistent verb endings or masculine or feminine endings that do not seem appropriate.

The opposite theory was that of the *anomalists*, who believed that language was full of anomaly, or irregularity in form. They were less concerned with consistency than with how language was actually spoken. They considered all forms of language acceptable as long as usage made them popular. The anomalists saw their function as that of students and recorders of the Greek language, whereas the extremists among the analogists felt their duty was to "correct" inconsistencies in language and to make them conform to a logical pattern.

This analogist-anomalist controversy grew largely out of the older nature-convention question, with analogists bearing a loose relationship to the naturalists. This question is very much with us in grammatical thinking today, for as we shall see in Chapter 2, it forms the basis of one of the major distinctions between the "traditional" and the "new" grammars.

Aristotle, like his predecessor, Plato, was a grammarian only in the sense that philosophers of the time considered in their bailiwick everything from the natural sciences to the social sciences, from religion to grammar. His works include a tremen-

---

[10] *Ibid.*, Section 435.

[11] *Ibid.*, Section 409c and d; 414.

[12] See, for example, Jowett's introduction to *Cratylus*, pp. 1 and 2.

dous variety of observations ranging through physics and biology to politics, ethics, and logic. He wrote no single essay on grammar, but referred to the structure of language in a number of works.

Aristotle's *Poetics* is a treatise on dramatic criticism, but it includes definitions of parts of speech and gender. Aristotle discussed types of letters (not differentiated from sounds), the division of sounds into vowel, semi-vowel, and mute (consonant), and presented a discussion of syllable, noun and verb, case, and sentence. He also defined masculine, feminine, and neuter nouns according to the letters from which they are composed.[13]

Throughout his grammatical comments, emphasis is placed on case, which is the changing of the form of a substantive as its position changes in the sentence. Case is important in the Greek language. In English a *tree* is called a *tree*, regardless of its position in the sentence, but this is not true of Greek, in which the form of a noun changes according to whether it is the subject or the object. One of the few surviving remnants of case in English is found in personal pronouns, as:

> *I* saw the dog.
> The dog saw *me*.

Note that the pronoun changes from the nominative to the objective case, but the noun, unlike its equivalent in Greek, remains the same.

In Chapter XXII of the *Poetics*, grammatical analysis was blended with a discussion of the "virtues" and "barbarisms" of various literary works. Grammar, then, can be clearly seen in its relation to Greek thinking, less as a study in itself than as an adjunct to literary analysis and criticism. In *De Interpretatione* Aristotle defined noun and verb, and discussed noun case and verb tense, as well as types of sentences. In the *Rhetoric* he added the *conjunction* to the classifications *noun* and *verb*. To Aristotle, conjunctions were all words that are not nouns or verbs. They differ from nouns and verbs in that they have no independent lexical meaning but are simply used to tie the utterance together. Although his definitions fail to distinguish adjective and adverb, Aristotle's division of words into those that do and those that do not have lexical meaning represents an early groping for the linguistic concept of form classes and function groups. (See Chapter 6, page 127.) Aristotle defined the *word* as the minimal unit of language, incapable of subdivision into smaller parts, a concept that our study of morphemics will reveal to be inadequate.[14] He also told us that words are not in themselves significant (cannot make a statement) but they must be used

[12] Aristotle, *Poetics*, Chapters 20 and 21.
[14] Aristotle, *De Interpretatione*, Chapters 2 and 3.

in combination with other words. This is related to our concept of a sentence and the need for completeness. It ignores, as many of our traditional grammarians do, the fact that some utterances are composed of phrases only: *What a storm!* or even a single word or two: *Hi, John.*

For our purpose, the most interesting work of Aristotle is probably the *Rhetoric.* Rhetoric is the art of persuasion, of using words *effectively* to convince, to influence an audience's thoughts or feelings. In most other works Aristotle took a conventionalist view, claiming that words are given, rather than discovered in the nature of things. But in the *Rhetoric* he tried to correct and improve usage. The foundation of good style, he claimed, is correctness, and he proceeded to discuss the proper use of number and gender.[15] Rhetoric, literary criticism, and grammatical analysis were not considered the same by the Greek philosophers. However, the tendency of classical writers to blend these areas, to jump from one to the other within the body of a single work, fostered the idea that it is the duty of the grammarian to improve the language, to formulate rules by which language usage will become more logical and more effective.

In the centuries following, and particularly during those Dark Ages between the fall of Rome and the Renaissance, the works of Aristotle came to be considered second only to the Bible as the final authority on all topics. Like Plato, Aristotle formulated his rules by *thinking about* language much more than by observing it.

Today the analogy-anomaly debate can be seen in the differing approaches of those who would teach correct usage (prescriptive grammar) and those who feel that grammar is a matter of studying language analytically to determine how it actually comes together (descriptive grammar).

Following Aristotle, other Greek grammarians, particularly those comprising the Stoic school of philosophy, developed and refined the parts of speech concepts, breaking language into additional categories and redefining previous ones. One writer of the latter part of the Greek period epitomized and summarized in one work all the grammatical thinking of his time. In the first century B.C., the *Téchnē Grammatikḗ* of Dionysus Thrax became the standard textbook on Greek grammar. Although it made no original contributions, it was the most comprehensive treatment of the Greek language to date, classifying and codifying the grammatical thinking of the time. It was so popular for so long that Gilbert Murray referred to it as one of the most successful school books in the world, mentioning its use in the Merchant Taylors' School, London, when his own great uncle was there.[16]

[15] Aristotle, *Rhetoric,* Book 3, Chapter 5.
[16] Gilbert Murray, *Greek Studies* (Oxford: Clarendon Press, 1946), p. 181.

The textbook of Dionysus discussed such topics as a definition of grammar, accenting, punctuation, letters and syllables, parts of speech, and declension and conjugation. He listed the *article* and the *participle* among the eight parts of speech, omitting the adjective and the interjection. Otherwise, his classifications are similar to those of many current grammar texts, except that many of his definitions have been revised. For example, his category for *nouns* included adjectives and demonstrative and interrogative pronouns. His *article* included relative pronouns, whereas his *pronoun* is limited to personal and possessive forms. Originally written in Greek, this volume was translated into Latin, from which form came many of the technical terms currently employed in formal grammar. It was largely through Dionysus that the Greek grammar of Plato and Aristotle, as well as a number of others, was transmitted to the eighteenth century.

Before we turn our attention to the Roman contributions, let us briefly summarize the major characteristics associated with classical Greek grammatical thought. First, living in an age of reason rather than in an age of science, an age in which problems were attacked by thinking them out instead of by gathering data in the field or in the laboratory, the Greeks did not examine their language with the scholarly detachment of a modern observer. Instead they *thought about* language, philosophized on the subject, and in their early groping for methods of analysis, often made limited and inaccurate observations. We have noted that the Greeks did not distinguish between sounds (phonemes) and letters (graphemes), and their definitions of the parts of speech have been changed over the centuries.

Second, they were interested in what language *should be*. The rhetorician and the literary critic were concerned with the *effective* use of language, hence some grammarians tried to improve usage by rules of grammar. Aristotle tells us that Protagoras wanted *anger* and *helmet* to be masculine, as this seemed more logical, and Zenodotus amended Homer to bring it into line with current Greek.[17]

Finally, Greek grammar was based on formal rather than informal language. Literature and oratory, not the everyday speech of men and women, were the concerns of the Greek grammarians. They visualized language as a constant, unchanging phenomenon rather than as a process of continual development. Those changes in language that they did recognize were thought to be the result of corruption and foreign influence.

---

[17] Aristotle, *de Sophisticis Elenchis*, Chapter 14.

THE RISE OF ROME

But it was not only through translation of Dionysus that classical concepts were transmitted to us. As Greek culture gave way to Roman, Latin became the dominant language of Western civilization. And the Romans, whose respect for Greek culture was tremendous, built their grammatical system on that of the Stoic philosophers, on Plato, and on Dionysus Thrax and his successors, superimposing Greek attitudes and Greek structure on the Latin language.

On the whole, this superimposition of the grammar of one language on the structure of another did not fare too badly, for the fabric of Latin is not unlike that of Greek, and the rules of grammar can be transferred with some degree of success. Greek had five case endings for nouns; Latin had six. Latin had no definite article, as did Greek. These minor differences had to be dealt with by the Latin grammarians, but they did not require a complete overhaul of the grammatical system. Perhaps it is unfortunate for grammatical thinking that it worked out so well, for this wholesale transfer of rules from one language to another established a precedent that plagues us to this day. It involves another controversy concerning language: the question of whether there is one universal grammar for all languages or if each language requires its own rules for analysis.

This question is tied to the analogy-anomaly controversy. If language is analogous to life—if people speak in patterns that are logical and consistent, and follow the rules of symbol-referent parallelism—then it would seem reasonable that one universal system of grammar would serve all languages. But if language is replete with anomalies, if it follows illogical patterns of whim and the needs of a particular society, it would seem unlikely that the same eccentricities would pervade all languages.

If Latin and Greek had contained major structural differences, the Roman grammarians might have been forced to look to their own language for its individual characteristics. But because the differences were minor, and because the Romans tended to accept Greek culture as a basis for their own, it seemed natural to assume that syntactic rules could be transferred from one language to another. Today the grammars of the Greeks and Romans have been refined and superimposed once more on still another language—English. But as we shall see in the pages to follow, the structure of English is not similar to that of Latin and Greek, and the transition has been considerably more painful.

One of the few Romans who studied the Latin language as an entity, without depending on Greek, was Marcus Terentius Varro, whose *De Lingua Latina* was published near the middle of the first century B.C. It contained twenty-five books on Latin structure, of which only Books V to X, plus a few fragments, have been preserved. Varro dealt with etymology, inflection, the anomaly-analogy controversy, parts of speech, and syntax. In the books that are preserved, Books V through VII dealt with derivation. In Book VIII, Varro revealed some very advanced linguistic thinking by dividing the words of the Latin language into four classes:[18]

1.   Those that have case forms (nouns).
2.   Those that have tense (verbs).
3.   Those that have neither case nor tense (adverbs).
4.   Those that have both case and tense (participles).

Although this system reflects the earlier thinking of Dionysus Thrax and is by no means complete, it represents an advance over those who defined the parts of speech according to meaning, for one can debate the meaning of the words *noun* and *verb*, but one cannot deny that Latin nouns have case and verbs have tense.

Varro went further into a discussion of the various parts of speech. He gave illustrations to show that nouns can be inflected according to gender (masculine, feminine, and neuter endings), number (singular and plural endings), and case.[19] He divided verbs into past, present, and future, and subdivided these into completed and incompleted actions, as well as active and passive.

On the subject of analogy-anomaly, Varro found some evidence for both sides. He argued, for example, that if a person assigns a name to a slave, this is a *voluntary* act, not following any universal laws, and that three different people might assign three different names under the same circumstances.[20] On the other hand, he continues, once the names are assigned, the use of these names in sentences would follow the *natural* (regular) rules.[21] (See Chapter 5 for rules of inflection.)

In Book X Varro divided all words into two classes, those that are inflected and those that are not.[22] This is in keeping with linguistic practice today, but he then went on to discuss words that change because of inflection and those that change because of etymological derivation, as if these changes were governed by the same laws.[23] (See Chapter 5.)

Varro's grammatical system, if incomplete and not entirely accurate by today's standards, represented advanced thinking for his time. He used the structure of a word (inflection) to classify it as to type, and based his observations on the Latin language rather than on Greek. He did observe that the same structure could be

---

[18] Marcus Terentius Varro, *De Lingua Latina*, Book VIII, Chapter 44.
[19] *Ibid.*, Book VIII, Chapter 20; Book IX, Chapters 96–99.
[20] *Ibid.*, Book VIII, Chapter 21.
[21] *Ibid.*, Book VIII, Chapter 22.
[22] *Ibid.*, Book X, Chapter 14.
[23] *Ibid.*, Book X, Chapter 15.

applied to Greek, but this was more of an afterthought than a source of reference.[24]

A century and a half later, Marcus Fabius Quintilianus wrote a treatise on the education of an orator entitled *Institutes of Oratory*. This document included a commentary on grammar, among other things, as part of the orator's training, and was one of the earliest works to consider the place of grammar in the education of the individual.

Quintilian assumed that a thorough grounding in grammar is necessary for effective use of language, an assumption that remains unquestioned by many English teachers to this day. He also saw grammar related to other academic disciplines, mainly literature. Not only did he believe a study of literature necessary for understanding grammar, but grammar was, according to Quintilian, the elementary stage of the study of literature.[25]

Quintilian stated that grammar should be based on reason, antiquity, authority, and usage.[26] Of these, he claimed that usage was the most dependable.[27] But much of his text was devoted to rooting out "barbarisms" (improper uses of a word) and "solecisms" (errors in syntax), and Quintilian's works gave impetus to the analogist (prescriptive) approach. He also placed great faith in authority and antiquity, for example, preferring to have a Latin orator educated by Greek grammarians.[28]

Quintilian's emphasis on correctness and respect for authority may have been the result of the widespread desire on the part of people throughout the Roman Empire for the capacity to use educated Latin. With Rome the center of the civilized world, it was natural that citizens throughout the diaspora would want to emulate the Romans. Many grammarians of foreign birth came upon the scene at this time. Quintilian himself was Spanish, and Priscian, of whom we shall speak presently, was from Mauretania, but lived much of his life in Constantinople.

The Roman heritage of Varro and Quintilian as well as that of other Roman scholars was transmitted to us by those grammarians who succeeded them, just as Dionysus Thrax preserved the grammar of the Greeks. The most famous of these late Roman grammarians were Donatus (c. 400 A.D.) and Priscian (c. 500 A.D.). It was for the work of these later grammarians that the Latins were famous, for they were the ones who gathered together the existing thoughts of their day and put them into single, comprehensive, organized works—works on grammar *per se*, rather than comments on the nature of language scattered throughout a number of essays on a variety of subjects.

[24] *Ibid.*, Book IX, Chapter 31.
[25] Marcus Fabius Quintilianus, *Institutes of Oratory*, Book I, Chapter 4, Section 3.
[26] *Ibid.*, Book I, Chapter VI, Section 1.
[27] *Ibid.*, Book I, Chapter VI, Section 3.
[28] *Ibid.*, Book I, Chapter IV, Section 1.

The age of Donatus and Priscian was an age of tradition, of respect for the classical heritage, particularly in literature. It was natural that their approach should be one of careful study of the works of the standard authors, of preservation of the literary heritage, of intolerance for anything that departs from the "standard." Priscian stated that he based his work on that of the Greek grammarian Appollonius Dyscolus of Alexandria (c. 140 A.D.) and that he considered the Greek scholars to be the authority.

In his *Ars Grammatica*, Aelius Donatus dealt with phonetics, syllabication, verse, accenting, and parts of speech. He followed with common sentence errors, then phrases favored by classical authors. His *Ars Minor*, describing the eight parts of speech, and his *Ars Maior*, a discussion of syntax, became standard texts throughout the Middle Ages. Peck tells us that the name *Donatus* became synonymous with grammar, as we might use the term *a Webster* for a dictionary.[29]

But the "most complete and systematic Latin Grammar that has come down to us from antiquity" is the eighteen books of the *Institutiones Grammaticae* of Priscianus Constantinople.[30] Some parts of this work show highly advanced thinking, whereas others typify the sort of armchair philosophy that for centuries has plagued careful inquiry into the nature of language. Priscian reasoned, for example, that in the word order of the sentence, nouns come before verbs because in the nature of things substances come before the actions they perform. On the other hand, his sections on syntax, declensions of nouns, and conjugations of verbs were highly satisfactory, although he claimed that words (except compounds) cannot be subdivided, an inaccuracy we have already noted. He followed Dionysus Thrax by defining the word as the minimal unit of utterance and the sentence as the expression of a complete thought.

In determining the parts of speech he claimed that meaning is the only clue, another point with which modern linguists disagree, but in practice his definitions drew from a number of sources. An examination of Priscian's parts of speech is interesting in that it reveals both the great strides that have been made toward definitions that come closer to our own and also the inconsistencies in thinking that have become part of our grammatical tradition. The following are a few excerpts:

1. *Noun:* "A part of speech assigning a common or specific quality to persons or things." This definition is based on the *meaning* of the word *noun*. It is the closest thing yet to the "person, place, or thing" definition still committed to memory by so many suffering and uncomprehending school children.

---

[29] Harry Thurston Peck, *A History of Classical Philology* (New York: The Macmillan Company, 1911), p. 185.

[30] *Ibid.*

2. *Verb:* "A part of speech with tense and mood, without case-inflection, signifying action or being acted on." This begins by examining the *form* of the verb, then concludes with its meaning.

3. *Participle:* Has "case-inflections and temporal significance together with active or passive 'meaning'." This again involves both form (case-inflections) and meaning (temporal significance).

4. *Pronoun:* "A part of speech used in place of proper nouns..." This definition is stated in terms of another standard, the *function* of the word in the sentence (to replace another word).

5. *Preposition:* "An indeclinable part of speech put before others either syntactically or in word formation." This definition rests partly on form (indeclinable) but depends mainly on function, or how it is used in the sentence.

6. *Adverb:* "An indeclinable part of speech by which meaning is added to the verb. (form and meaning)."

7. *Interjection:* "no syntactic union with the rest of its sentence... 'signifying a state of mind.'" (function [no syntactic union...] and meaning).

8. *Conjunction:* "An indeclinable part of speech connecting other words, giving them added meaning or exhibiting their mutual relationship." This definition combines form (indeclinable), function (connecting other words), and meaning ("giving them added meaning").[31]

These definitions reveal that much of our grammatical thinking was formulated fifteen hundred years ago, and that only minor refinements have been added to this basic concept of the classification of words. They also reveal the unscientific nature of our grammatical thinking. As W. Nelson Francis has stated, the use of three separate standards (form, function, and meaning) can be compared to the practice by a zoologist of classifying animals into invertebrates, mammals, and beasts of burden.[32]

AFTER THE FALL

Tracing the flow of grammatical thought after the fall of Rome becomes more complicated. During the early Middle Ages, the works of the Greeks were not commonly known, and the standard grammar texts were Donatus and Priscian. Grammar

---

[31] Quotations are from Robins, *Ancient and Medieval Grammatical Theory*, pp. 65–67. Comments are by the author.

[32] W. Nelson Francis, "Revolution in Grammar," *Quarterly Journal of Speech*, Vol. 40, October 1954, p. 305.

became firmly established as one of the major subjects for study, the leader of the *trivium* of grammar, rhetoric, and dialectic. The Middle Ages was hardly an age of discovery or innovation, but was rather one of slavish adherence to tradition, of picayunish debates concerning obscure grammatical points. The seventh-century grammarian Virgilius Maro tells about scholars "wrangling for a fortnight over the vocative of *ego*," and drawing their swords in fury "after an equally long discussion on inchoative verbs."[33]

The Middle Ages was also dominated by Christian theism, and no authority was given credence if his work was in any way in conflict with the Scriptures. For example, although Donatus and Priscian's texts were the leading authorities on Latin grammar, their language references were taken from the writings of classical authors. But the grammar of the Vulgate (the Latin Bible of Saint Jerome, translated between 383 and 405 A.D.) was that of the fourth century. Medieval grammarians were not aware that language is in a constant state of flux, and that grammatical rules common to one period may not be applicable in another. They criticized Donatus and Priscian for failing to recognize the superior authority of the Scriptures. Thus may be seen another failing of grammarians to date—a tendency to try to find grammatical rules that are universal and unchanging, despite the constantly changing nature of language.

The rise of Christianity in Europe during the Middle Ages gave impetus to grammatical study, as missionaries set out to Christianize the world. With Latin firmly established as the language of the Church, with monasteries scattered throughout Europe, the teaching of Latin took on renewed importance to the missionaries who brought Christianity to non-Latin speakers.

Around 1000 A.D. Aelfric, Abbot of Eynsham, England, wrote a Latin grammar for English speakers. Based on the works of Priscian and Donatus, this text was presumed by the author to be applicable to Old English as well as Latin. Thus the tradition of adapting the grammar of one language to another was carried into English, and as this was one of the earliest grammars for English speakers, it set the style for many years of scholarship.

Unfortunately, the grammatical journey from Latin to English by way of Old English was not as happy as that from Greek to Latin. Latin nouns, for example, have six case endings, Old English only four, with prepositional phrases making the proper distinctions. Modern English nouns have only one case ending—the genitive, or *'s* (see Chapter 5). In addition to prepositions, modern English employs *word order* to distinguish between the various forms of subject and object. As early as

---

[33] Sir John Edwin Sandys, *A History of Classical Scholarship* (New York: Hafner Publishing Company, 1958), Vol. I, p. 450.

Shakespeare's time, Grumio could get a laugh by yelling, "The oats have eaten the horses."[34] Improbable as such an occurrence sounds, word order in English is so rigid that there could be no doubt in anyone's mind just what had eaten what.

After the eleventh century, Greek language and literature were rediscovered and translated. New authority was given to classical authors, particularly Aristotle, and grammatical thinking throughout Europe became more prescriptive, more logical, and more authoritative as grammarians renewed their search for a *final, certain* system.

The assumption of a single, universal grammar was part of the dominant thinking of the age, generally known as *scholasticism.* This term is frequently applied to the attempt to reconcile all fields of study with religious dogma, to find in the teachings of the learned some over-all form, purpose, and reason for the universe. Thus Donatus and Priscian, although accepted as the authorities on grammar, were criticized for not going far enough—for stopping short at merely looking at language and analyzing its forms. The scholastics wanted grammar to contain some evidence of logic, some proof of a Divine Plan, some philosophical basis for grammatical study.

About the middle of the twelfth century, Peter Helias, of the University of Paris, wrote a commentary on the grammar of Priscian, seeking a philosophical explanation of Priscian's rules. Helias stated that each language had its own grammatical system. But the views of Helias did not typify the period. His contemporary Roger Bacon claimed that "the grammar of all languages is *substantially* the same, although there may be *accidental* variations in each."[35]

Bacon's faith in a universal grammar typified the school of grammatical thinking that dominated the late Middle Ages. A number of writers of that time wrote commentaries entitled *De Modis Significandi*, from which they became collectively known as *The Modistae*. Most writers of the *Modistae* believed in one universal grammar for all languages, which was dependent upon the nature of reality and on human reason. They believed that philosophers, not grammarians, must be the dictators of correctness. They criticized Priscian for not improving the language, for not making it conform to logic. Robins sums up the thinking of the *Modistae*:

Grammatical rules in other words are to be founded on extra-linguistic premises, the 'laws of thought' or the 'nature of things,' which are the concern of the philosopher. Where he cannot justify it by appeal to logic, a philosopher, and he alone, may emend it and so improve the existing grammar of the language as an instrument of human thought and intercourse. It will be seen that the issues raised and involved here are of the same order as those involved between the 'analogists'

[34] William Shakespeare, *Taming of the Shrew*, Act III, Scene 2.
[35] Sandys, *A History of Classical Scholarship*, Vol. I, p. 595.

and the 'anomalists' in antiquity: to what extent if at all should a grammarian as such seek to alter the structure of his language, either in the interests of greater regularity of patterns or to bring the forms of language more into line with the forms, observed or hypothecated in the world of things and thought?[36]

Since grammar was thus to be based outside language, a universal grammar for all languages was believed possible. The Modistae refined and systematized grammatical thinking, classifying language phenomena according to regular patterns. They even rejected literature if it stood in the way of logic. Although as a group they did not outlast the Renaissance, the thinking of the Modistae left its imprint on modern grammar, strengthening the philosophical framework that held that grammar should be analogous to logic, and giving new impetus to the search for a universal system.

THE RENAISSANCE

The Renaissance was a period of expansion of learning, of greater tolerance for divergent ideas, appreciation for the work of foreign scholars, and emphasis on man rather than on the Divine, and on the here-and-now instead of on the hereafter. Hitherto grammar had consisted of the study of Latin, with a system based on Greek. No other language had been considered worthy of study. During the Renaissance, however, the works of scholars throughout the world came to be known, and other languages were also scrutinized.

Hebrew, as the language of the Bible, was given particular attention. Closely related to Hebrew studies was Arabic, both because Hebrew and Arabic are related languages (See Chapter 8) and because of the expanding influence of the Islamic Empire in the Near East and North Africa. Much work in these languages was done by Jewish and Arabic scholars who were not involved in the tradition of Greek and Latin grammar and were thus free to study their own language and work out its rules of structure.

Interest in Semitic languages helped break the exclusive hold of Latin on the attention of European scholars, and by the fifteenth and sixteenth centuries, grammars of vernacular languages were beginning to appear. Frequently these grammars reflected pride in one's nation or region or the desire to promote a particular language or dialect, as expanding commerce created great rivalries among men and nations.

---

[36] Robins, *Ancient and Medieval Grammatical Theory*, p. 78.

Although language study during the Renaissance concentrated on the literary heritage, this heritage frequently involved the same language as everyday speech, at least that of the educated classes. This reawakened interest in the study of spelling and sound-letter relationships. Few grammarians, however, properly distinguished between the sound system of the language and the spelling system, although the advent of the printing press led to intense efforts to standardize spelling.

The new interest in vernacular languages changed the position of Latin, which was no longer spoken, except in religious services. Latin came to be studied strictly as a literary and ecclesiastical language, with emphasis on the classical authors. Most of the Latin grammars (as well as the Greek) in use today are direct outgrowths of Medieval texts, which are based largely on Priscian. Such changes as the separation of the adjective and noun into distinct classes have been made since, but the essential philosophy of the study of Greek and Latin as classical, unchanging, literary media remains to this day.

Among the spoken languages that came to be studied was English. Some of the work of this period, such as W. Holder's *Elements of Speech* (1669) sounds remarkably modern in its description of the physiology of the speech mechanism. In the area of syntax English grammarians tended to begin with Priscian's eight parts of speech. Some, following the tradition of Aelfric, accepted these categories unquestioningly, as most Latin grammarians had accepted Greek grammar as a form for Latin. However, with the growth of empirical scientific studies generally, there came an increasing tendency to look closely at language and determine by observation whether preestablished rules were applicable.

Thus after the Renaissance, grammatical studies developed into something of a debate between the advocates of a single universal grammar and those of an empirical study of English (and every other language) as a separate entity. The ghosts of analogy-anomaly continued to walk.

Thus developed the discipline that we know today as "traditional grammar." Just as the Roman grammarians superimposed the rules of Greek upon Latin, so these rules were superimposed upon English, and many of today's grammar textbooks are the children of Priscian and Dionysus Thrax. This tradition came to us through a succession of eighteenth- and nineteenth-century grammarians.

Samuel Johnson, whose *Dictionary of the English Language* of 1755 was a combination of careful observation and prescriptive dogmatism, set the stage for many excellent lexicons that were developed to record the English language. In 1761, Joseph Priestley's *Rudiments of English Grammar* pointed out the ridiculousness of some of the customs and traditions of grammatical thought, many of these customs being with us to this day:

I own I am surprised to see so much of the distribution, and technical terms of the Latin grammar, retained in the grammar of our tongue; where they are exceedingly awkward and absolutely superfluous....[37]

we have no more business with a *future tense* in our language, than we have with the whole system of Latin moods and tenses; because we have no modification of our verbs to correspond to it; and if we had never heard of a future tense in some other language, we should no more have given a particular name to the combination of the verb with the auxiliary *shall* or *will*, than to those that are made with the auxiliaries do, have, can, must, or any other.[38]

Priestley's reference is to the fact that in English we have no verb inflection for the future tense, as we have a $\{D_1\}$ morpheme for the past tense. (See Chapter 5.)

On the subject of prescriptivism, Priestley says:

the custom of speaking is the original, and only just standard of any language.[39]

But the following year *A Short Introduction to English Grammar*, by Robert Lowth, said of language usage:

a faculty solely acquired by use, conducted by habit, and tried by the ear, carries us on without reflection; we meet with no rubs or difficulties in our way, or we do not perceive them; we find ourselves able to go on without rules, and we do not so much as suspect that we stand in need of them.[40]

Lowth further concludes that:

the Principal design of a Grammar of any language is to teach us to express ourselves with propriety in that language, and to be able to judge of every phrase and form of construction, whether it be right or not. The plain way of doing this is to lay down rules, and to illustrate them by examples.[41]

Among the popular textbooks of the period were Lindley Murray's *English Grammar Adapted to the Different Classes of Learners*, published in 1795 and his *English Exercises*, published in 1797. Like Lowth, Murray believed it was the duty of the

---

[37] Joseph Priestley, *Rudiments of English Grammar* (London: J. Johnson and F. and C. Rivington; G. G. and J. Robinson; J. Nichols, and W. Lowndes, 1798), p. iii. The edition I am quoting was published on the date given. It is the only edition I have seen.

[38] *Ibid.*, p. iv.

[39] *Ibid.*, p. v.

[40] Robert Lowth, *A Short Introduction to English Grammar* (London: Printed by J. Hughs for A. Miller and R. and J. Dodsley, 1762), p. vi.

[41] *Ibid.*, p. x.

grammarian to purify language by casting out all forms of incorrectness, and he based his grammatical system on that of Latin. And it is in the Latin tradition of Lowth and Murray, rather than on the observations of Priestley that many of our current text-books are based. But the grammatical journey from Latin to English is fraught with shoals, for English is not the direct descendant of Latin, but a Northern European language with a heavy infusion of Latin words, having a syntactic pattern distinctly its own.

Today, as we look back on the evolution of English grammar, one fact stands out: that the grammatical system of every major period was appropriate for and served the needs of its time. To the Greeks, with their emphasis on order, with their sensitivity to aesthetic quality, grammar represented a search for structure, for logic, and for the same dignified beauty that characterized Greek architecture and sculpture. With Greek curiosity regarding the nature of the universe, they examined lang   but with Greek emphasis on the capacity of the mind to solve all probl   y were more concerned with philosophizing about its nature than examining it in minute detail.

To the Romans, who were used to translating Greek culture into Latin forms, the transition came easily. But the Romans were great pragmatists, and anything worthy of attention served a useful need. What could grammar tell us about becoming a great orator, they wanted to know; how could language be used most effectively to plead a case in court or in the Senate?

In the Middle Ages, respect for authority, antiquity, and most of all theology dominated grammatical thought. If God was omnipresent, and if man was created in His image, does not the entire universe, including the family of languages, operate on a single standard, a single set of rules for all human utterances?

Since then we have seen a tremendous expansion and exploration of grammatical thinking, accompanying a knowledge explosion everywhere. A new tolerance for divergent ideas and a new interest in the universe of man prevailed in all phases of thought. But grammatical scholarship throughout the seventeenth and eighteenth centuries was firmly rooted in classical tradition, and a new school of thought would be required to do what Euclid did for geometry and Newton did for physics.

Today the New English is the twentieth century's answer to a system that has not progressed sufficiently beyond the Middle Ages. It is the Renaissance of language instruction, come a bit tardy upon the scene. It is appropriate for an age of exploration, an age of iconoclasm, an age of careful scientific observation. From the electron microscope to the two-hundred inch lens, the twentieth century is, above all, a time of meticulous examination of every facet of the universe. And with it has come a new breed of language students. Calling themselves "scientific linguists," they have looked at language with scholarly detachment. Although recent years have seen a tendency by some linguists toward a more philosophical approach and a return to the search for universal principles of language, compared to their classical ancestors, modern linguists are less closely related to the philosophers and aesthetes than they are to physicists and biologists.

The presence of linguistics in school curricula is still in an early stage. What its ultimate impact will be on the teaching of language can only be conjectured at the present time. But the movement is too widespread for the professional to ignore, and thus it behooves all teachers of language to examine it, consider it, and evaluate it. For it is a search for a method of describing language that conforms to the thinking of the twentieth century.

2

the challenge
a tradition falls

The modern era in the science of linguistics is frequently dated from 1786, with the speculations of the oriental languages scholar Sir William Jones, who focused attention on some interesting similarities between the ancient Sanskrit language of India and most of the languages of Europe. Jones demonstrated that these modern languages and Sanskrit could be traced back to a common ancestor. Although this had been previously noted by other scholars, Jones set off a wave of speculation that stimulated much interest in the nature of language.

Attention was directed not only to the historical relationships between languages but also to the entire tradition of linguistic studies that had been going on in India since about 1000 B.C. This tradition had much in common with European scholarship, but it also had some points of difference. European linguists, for example, had concentrated on the *word* as a linguistic unit; some Indian scholars were more concerned with the sentence as a whole. European scholars in general had taken an analytic approach, one concerned largely with the *structure* of language; Indian scholarship had delved deeply into *meaning*, or semantic implications. As early as 800–1000 B.C., Indian grammarians had also done highly advanced work in the physiology of speech sounds, describing them more precisely than anyone in Europe had done prior to the nineteenth century. The most famous of these Sanskrit manuscripts, the *Eight Books* of Pānini, is also the earliest of these extant works. Its date has been variously estimated from 300 to 600 B.C., and it is clearly the culmination of much that had gone before. From this ancient manuscript have come such modern linguistic devices as the zero morpheme, the purely theoretical form that is added to such words as *deer* to change from singular form *deer* to plural form (*deer* + ϕ) [zero plural]. See Chapter 5.

In 1867 William Whitney, an American linguist and Sanskrit scholar, published a series of his lectures entitled *Language and the Study of Language: Twelve Lectures on the Principles of Linguistic Science.* Although many of the ideas expressed by Whitney originated with other linguists, notably certain German scholars, Whitney's publications did much to popularize the more recent linguistic thinking. Many grammarians of Whitney's time concentrated on the written language, and placed special emphasis on the works of leading authors, with careful attention to developing the ideal of correct usage. Whitney wrote:

> The material and subject of linguistic science is language, in its entirety; all the accessible forms of human speech, in their infinite variety, whether still living in the minds and mouths of men, or preserved only in written documents, or carved on the scantier but more imperishable records of brass and stone. It has a field and scope limited to no age, and to no portion of mankind. The dialects of the obscurest and most humbly endowed races are its care, as well as those of the leaders of the world's history. Whenever and wherever a sound has dropped from the lips of a human being, to signalize to others the movements of his spirit, this science would fain take it up and study it, as having a character and office worthy of attentive examination. Every fact of every language, in the view of the linguistic student, calls for his investigation, since only in the light of all can any be completely understood.[1]

In the introduction to Whitney's volume, Reverend R. Morris exploded the myth that English is an inferior language, unworthy of scholarly devotion, because it lacks the extensive inflectional systems of Latin and Greek.[2]

This tendency to look down on English is not dissimilar to the position of many grammarians of the past toward the vernacular of their own time. According to Whitney, however, all phases of all languages are to be considered equally worthy of scholarly attention. Once the basic fact was recognized, Whitney tells us, that "no dialect, however rude and humble, is without worth, . . ." linguistic science progressed rapidly.[3]

Much of Whitney's volume discussed another concept often unrecognized by his predecessors: that language is in a constant state of change. Whitney saw language change take place through the addition of new words that would fit new conditions

---

[1] Quoted from a later publication of Whitney's work, *Language and Its Study* (London: Trubner and Company, 1876), p. 6.

[2] *Ibid.*, p. vii.

[3] *Ibid.*, p. 3.

and products, and through the inevitable alteration of words and phrases as they pass from one generation to another. He described these changes that tend to occur as having two motivations:

First is the tendency to make speech as easy and economical as possible, which results in a shortening or combining of forms, as in the development of silent letters that were once pronounced (knight, sword).[4] Also, we tend to rid the language of irregular forms. A child may say *foots* and *mouses*, *gooder* and *goodest*. An adult, inspired more by tradition than logic, may "correct" him. But even the adult world moves, albeit slowly, through the path of linguistic change. For example, witness the change away from the older *holpen* to *helped*, from *wrought* (obsolete, except in special uses) to *worked*.

Despite his forward-looking approach to grammar, in the area of usage, Whitney was in some respects a follower of tradition. For example, he referred to "bad English" and "best usage," and stated that language changes take place "among the speakers of English who do not take sufficient pains to speak correctly...." assuming that although all English forms are worthy of study, some are more correct than others.[5]

In 1892, Sara Lockwood adapted Whitney's *Essentials of English Grammar* into a text for use in secondary schools. By modern standards it would seem quite out of date, but it was one of the first linguistically oriented texts for this grade level. She stated that "Grammar does not make the laws for language. It merely states the facts in regard to the right use of language...."[6] Here a step forward had been taken, but her term *right use* indicates that the step was a small one. Lockwood's text abounds with such phrases as "people who use the language correctly"[7] and "people who are careless or ignorant about correct usage."[8] She stated, "The study of grammar is useful to us because it helps and hastens the process of learning to use good English, since it sets before us the rules of good usage, with illustrations and exercises." The text also defines good and bad English: "By 'good English' we mean such as is used by the *most careful* writers and speakers, the people of best education; and 'bad English' is simply such as is not approved and accepted by them."[9] Thus some assumptions are perpetuated that remain unquestioned by many people to this day. These assumptions are that there is a "right" and a "wrong" way to use language, that the language of people of prestige is better than that of the less educated or less affluent, and that

---

[4] *Ibid.*, p. 28.

[5] *Ibid.*

[6] Sara E. Lockwood, *An English Grammar*, Adapted from *Essentials of English Grammar*, by William Dwight Whitney (Boston: Ginn and Company, 1892), p. 6.

[7] *Ibid.*, p. 5.

[8] *Ibid.*, p. 6.

[9] *Ibid.*, p. 5.

teaching grammatical rules can change the way language is used. She also declared that grammar is valuable because it is useful in learning to speak a foreign language,[10] a claim that seems to have some validity, but is interesting, considering the many times it is claimed that the study of foreign language is valuable because it helps the student understand English grammar.

William Whitney was one of two great linguists of the late nineteenth century, but it was his British contemporary, Henry Sweet, who took a giant step toward the development of a scientific attitude. Sweet, whose grasp of phonology was so precise he could recognize one-hundred twenty different vowel sounds (an exceptional feat at that time), is generally considered to be the model for George Bernard Shaw's Henry Higgins in *Pygmalion* and the Broadway adaptation, *My Fair Lady*, by Lerner and Loewe. In his *New English Grammar* of 1892, Sweet stated:

We do not study grammar in order to get a practical mastery of our own language, because in the nature of things we must have that mastery before we begin to study grammar at all. Nor is grammar of much use in correcting vulgarisms, provincialisms, and other linguistic defects, for these are more dependent on social influence at home and at school than on grammatical training.[11]

Now this is rather strong stuff. After all the years of studying parts of speech to obtain a mastery of the language, along comes a professor of philology who claims that, on the contrary, mastery of language comes *first*, as a prerequisite to the study of grammar. The language we use, he tells us, is learned not by a process of analysis and synthesis of syntactic rules, but simply by *social influence*, by hearing, reading, speaking, and writing the language that surrounds us. But if each individual learns his language from those around him, and if language competence cannot be obtained by a study of form, how can any standard of correctness be established? How is one to distinguish good English from bad if he learns only by imitation and is not trained in school to improve his usage through study of grammar? Again I quote from Sweet:

In considering the use of grammar as a corrective of what are called 'ungrammatical' expressions, it must be borne in mind that the rules of grammar have no value except as statements of facts: whatever is in general use in a language is for that very reason grammatically correct.[12]

This is probably the most important difference between traditional and linguistic grammars. Traditional grammar tends to be *prescriptive*. It *prescribes* which form of

[10] *Ibid.*, p. 7.
[11] Henry Sweet, *A New English Grammar* (Oxford: At the Clarendon Press, 1892), p. 4.
[12] *Ibid.*, p. 5.

the verb is to be used with a plural subject and when to use *sit* and *set*. *Descriptive grammar*, as Henry Sweet defined it, has as its object "to observe the facts and phenomena with which it has to deal, and to classify and state them methodically."[13] The linguist, then, is similar to the chemist who observes the elements of the universe, classifies them, gives names and symbols to each, and notes their properties. The chemist does not try to make value judgments about whether oxygen is a better substance than helium. Like the chemist, the linguist observes phenomena (in this instance language) but does not sit in judgment on what he observes.

A linguist can, however, make certain observations. Just as a chemist can legitimately observe that oxygen is inflammable and helium is not, so may the linguist observe that certain *forms* are characteristic of certain language communities. He may note that *lie down* is more likely to be used in formal, written English; and that *lay down* may predominate in informal conversation. He observes and records these phenomena, as a botanist observes and records the families of the plant kingdom and leaves it to the horticulturist, the florist, the forester, and the farmer to decide which plants are most valuable for which purposes.

Of course, with his expertise in language, the linguist, as any scientist, is frequently *called upon* to make judgments. But these judgments do not concern superior or inferior qualities of various language forms. They refer to how the data revealed by the study of language can be used.

Education is an excellent example. Linguists have written textbooks on the teaching of reading and spelling. They have attacked practices in grammar and foreign language instruction. They are frequently consulted in curriculum planning and textbook writing. But this is *applied linguistics*. Practical applications of any scientific findings are a natural outgrowth of theoretical research. Such work should not be confused with that of the grammarian who decided that henceforth we are to adopt certain rules for using *shall* and *will*.

Henry Sweet defined a number of areas of study for the linguist: Once we have a clear statement of *what* a particular linguistic phenomenon is, we may want to investigate *why* it is that way. The study of the explanation for language he calls *explanatory grammar*, and divides this area into three phases:

1. *Historical grammar*: Tracing language back to its origins in other languages.
2. *Comparative grammar*: Comparing phenomena of one language with those of related languages.
3. *General grammar*: The study of general principles of language, not necessarily of a single language.[14]

[13] *Ibid.*, p. 1.
[14] *Ibid.*, p. 2.

(Today most linguists prefer to study each language separately to find those characteristics that are applicable to the particular language under study.)

In his grammar text, Sweet deals with grammatical definitions, parts of speech, word group and sentence construction, the changes that take place in language, history of the English language, and phonology, and in a second volume, published in 1898, syntax. His parts of speech are defined three different ways—by form, function, and meaning. For example, he defines nouns:

1. *Form*: Nouns are inflected for number (singular and plural) and case.[15] Possessive ('s or s') is the only case remaining in English nouns. (Nevertheless, he runs through all the Latin cases, simply mentioning that the English noun does not change.)
2. *Meaning*: Nouns "express substances."[16] Here he lists the various subdivisions of nouns, such as common and proper, individual and collective, concrete and abstract.
3. *Function*: Nouns serve as "head-words."[17] They are, in other words, the core of an expression, complete with modifiers and other related words, which some later grammarians have come to call "noun phrases."

Note that he is still classifying parts of speech by the three systems of form, function, and meaning, as did Priscian fifteen hundred years earlier, but Sweet has sorted out the three methods, separated them, and shown that there is more than one way to define grammatical terms. His other parts of speech are adjectives, pronouns, verbs, numerals, verbals, adverbs, prepositions, conjunctions, and interjections.[18]

Linguistic thinking in the nineteenth century had centered largely around historical and comparative studies, as linguists began to piece together a picture of the evolution of languages—tracing, comparing, and classifying them into families. The results of these studies are discussed in Chapter 8 of this volume.

Early in the twentieth century a number of American linguists directed the movement more toward descriptive analysis. Edward Sapir discussed the intimate and subtle relationships between a native tongue and the culture in which it develops, pointing out that everything from geography to economics will influence language.[19] Leonard Bloomfield was less interested in cultural influences than in a detailed, objective study of language itself. In 1933 Bloomfield's *Language* codified English so comprehensively that it ushered in what is frequently referred to as the Bloomfieldian Era. Bloomfield based his presentation on the system of phonemes and morphemes

---

[15] *Ibid.*, p. 49.
[16] *Ibid.*, p. 54.
[17] *Ibid.*, p. 62.
[18] *Ibid.*, pp. 65–153.
[19] Edward Sapir, *Language* (London: Oxford University Press, 1921). Especially Chaps. I and X.

that comprise the component parts of language as well as the manner in which these components form sentences. Chapters 4, 5, and 6 of this book discuss Bloomfieldian linguistics as modified by his successors in the field.

STRUCTURAL LINGUISTICS

But it remained for Charles Carpenter Fries to change the face of English teaching in America. In 1940 his landmark study, *American English Grammar* appeared. Commissioned by the National Council of Teachers of English to recommend what course language instruction should take, Fries made an intensive grammatical analysis of three thousand letters written by Americans from all walks of life, who did not know that their writing would be studied grammatically. He wanted to find out first the actual characteristics of American English and second in what ways the writing of educated Americans differs from that of the uneducated.

Fries divided his contributors into three groups.[20] "Vulgar" English was from writers with: (1) no more than an eighth grade education, (2) manual and unskilled occupations, and (3) a writing style that included "spelling, capitalization, and punctuation which clearly demonstrated that the writer was not accustomed to writing at all, that he was semi-literate."[21] "Standard" English was written by college graduates in the high levels of professional life whose writing met the usual formal standards. There was also a "common" group in the middle.

Fries' conclusions were startling. He found that our precepts of "correct" and "incorrect" usage do not really describe the differences between how educated and uneducated Americans use their language. And if the users of standard English consist of "college professors, physicians, lawyers, judges, clergymen, commissioned officers of the United States Army above the rank of lieutenant, and, from cities of more than 25,000 inhabitants, the superintendents of schools and the editors of newspapers,"[22] how can schoolteachers claim that the English of these successful people is incorrect? And if their English does not differ markedly on certain points from that of unskilled manual laborers with less than nine years of schooling, perhaps we had better accept the realities of common usage.

For example, he found that both groups use *everybody* and *everyone* as well as *none* with a plural verb. Both groups use the indicative case with non-fact clauses (*if I was*

---

[20] Charles Carpenter Fries, *American English Grammar* (New York: D. Appleton-Century Company, 1940), p. 29.

[21] *Ibid.*, p. 30.

[22] *Ibid.*

you...)[23] and the rules for *shall* and *will*[24] and *It is I*,[25] as traditionally given in the texts, simply do not describe the usage of either group. Fries concluded that there were only minor differences in the formal characteristics of the English of the two groups, but that the real difference between the writing of educated and uneducated English speakers resided in the *poverty* of language of the uneducated. Both in vocabulary and in variety of form, the educated group showed far greater familiarity with the many possibilities available to the skilled user of language.[26]

Fries suggested that English programs stop trying to *alter* language habits and simply *observe* them, in other words to stop trying to do the impossible.[27] If, instead of concentrating on correcting errors, the English teacher helped his students to develop *sensitivity*[28] to the power of language and a knowledge of the great variety of form and vocabulary available, far more may be accomplished. For we have no evidence that learning grammar increases skill in language. On the contrary, Fries asserted, *it may very well be that the continued concentration on errors may eventually dull the very sensitivity to language that our program should be designed to develop.*[29] Furthermore, he suggested that we stop using literary language to teach school-children and concentrate on the standard but *informal* usage that characterizes the everyday speech and writing of sensitive, educated men and women.[30]

Twelve years later, in *The Structure of English*, Fries compared the language of great literature to a hothouse flower. It may be very beautiful, but just as a botanist would not think of confining his study of the plant kingdom to hothouse flowers, so the linguist is interested in all phases of language.[31] And Fries found the everyday conversations of ordinary men and women infinitely more interesting than the polished works of the masters.

The Structure of English was based upon recorded conversations, and attempted to find in everyday utterances some structure upon which the English language is based. Published in 1952, this volume was instrumental in bringing to the attention of many teachers of grammar some of the basic concepts of Bloomfieldian linguistics. His pattern for organizing language phenomena has come to be known as *structural linguistics.*

[23] *Ibid.*, p. 287.
[24] *Ibid.*, p. 154.
[25] *Ibid.*, p. 287.
[26] *Ibid.*, p. 288.
[27] *Ibid.*, p. 289.
[28] *Ibid.*, p. 285.
[29] *Ibid.*, p. 286.
[30] *Ibid.*, p. 289.
[31] Charles Carpenter Fries, *The Structure of English* (New York: Harcourt, Brace, and World, Inc., 1952), p. 4.

To begin with, Fries challenged again the assumption that *meaning* is a valid tool of analysis.[32] He used nonsense words to illustrate his point:

Woggles ugged diggles[33]

Here is an utterance that is composed of three nonwords. It has absolutely no meaning, but any native speaker of English, looking at this utterance and assuming it follows the usual patterns of the English language, can tell that the words *woggles* and *diggles* are nouns, and *ugged* is a verb. Yet it would be impossible to define any of these words or tell what the sentence means. Therefore, an attempt to define the term *noun* according to meaning is futile. We can, on the other hand, describe a noun as a word that occupies a certain place in a model sentence and state that any other word that can be put in its place is a noun. We can say, for example, that a noun is a word that can be substituted for *concert* in the utterance:

The concert was good.

The food was good.
The coffee was good.
The taste was good.
The container was good.
The difference was good.
The privacy was good.
The family was good.
The company was good.[34]

Thus, the structure of utterances becomes the key to analysis of language. A sentence no longer is defined as having a subject and predicate, but, as a practical, working definition he suggests, "A sentence is a word or group of words standing between an initial capital letter and a mark of end punctuation or between two marks of end punctuation."[35] What a reversal! No longer is it the end of a sentence that motivates the punctuation, but the existence of the punctuation that describes the content as a sentence. Later in his volume, Fries restructures his concept of the sentence by paraphrasing an earlier definition by Leonard Bloomfield:

Each sentence is an independent linguistic form, not included by virtue of any grammatical construction in any larger linguistic form.[36]

For example, observe the utterance:

The little brown dog ran up the hill.

---

[32] *Ibid.*, p. 7.
[33] *Ibid.*, p. 71.
[34] *Ibid.*, p. 76.
[35] *Ibid.*, p. 9.
[36] *Ibid.*, p. 21.

The little brown dog is not a sentence because it is part of a "larger form." Neither are *up the hill, brown dog,* nor any other *part* of the utterance. But the complete utterance is a sentence, as it is not part of any longer form.

Even this is subject to interpretation. *Structurally* it is true that a sentence is not part of a larger form, for most of our common pronouncements about the "structure" of a paragraph—or of other literary forms—break down under an examination of an assortment of these forms. But *semantically*, a sentence, particularly a written sentence, is frequently part of a larger form—a paragraph, story, essay, drama, or poem.

Fries' emphasis on the structure of the language brought out one very important point. As mentioned previously, grammatical tradition in English developed from Latin, which was an outgrowth of Greek. But Latin is an inflected language, in which changes in *word endings* constitute much of the grammar, whereas in English such devices as prepositional phrases and auxiliaries are used to indicate mood and tense. Therefore, the old "parts of speech" grammar is not well suited to the needs of English. English is best described by a grammar based on *word order*—on the position of the word in the utterance. In order to achieve this new point of view, Fries literally threw out most of our traditional grammar and started over.

In his zeal to find a new method of describing the English language, Fries eliminated much of our conventional terminology. His grammar consists largely of a series of "test frames," or pattern sentences illustrating the various constructions into which words of the English language can fit. Instead of the usual eight parts of speech, he divided most English words into four *Classes*. Words of Class I, Class II, Class III, and Class IV relate roughly, but not exactly, to the traditional noun, verb, adjective, and adverb. Those few words that do not fall into one of these classes were put into fifteen *Function Groups*, designated A to O.[37]

Fries also dealt with intonation patterns (pitch and stress), formal characteristics of words (inflections), and the relationships between utterances in a dialogue— relationships by which one human being elicits a response from another. He was also concerned with the English sentence—its structural patterns and how these patterns can be analyzed and systematized.

CHOMSKY AND TRANSFORMATIONS

The story of the development of linguistics cannot be told without one more episode. In 1957 a new theory of analysis appeared that was destined to have as

---

[37] This system is examined in more detail in Chapter 6.

profound an effect on linguistic thinking as the structuralism of Charles Fries. The book was *Syntactic Structures*, and the author was Noam Chomsky. It was Chomsky's theory that it is not sufficient to investigate sentences as static, isolated bits of linguistic phenomena. The structures of the sentences of a language bear certain *relationships* to each other, and these relationships interested him. By what process, he asked, is a sentence changed from active to passive voice, from simple to compound, from singular to plural, from present to future?

Variety of language structure is obtained by *transforming* certain elements of the sentence—by interchanging, adding, or deleting linguistic forms; by reversing word order; or by combining two or more structures into one. Thus, beginning with a simple declarative sentence one can *generate* an infinite variety of new sentences. This theory is known as *transformational grammar*, or *generative grammar*.

According to transformational-generative theory, one can begin with a kernel sentence:

> *Porcupines were pushing peanuts in the parlor.*

By means of syntactic rules (See Chapter 7.), this sentence can be transformed to:

Negative:	*Porcupines were not pushing peanuts in the parlor.*
Echo:	*Porcupines were pushing peanuts in the parlor?*
Yes/No:	*Were porcupines pushing peanuts in the parlor?*
Tag:	*Porcupines were pushing peanuts in the parlor, weren't they?*
Who:	*Who were pushing peanuts in the parlor?*
Where:	*Where were porcupines pushing peanuts?*
What:	*What were porcupines pushing in the parlor?*
How:	*How were porcupines pushing peanuts in the parlor?*
When:	*When were porcupines pushing peanuts in the parlor?*
Do:	*Do porcupines push peanuts in the parlor?*
Passive:	*Peanuts were being pushed (by porcupines) in the parlor.*

Simple sentences can also be combined with other sentences:

Compound:	*Peter pushes peanuts, and porcupines push Peter.*
Possessive:	*Peter's porcupines push peanuts.*

This list could continue until a great variety of sentences are generated. If all possible variations of all kernel sentences are accounted for, a complete grammar of the language is obtained.

No further comment will be made concerning transformations at this time, partly because the structures of Noam Chomsky are too complex for this brief introduction, and partly because all of Chapter 7 is devoted to transformational theory. Just as structural grammar changed the direction of linguistic thinking in America during the 1950's, so in the 1960's the transformations of generative grammar have been the basis for much of our work in linguistics.

SUMMARY OF DIFFERENCES BETWEEN TRADITIONAL AND LINGUISTIC APPROACHES

Linguistics is still in a formative stage. New discoveries, new approaches, and new systems are constantly emerging. Terminology has not been standardized, and linguists do not always agree among themselves. Yet linguistics has developed sufficiently to present a few major characteristics that distinguish this new movement from most of the established tradition.

Traditional	Linguistic
Based on reason, authority, philosophy	Based on careful observation of language data
Concerned with written language, especially great works of literature	Concerned with all phases of language: spoken, written, recorded in any form. Often emphasis on spoken
Until recently, considered the language of the vernacular inferior. Especially disparaged English because it had few inflections	Considers the language of all communities of equal value
Attempts to "fix" language into one, un-changing form	Views language as a constantly changing phenomenon
Has as its purpose the eradication of errors in usage (prescriptive approach)	Investigates language as it is actually used (descriptive approach)
Syntax based on Latin-Greek inflection system	Syntax based on English word-order system
Uses form, function, and meaning indiscrimin-ately in defining terminology	Separates form, function, and meaning into different systems, tends to favor form and function over meaning

LINGUISTICS AND THE SCHOOL

Meanwhile, back in the classroom, teachers and students continued to busy them-selves with ferreting out split infinitives and dangling prepositions. For years English courses in the public schools and colleges were hardly touched by the linguistics movement. It was as if the physics teachers continued to teach that the Earth is the center of all things, and that the sun, moon and stars revolve around it. For the linguists of whom we have spoken were not school teachers. They were professors in leading universities who were prominent in the field of linguistic knowledge and discovery. They were interested in linguistics *per se*, and were usually no more concerned with classroom applications of their discipline than a medical researcher would be concerned with a course in high school biology. Charles Fries summed up this attitude:

> As a scientist the linguist is searching for pure knowledge. To know the facts and to understand the language processes are to him ends in themselves. He usually leaves to others the business of applying practically the knowledge he has won.[38]

Despite this statement, his book contains a chapter on "practical application," but concludes that the most important value of linguistics lies not in any use to which it can be put, but in the broadening it bestows upon the individual who gains insight into the nature of his language.[39]

But in recent years, and particularly since the Woods Hole Conference, there has been an increasing tendency to call into the educational scene scholars on the forefront of knowledge to update and upgrade our elementary and secondary school offerings to bring them more into line with the knowledge explosion.[40] The "new" science programs are the direct result of this effort, and the new mathematics curricula are closely related. Thus far in America linguistics has had a more far-reaching effect on the teaching of foreign language, with its current emphasis on the spoken word, than it has had on the teaching of English.

But the new classroom grammar has arrived, and its impact on education may be even more far-reaching than the new curricula in science and math, for it carries with it implications that affect our attitudes toward the most universal and basic of all human activity—language.

For many years the lack of suitable textbooks effectively kept linguistics out of the classroom. The writings of the linguists were far too complex and abstruse for use in the public schools. Textbooks were too concerned with differences between subordinating and coordinating conjunctions to bother with form classes and transformations. The Project English Centers at the University of Nebraska and the University of Oregon, pioneers in the field of teaching linguistics in the public schools, had to develop and print their own material.

[38] Fries, *The Structure of English*, p. 4.

[39] *Ibid.*, p. 296.

[40] Thirty-five scientists and educators were called together in September 1959 to discuss improvement of science education programs in the schools. Under the auspices of the National Academy of Science, this conference was one of the most influential of a number of efforts to upgrade the teaching of mathematics and science.

In 1959, however, James Sledd's *A Short Introduction to English Grammar* appeared for use in college freshman English. It was not the first of its kind, for three years earlier Harold Whitehall had published *Structural Essentials of English*,[41] and Donald Lloyd and Harry Warfel had brought out their *American English in Its Cultural Setting*.[42] Sledd took a descriptive approach, stating in his introduction: "Unfortunately there is no substantial body of experimental evidence that a conscious, organized knowledge of the structure of English makes students speak better or write better."[43] Syntax, then, is to be studied as an aspect of human culture, not as an aid to better usage. Sledd also made the point that the science of linguistics is still in its early period of discovery, and that "current linguistic doctrines, like the traditional pronouncements, are treated as hypotheses to be tested, not as ultimate truths."[44]

The syntax of Sledd is based mainly on that of Fries,[45] and his phonology is based on George Trager and Henry Smith's *An Outline of English Structure*.[46] Sledd takes something of a middle ground in using traditional terminology of *subject* and *predicate*, *simple* and *compound sentences*, *independent* and *dependent clauses*, and many conventional parts of speech to explain the phenomena of structural linguistics. He also emphasizes phonology, including intonation, stress, transition, and the mechanics of voice production.

Until recently, publishers had been slow in presenting scientific concepts of syntax in school texts because so many teachers were dedicated to the traditional grammar. Teachers were reluctant to offer, or even learn, the new grammars until textbooks were available.

In recent years, however, many linguistically-oriented English textbooks have been published covering every grade level from primary through university. Some are actually traditional grammar texts with a little of the "new" terminology or methodology added to give the illusion of being up-to-date. Others are truly based on the work of Bloomfield, Fries, and Chomsky. A selected list of school textbooks in linguistics is included in the bibliography at the end of this volume.

One of the popularizers of Fries and Chomsky was Paul Roberts. His early books, intended for use in secondary schools, were quite complex, and their effectiveness in

[41] Harold Whitehall, *Structural Essentials of English* (New York: Harcourt, Brace and World, Inc., 1956).

[42] Donald J. Lloyd and Harry R. Warfel, *American English in Its Cultural Setting* (New York: Alfred Knopf, Inc., 1956).

[43] James Sledd, *A Short Introduction to English Grammar* (Chicago: Scott, Foresman and Company, 1959), p. 6.

[44] *Ibid.*, p. 11.

[45] *Ibid.*, p. 8.

[46] George Trager and Henry Smith, *An Outline of English Structure*, Studies in Linguistics: Occasional Papers, 3 (Norman, Oklahoma: Battenburg Press, 1951).

the classroom was dependent on the teacher's skill in presenting and explaining.[47] But his 1966–67 series, composed of six books for use in grades three to eight, plus a "complete course" in one volume presents, in carefully sequenced programs, a series of textbooks designed to cover the language arts.[48] The Roberts system is a combination of the old and the new. Traditional and linguistic terminology are blended, and the lessons contain an element of prescription, which is intended to develop language competence. Although literature and composition are included, the emphasis of Roberts' system is on a systematic, descriptive approach to structural and transformational grammars. A student progressing through this series should come out with a fairly good grasp of the essentials of phonology, morphology, historical linguistics, and syntax. Roberts' major thrust, however, is a system of generative-transformational grammar based on Noam Chomsky.

Today other writers and other publishers are showing an increasing interest in linguistics in the public schools. The Postman Series, with less emphasis on learning linguistic data and more on an inquiry approach to the *methodology* of linguists, is also available.[49] Many of the more traditionally oriented secondary textbooks either contain a separate section on linguistics, stating that there is more than one grammatical system in English,[50] or use some of the findings of the linguists in the body of the texts.

What the future will be is still difficult to predict. Some teachers have already launched full-scale campaigns, from phonology to transformations. Others are still tracking down errors in *shall* and *will.* With still others, the rules of phrase structure have become a sort of academic status symbol, pursued with the same blind devotion once lavished on *It is I.*

Today's English teacher stands at the crossroads. The tradition, born of the greatest minds of the classical age, is being challenged. The choice is clear : tradition or science? Linguists will undoubtedly continue their scholarly analysis of language while the Don Quixotes of the classroom joust at the dastardly double negative.

Yet even the new grammar is undergoing its difficulties. In challenging the old assumptions, linguists have opened up a Pandora's box of new problems. After criticizing the tradition for being inconsistent, overly complex, and useless, linguists, as we shall presently see, have had difficulty standardizing their terminology, simplifying

---

[47] See Paul Roberts, *Patterns of English*, 1956; *English Sentences*, 1962; *English Syntax*, 1964 (New York : Harcourt, Brace and World, Inc.).

[48] This series is now extended downward to the first grade.

[49] Neil Postman, Harold Morine, Greta Morine, and Howard C. Damon, *The Postman English Series* (New York : Holt, Rinehart and Winston, Inc., 1963, 1965, 1966, 1967). Six volumes grades 7–12.

[50] See Thomas Clark Pollack *et al.*, *The Macmillan English Series* (New York : The Macmillan Company, 1961, 1964, 1967).

their discipline to a level realistic for school use, and demonstrating that learning the new grammar will help the schoolchild improve his reading or composition.

The selection of subject matter for English is therefore far from clear-cut. Much of this dilemma stems from the origin of the teaching of grammar. Rather than developing in response to a real educational need, grammar teaching grew out of ancient philosophical discussions, then calcified in the textbooks until it was challenged in recent years. Now, with the tools of modern language investigations available for the first time, a serious reappraisal of the role of language instruction is being undertaken.

The vital question of what to include in a school language program is unanswered at this point. Ultimately, the final decision must rest with the teaching profession. In the following chapters, let us look at some of the possibilities.

3

an overview
let's be linguists

LANGUAGE AND THE UNIVERSE OF MAN

Language is man's principal link with man, and *linguistics* is the study of language. This chapter provides a quick survey of those studies that make up linguistic science. Therefore, let us temporarily assume the role of linguists and look at the many ways we could go about the study of our discipline. The first thing that we observe is that from early speculations about the similarity of certain English and Sanskrit words, linguistics has developed into a full-blown academic discipline, with many specialized areas, important contributions to education, and data capable of filling a substantial library. It has, in other words, taken its place in the gallery of modern sciences.

Today our fellow linguists are everywhere. Few university departments of anthropology do not include linguistics in their course of study. English departments of public schools as well as universities are looking to linguists for help in the teaching of reading, spelling, composition, and literature, as well as grammar. Linguistic contributions to the teaching of foreign language, with current emphasis on conversation, have been tremendous. Businesses, missionary and scientific expeditions, and many other activities that involve lands where little-known languages are spoken have employed linguists or used knowledge gained from linguistic study to help establish communication. Wherever language is spoken, written, or dug up among the ruins of ancient civilizations, we find material for study. Linguistic implications exist in so many other academic disciplines that it is now difficult to tell where linguistics leaves off and psychology, philosophy, speech pathology, educational methodology, history, and many other studies begin.

There is, of course, nothing unusual about this. Most modern sciences are multi-faceted and overlapping. Chemistry, physics, mathematics, astronomy, geology, meteorology, and others are interwoven to the point where there are no clearly marked boundaries, and competent scientists must dip into many disciplines to function in their own.

The complexity of linguistic science, therefore, is in no way unique, and beginners should no more be deterred from taking elementary courses by the enormity of the field than beginners in astronomy should become discouraged by the impossibility of learning the name of every heavenly body.

A brief overview of the many areas that we, as linguists, can investigate is contained in Figure 3-1. In the center of this chart is the word MAN, indicating that man is the center of things. Whether this is true in the ancient theological sense is not our concern; what the chart indicates is that *man should be the center of his own institutions.* That is, whatever man builds should work ultimately for his benefit. Unfortunately, many of us can become so intrigued with an idea, a custom, a project, or a commitment, that, like the British soldiers in *The Bridge on the River Kwai*, we frequently fail to look at the ultimate effect of our activities.

The basic assumption of this volume is that schools must exist for the benefit of the students. At first glance, this would seem axiomatic, but even a brief survey of many of our institutions indicates that we do not always build with our own welfare in mind. Cities, for example, seem better adapted to the needs of the motor car than to the needs of the people living there. Political systems are perpetuated out of loyalty long after their service to humanity is questionable. And many of the institutions that were developed to serve a human need have ultimately served an idea, a special interest, or simple administrative convenience.

In some ways the school has served society well; in others it has fallen into this trap. Chapter 1 discussed how teachers of grammar became intrigued with a tradition, failing to ask the question—what good is this to our students?

The New English, then, must be viewed from the point of view of the student. Does it make a contribution to the student's grasp of the fundamental skills, help him understand himself and his relationship with the larger group, earn his paycheck, enjoy life more fully, or be a more responsible citizen? Or does it merely exchange new traditions for old? Language teachers have frequently assumed that by helping the student to understand the structure of language, grammar instruction provides one of the basic tools. As we investigate the linguistics movement, let us measure it against this standard to see if the claim is valid.

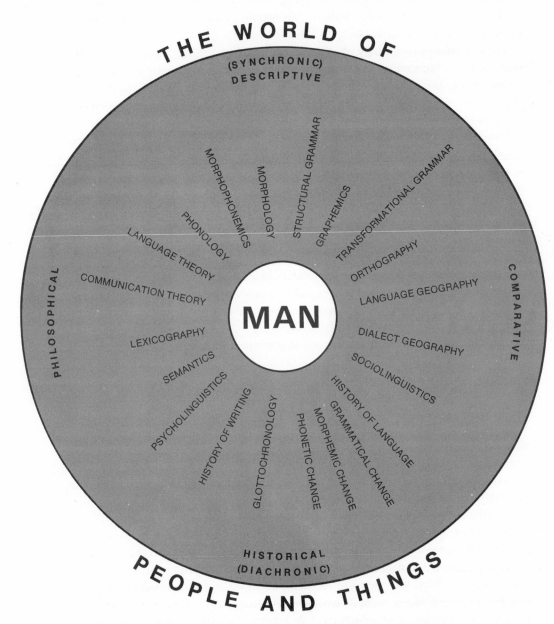

THE WORLD OF

(SYNCHRONIC) DESCRIPTIVE

MORPHOPHONEMICS

MORPHOLOGY

STRUCTURAL GRAMMAR

GRAPHEMICS

TRANSFORMATIONAL GRAMMAR

PHONOLOGY

LANGUAGE THEORY

ORTHOGRAPHY

PHILOSOPHICAL

COMMUNICATION THEORY

LANGUAGE GEOGRAPHY

COMPARATIVE

MAN

LEXICOGRAPHY

DIALECT GEOGRAPHY

SEMANTICS

SOCIOLINGUISTICS

PSYCHOLINGUISTICS

HISTORY OF WRITING

HISTORY OF LANGUAGE

GLOTTOCHRONOLOGY

GRAMMATICAL CHANGE

PHONETIC CHANGE

MORPHEMIC CHANGE

HISTORICAL (DIACHRONIC)

PEOPLE AND THINGS

Figure 3-1. LANGUAGE: MAN'S LINK WITH MAN

Returning to Figure 3-1, we find that the inscription around the outside reads: THE WORLD OF PEOPLE AND THINGS. Man is surrounded by his environment, but to reach his environment, to function with it, he needs language. Language forms a series of bridges that man must cross in order to meet his destiny in the world around him. He cannot dig the minerals from the earth, grow his daily food, or build houses, stores, or factories without some system of communication with his fellow man.

This is not to imply that language is the only necessary medium. Science, mathematics, social science, art, and many other endeavors also play a vital function, but language is a prerequisite for most organized human activity.

Because language is one of the most complex of man's activities, linguistics must necessarily be complex and multifaceted. Arranged on the chart like spokes of a wheel, forming a series of paths on which man can reach the world of people and things, are the many areas of study that we as linguists can investigate.

The names of the studies depicted on the chart are by no means definitive. Each of these categories overlaps some of the subject matter of other categories. Even the names of the branches of study are by no means standardized. What some call *semantics* others insist must be designated *general semantics*, and *psycholinguistics* and *communication theory* are also concerned with much of the same subject matter.

But this lack of clear definition of areas should be no obstacle. In this fast-changing society the distinguishing characteristic of the New English Teacher is his ability to operate comfortably and effectively without the artificialities of rigid rules, unchanging values, and neat little categories. These, he realizes, exist only in the mind of the individual. The New English Teacher can operate in a fluid, dynamic, and free-flowing system.

As linguists, we find that we can take certain approaches to the study of language. First, there is the *synchronic* approach, in which language is viewed as it exists at some particular point in time without reference to the changes that are part of the development of any language. *Descriptive linguistics*, to which Section Two of this volume will be devoted, is essentially a synchronic view of language study, examining linguistic data with little reference to what came before or what exists elsewhere.

Languages, however, do not develop in isolation. English, like most languages, has a long history, evolving slowly out of older protolanguages. It also contains a complex family of related languages spoken in many parts of the world. Therefore, linguists can also take a *diachronic* approach, viewing language from a historical perspective and concerning itself with how linguistic phenomena developed from earlier forms. Included in this area, also known as *historical linguistics*, would be the origin and development of the sound structure of a language, of individual words, of the grammatical relationships between words, of the written system, and all other data pertaining to language. In other words, any phase of linguistics that can be studied descriptively can also be studied historically.

A third approach to language study, the *comparative*, could be taken, in which we would investigate how the sound system of English compares with that of Spanish, how the grammatical system of Chinese is similar to or different from Sanskrit, or how Hebrew writing compares with Greek. Comparative linguists are also interested in variations within a language, in comparing the English of a Yorkshireman with that of a Welshman, or noting that a *drug store* in America is a *chemist's shop* in England, that cowboys of the Southwest have a *row-DAY-oh* and then go East for a *ROAD-ee-oh*.

Finally, we become aware of a fourth approach to the study of language, one that does not fit any of the categories mentioned previously. For want of a commonly accepted term, I shall call this the *philosophical* approach, in which we are more concerned with the *meaning* of language than with its structure. Such studies are more subjective and difficult to reduce to charts, graphs, and formulas. Consequently, most of the philosophical areas are not as advanced or as well recognized in academic circles as the other three. Yet to leave meaning out of linguistic study is to leave the reason for its existence out of language.

Let us now turn to the individual studies depicted on the chart. We shall describe each one briefly in this chapter, and then in succeeding chapters investigate more thoroughly those that are commonly dealt with in the new school textbooks. We could begin anywhere around the "wheel" we have created, but inasmuch as the following chapter has to do with phonology, let us begin there.

DESCRIPTIVE LINGUISTICS

Phonology is the study of the sound system of language. As phoneticians we listen to speech and break it into its constituent sounds, discovering that the sound represented by *f* in *focus* is similar to that represented by *ph* in *phony*, but not identical to the *f* in *surface*. We discover that at one time the word *wind* rhymed with *find*, whereas today it rhymes with *sinned*. We also find that the letter *r* in *here* is pronounced quite differently in Connecticut, in Texas, and in Illinois, and that even in any single locality different people have diverse speech patterns.

Notice the three approaches to linguistics given in the examples. In studying the nature of the *f* sound and noting its variation from one word to another, we are taking a descriptive approach. In tracing the changes that have taken place in the pronunciation of *wind*, we are studying linguistics from a historical point of view. Finally, by contrasting the ways in which the letter *r* is pronounced in different localities, we are making a comparative study. Phonology is studied in more detail in the next chapter. With morphology and grammar, phonology is placed at the descriptive end of the chart because it is generally considered as part of descriptive linguistics, but it should be understood that most of these categories could be shifted to any part of the chart, depending upon the approach taken.

Let us temporarily skip morphophonemics and look at *morphology*. As morphologists we are interested in the particles of meaning, or *morphemes*, that are put together in various combinations to form words. The closest thing to morphology in the traditional English textbooks is the "prefixes, suffixes, and roots" approach to word analysis. But, as Chapter 5 reveals, linguists have refined word analysis to the point of finding the *morphological structure* of the language and comparing the units of meaning (morphemes) of our language with similar forms in other languages.

Some linguists have even classified languages according to the way in which morphemes are put together to form words. *Agglutinative* languages are those that have a tendency to combine long strings of morphemes into a single word. In Swahili, for example, a word that sounds something like *atanipenda* means *he will like me*, but a change to *atakupenda* makes it *he will like you*. Gleason gives us an interesting illustration of how speakers of this East African language put together strings of morphemes to form words. A few examples from his chart are reproduced as follows:

Swahili	English
atanipenda	*he will like me*
atakupenda	*he will like you*
atampenda	*he will like him*
atatupenda	*he will like us*
atawapenda	*he will like them*
nitakupenda	*I will like you*
nitampenda	*I will like him*
utampenda	*you will like him*
tutampenda	*we will like him*
watampenda	*they will like him*
atakusumbua	*he will annoy you*[1]

Isolating languages, such as English, tend to use shorter words. A speaker of English may require a phrase or even a complete sentence to say what a speaker of Swahili may say in a word. Isolating languages depend more on word order to achieve meaning. *Polysynthetic* languages are similar to agglutinative, only more so. Robert Hall cites a classic example of a word from a polysynthetic Eskimo language that means *I am looking for something suitable for a fish line.*[2] *Inflectional* languages, such

---

[1] Henry Allen Gleason, Jr., *Workbook in Descriptive Linguistics* (New York: Holt, Rinehart and Winston, Inc., 1966), p. 26.

[2] Robert A. Hall, *Introductory Linguistics* (Philadelphia: Chilton Company, 1964), p. 148.

as Latin, have an elaborate system of word endings for nouns, verbs, and certain other parts of speech. These endings indicate such things as tense, number, gender, and case.

Today this method of classifying languages is not popular, as such classifications are too vague. Most languages have some characteristics of all these types, and arbitrary classification into a category fails to adequately describe languages.

Those who use the term *morphophonemics* refer to the relationships between the sound structure and the word structure of the language. Because of the irregularity of English, this can be an important area to consider, and because both morphology and phonology are involved, some linguists feel the need for a term to describe this study. An example of one type of morphophonemic relationship is in the sentences:

> *A tiger is dancing on the table.*
> *An elephant is dancing on the table.*

In these sentences the initial sounds (phonemes) of *tiger* and *elephant* determine which variation of *a ~ an* (morpheme) will be used. The usual practice in English is to have words beginning with a consonant sound preceded by *a* and words beginning with a vowel sound preceded by *an*. Thus the sound pattern of one word governs the morphemic structure of the preceding word. Morphophonemics is discussed more fully in the next two chapters.

Morphology is concerned with the structure of the word, but *syntax* deals with how words are put together to form meaningful phrases, clauses, and sentences. *Grammar* is sometimes used synonymously with *syntax*, sometimes as an over-all term for phonology, morphology, and syntax. *Structural grammar* is largely the successor of traditional grammar, and is frequently a rebellion against traditional grammar. It deals with many of the same concepts, and even shares much terminology with traditional grammar. But as structural grammarians, we use words such as *noun*, *phrase*, and *sentence* with somewhat different implications. Structural grammar is discussed in Chapter 6.

Because traditional and structural grammars are so closely related, traditional grammar could have been placed on the chart in Figure 3-1. When the traditional grammarian observes that the common pattern of the English sentence is *subject-predicate*, he is as much a linguist as anyone. But when he insists that this is the *only* possible way to write understandable English, he is stepping out of the realm of linguistics by substituting subjective judgment for evidence.

Transformational, or *generative grammar* as it is frequently called, is one of the newer branches of linguistics and has achieved a popularity that makes it currently the most important phase of language study. As transformationalists, we are able to conduct grammatical analysis on a more detailed level than was possible before

Noam Chomsky presented this system to the linguistic world. (See Chapter 2, page 35.) Since that time, transformational linguistics has gained enough popularity to give the impression that linguistics and transformational grammar are the same thing. One of the major purposes of this chapter, however, is to point out that although transformational grammar is receiving the bulk of attention today, it is just one phase of the total science of linguistics. Chapter 7 deals with transformational analysis.

With the addition of *graphemics*, the study of writing systems, and *orthography*, another name for spelling, we have discussed the most important areas of descriptive linguistics. Because modern linguists tend to stress the "primacy of speech," we give graphemics and orthography comparatively scant attention.

As teachers, however, we have an unusual interest in what linguistics has to say about the relationship of English sounds to the way they are spelled. Among linguists, however, there seems to be more interest in the *historical* study of writing systems than in any other phase of graphemics.

In this volume all of Section Two is devoted to descriptive linguistics because these are the systems most popular in the new school textbooks. In Section Three, however, some alternate methods of language study are discussed.

HISTORICAL APPROACHES

At the bottom of Figure 3-1 directly opposite the descriptive, we find the diachronic, or historical point of view. This is placed at the opposite end of the chart to contrast the synchronic with the diachronic approach. In practice, however, these approaches use the same phonological, morphological, and grammatical methods. In other words, phonology could be studied from either a descriptive or a historical point of view. The same is true of the other studies listed as descriptive linguistics. As historical linguists, we are interested in how language began, how it developed, and how it came to be what it is today. We may even speculate on what it will be like tomorrow. Chapter 8 traces the history of language from the beginning of our knowledge to the present day. Obviously, with the use of language extending into prehistoric times, we know almost nothing about its origin. Speculations range from traditional religious concepts, such as the one in Genesis, to a number of carefully thought-out but purely speculative theories.

By comparing the word-stock of the various languages of the world, linguists have discovered that many seemingly dissimilar languages have a common ancestor, which may or may not be in use today. It probably is not, for languages change constantly, and if a language is old enough to have had other languages branch from it, the chances are that it has changed too much to be recognizable. English, for example, can be traced back to Old English, commonly called Anglo-Saxon. Today the closest thing to Anglo-Saxon is *Frisian*, a language spoken by a small group of people who have lived in isolation along the coast and on islands in the North Sea. Our main contact with Anglo-Saxon, however, is through written manuscripts such as the epic poem *Beowulf*.

Anglo-Saxon, in turn, can be traced back to an ancient language generally called *Proto-Germanic*, the ancestor of many languages of northern Europe. We know much less about *Proto-Germanic* than about Anglo-Saxon, and even less about *Indo-European*, which is believed to have been spoken in prehistoric central Europe, and is generally considered the common ancestor of most European languages as well as those of northern India.

It is this type of historical study with which we, as language historians, or *philologists*, are concerned. Philology is not listed on the chart because it is really another name for the study of the historical and comparative aspects of language. Historical linguists use the tools of descriptive linguistics to analyze ancestor languages on the basis of their phonology, morphology, graphology, and syntax, tracing the development of the sound system, the vocabulary, and the written system. We also note that language changes usually take place according to regular patterns, or as the result of historical events, such as intermingling with other people or the invention or discovery of new things that require new names.

COMPARATIVE METHODS

Differences between languages and between dialects are the direct outgrowth of their historical development. As philologists we are both historians and geographers, for in looking at the similarities and differences in speech habits, we are also concerned with how a language developed into its current form.

Language geography concerns the gathering of data that tell which languages are spoken in which parts of the world, how many speakers each has, and which language speakers have the greatest social and political impact. *Dialect geography* deals with the variations within language. As language geographers we may compare the English word *carnal* with the Spanish *carne* (meat), while the dialectician compares the *greasy* speakers with the *greazy* speakers.

But how can a linguist tell whether he is comparing two similar languages or two highly diverse dialects? The answer is not always simple and clear. Obviously, German and English are different languages, while the speech of Tallahassee, Florida, and Sacramento, California, represent dialects of English. But more frequently, the differences are not so clear-cut. In the Bantu area of Central and Southern Africa, dialectal differences in some locations occur so gradually that one can travel from place to place and not be sure at what point he has stopped hearing dialectal differences and started hearing a completely different language. Leo Rosten quoted Max Weinreich's playful remark that "A language is a dialect that has an army and a navy."[3]

In addition to geographic dialectology there is a *social dialectology*, or *sociolinguistics*, which is the study of differences in dialect resulting from age, sex, occupation, education, personality, and other factors. Frequently social dialects involve not only differences in pronunciation but also in word selection and sentence patterning. A linguist may discuss *conventional orthography*, but to a layman it is just a matter of *correct spelling*. A botanist may call it *aucuba japonica variegata* and a gardener *gold dust*, but to me it is that pretty bush with the speckled leaves.

One important axiom of comparative linguistics is that everyone speaks a dialect. The only possible exception would be the case of an isolated language spoken by too small a language community to have any significant variations. But you cannot speak English—or any language—without speaking it as it is commonly spoken in *some* language community. And that is your, or my, dialect. In other words, to a linguist there is no such thing as "pure" language; neither are some dialects "corruptions" of others.

Frequently, a particular dialect will be thought of as the "best" or most prestigious variety of a language, which may be because it contains the greatest number of features common to all or most of the dialects of the language. Or it may be considered the best dialect simply because the speakers of the dialect constitute an elite, prestigious group, such as the educated class or the residents of a royal court or a capital city. But existing languages and dialects evolved from an earlier form, and will continue to change either to meet new circumstances or to follow the general tendency of languages to evolve new sound and grammatical structures. The comparative linguist records language *as it is spoken* and studies the likenesses and differences between language communities.

Another interesting discovery of comparative linguistics is that there are no "primitive" languages. Linguists have searched the world over—have studied language among the most remote and primitive people—but have not found any language anywhere that is not fully developed and well suited to the needs of its speakers. The popular belief that some languages consist of "just grunting" is completely false. Frequently a language that is not closely related to English will be *heard* by us as a series of grunts, but this is just an example of our own cultural deafness. Our ears

---

[3] Leo Rosten, *The Joys of Yiddish* (New York: McGraw-Hill Book Company, 1968), p. 85.

simply are not trained to make distinctions between many of the sounds that do not occur in English, just as a Japanese may have difficulty differentiating between the English *l* and *r* sounds because they do not occur in Japanese. The Kru language of Liberia, for example, has two plurals to our one, differentiating with an inflection (word ending) between related and unrelated items. Many languages, such as Cree of an American Indian tribe, have inflectional categories differentiating between animate and inanimate. The study of those inflectional, grammatical, sound, and other linguistic patterns that are completely unknown to speakers of English leads inevitably to the conclusion that if there ever was a primitive, undeveloped language, there are none discovered today, and all contemporary languages are mature, complex in structure, and well adapted to the requirements of the culture.

It is interesting to note the cyclic nature of many things. After centuries of debate between the advocates of a universal grammar and those of a separate grammar for each language, and after the battle has been firmly won by the advocates of a separate grammar, some of our leading linguists are once again asking questions about universal principles. But this time they are questioning scientifically, with masses of data indicating that a comparison of any two languages will reveal both differences and similarities, with greater similarities usually (but not always) being seen between closely related languages.

The question being asked is: Is there, in this mass of linguistic data, anything at all that is universal, any principle that is applicable to all languages? More broadly stated, are there any universal tendencies in human communication? At this writing, we shall have to wait for an answer.

LINGUISTICS AS PHILOSOPHY

After analyzing language and spreading its parts out for inspection, and after investigating the multiple variations from one place to another, from one social class to another, and from one individual to another, we are left with the biggest question of all: What is language? What does it mean? Armchair speculation about language did not disappear with the Greeks and Romans. In those areas in which language can be examined objectively, we proceed with scholarly devotion, but where it cannot, we turn again to speculation. Inasmuch as we shall not have a chance in later chapters of this volume to delve deeply into some of the theorizing that has been done about language, let us look at some examples here.

Sign and Symbol

Leslie White is among those who have thought deeply about the significance of the spoken word. In *The Science of Culture* he discussed the differences between man and animal: Darwin, he reminded us, noted that mental differences are differences in degree, that all animals are endowed with intelligence; man simply has more than other forms.[4] White pointed out that man is capable of using words as *symbols*; animals can use words only as *signs*. The difference between sign and symbol is significant: "A symbol may be defined as a thing the value or meaning of which is bestowed upon it by those who use it."[5] A sign, on the other hand, is:

a physical thing or event whose function is to indicate some other thing or event. The meaning of a sign may be inherent in its physical form and its context, as in the case of the height of a column of mercury in a thermometer as an indication of temperature, or the return of robins in the spring. Or, the meaning of a sign may be merely identified with its physical form as in the case of a hurricane signal or a quarantine flag. But in either case, the meaning of the sign may be ascertained by sensory means.[6]

White pointed out that a thing may be a symbol in one context and a sign in another. A thing (including a word) may be a symbol as long as there is no physical connection between it and the thing it symbolizes. The word *tree* may symbolize a certain thing in English; in French the word *arbre* and in German the word *Baum* have the same meaning. None of these words bears the faintest resemblance to the object it symbolizes. We understand by *prearrangement* that a particular combination of sound frequencies emitted vocally or a particular arrangement of marks on paper or other writing surface carries a particular symbolic value.

As human beings, you and I have the power to alter symbolic values. If we decide to use the words *frying pan* in place of the French *arbre*, German *Baum*, or English *tree*, we can do so, and anyone else who agrees to use our system can derive the same symbolic value from the same thing. It is all a matter of consensus, arrived at by prearrangement.

Contrast this with animal behavior. A dog can be trained to *respond* to a word. You can teach a dog to *lie* on command, or you can use the word *tree* or the Spanish *árbol* or any word or gesture that can be seen and distinguished from other words or gestures. This much is also true of man, but the significant difference is that man

---

[4] Leslie A. White, *The Science of Culture* (New York: Farrar, Straus and Company, 1949), p. 22.

[5] *Ibid.*, p. 25.

[6] *Ibid.*, p. 27.

can perceive the word as a symbol, can make up the word himself or change the signal if he wishes (by consensus), and can be the author of his own symbolic system.

But to an animal this is out of the question. Fido lies, sits, or speaks because some intricate connection between stimulus and response is established, so that a change of inflection, pitch, or volume might not be perceived as the same stimulus at all. The word, to an animal, has some intrinsic connection with its referent. He hears the word; he performs on command, simple stimulus-response. The word, then, is not a symbol but a sign—a sign that something should be done—in the sense that the return of a robin may be taken as a sign of the return of spring. Even man cannot create new signs of the return of spring, although he may symbolize the concept in art, music, or words. White's thesis may be summed up in the following excerpt:

> The Statements, "The meaning of a word cannot be grasped with the senses," and "The meaning of a word can be grasped with the senses," though contradictory, are nevertheless equally true. In the symbol context the meaning cannot be perceived with the senses; in the sign context it can. This is confusing enough. But the situation has been made worse by using the words 'symbol' and 'sign' to label, not the different contexts, but one and the same thing: the word. Thus a word is symbol and a sign, two different things.[7]

Leslie White is among those whose interest in language lies not alone with examining its form or origin, or even with comparing one man's speech with another's. He is concerned with the place of language in the culture of man—its contributions, its general characteristics, its limitations. As linguists, we may find this type of speculation as interesting as the purely analytic approaches.

The Design Features of Language

Writing in *Scientific American* in 1960, the American linguist Charles Hockett presented his thoughts concerning our attempts to develop a theory about the origin of language and its development out of animal sounds and signals. This is usually done by tracing languages back to their ancestor languages, as described earlier in this chapter. Hockett suggested, however, that the use of comparative methods to investigate the origin of language could be extended only to a point, beyond which knowledge was lost in antiquity. He suggested another method, that of comparing languages not with each other, but with non-human forms of communication.[8]

---

[7] *Ibid.*, p. 30.
[8] Charles F. Hockett, "The Origin of Speech," *Scientific American*, 203:1 (September 1960), pp. 89–90.

Hockett listed those characteristics that human speech—all human speech—has in common, as contrasted with much of the communication of other forms of life. His result was thirteen "design features" of language, features that are not completely shared by other members of the animal kingdom.

These features include the following:

Vocal-auditory channel is simple and obvious. Language is transmitted from the vocal mechanism of the sender to the auditory system of the receiver. In the final section of this volume we shall discuss some other types of communication that *could have* developed instead and some probable reasons why language as we know it was preferred. This feature is shared by many other types of animal communication, such as a dog's bark or any vocal animal sound. But a dog can also silently show his teeth or wag his tail, and a human being can gesture. Other channels of communication (such as visual) are also open, but human speech is vocal-auditory.

Broadcast transmission and directional reception stem from the first characteristic. The signal is broadcast from the vocal system of the sender, and anyone within hearing can pick it up. Directional reception is the ability of the two ears to sense the direction from which a sound is coming by means of binaural direction finding.

Rapid fading refers to the transitory nature of sound. Once an utterance is spoken, it exists momentarily, and then is gone. The characteristics discussed thus far are shared by many nonhuman forms of communication. Writing, of course, does not contain the same design features as speech, but writing is a recent development in the culture of man. It is generally not considered part of the language-formation process, but was superimposed on language at a later time.

Interchangeability means that if you can say *hello* to me, I can say the same to you. Human beings can interchange their respective roles and reproduce any utterance they can understand. This contrasts with such communications as courtship rites of many members of the animal kingdom, in which neither can produce the patterns of the other.

Because of *total feedback* the sender as well as the receiver hears what is said. Thus he understands his own signal, internalizes the message, and is conscious of having communicated.

Specialization implies that sending a message is done as a separate process and not incidentally as part of some other body function. A dog showing his teeth transmits a message, but baring the teeth also prepares them for action. Human speech is closely connected with the respiratory system, speech sounds being produced on the exhalation and in some rare cases on the inhalation. Nevertheless, the vibration in the vocal cords and the modification of the air stream in the oral cavity and in other areas are specialized functions of speech which accomplish no purpose other than communication.

Semanticity is similar to what Leslie White calls symbolism. Particular words can symbolize certain things. Animal calls are semantic to a very limited extent: a dog may yelp or growl or wag its tail. Each of these messages has a different semantic meaning, but we have no evidence of any animal with the extensive semantic repertoire of man.

Closely related to semanticity is *arbitrariness*, the lack of connection between the word and its referent. When an animal yelps, his yelp is part of the pain process (lack of specialization). Animals from another part of the world do not yelp in another language, but *pain* and *dolor* have the same meaning in different languages without having any resemblance to each other. Hockett's example is a classic: A little word such as *whale* can be used to name the world's largest living things, but *microorganisms* names the smallest. Obviously, there need be no connection between symbol and referent. Here a modern linguist takes a position on the ancient analogy-anomaly controversy.

Discreteness is the capacity of the human being to make fine distinctions in the sounds he uses. The words *die* and *tie* are exactly alike except for a bit of vibration in the vocal cords at the beginning of *die*. Yet we can produce and hear such fine discriminations without difficulty. There may be a greater difference in the sound patterns of two people saying the same word than between the same person saying *tie* and *die*, but it is the differentiation within the sound system of our language that we recognize.

Also, we differentiate on an either-or basis. Either we hear *tie* or we hear *die*. We have nothing in the middle.

The opposite of discreteness would be continuousness. A dog may bare his teeth slightly or fully or any degree in between, and the degree to which he performs the act is the degree to which he gets across the message of danger. When bees perform their ritualistic dance to inform other bees of the source of food, they dance faster if the source is closer, and more slowly if it is far away. The speed of the dance can be regulated to indicate the distance. The snarling dog and dancing bee are using a nondiscrete, or continuous system of communication, as opposed to human speech, which may signal *Margie will be fine* or *Margie will be mine*, but nothing in the middle.

This does not imply that the human articulatory mechanism could not produce a sound with so little vibration in the vocal cords that it could be considered somewhere between *tie* and *die*. This happens regularly in the course of individual differences in speech production, but such in-between sounds have no discrete meaning, and therefore would be *perceived* as one word or the other. The hearer, in other words, compensates for these differences by assigning an absolute interpretation whenever there may be ambiguity in the sound itself. If the *Margie* of the previous example cannot tell whether she heard *fine* or *mine*, she will not know whether the comment concerned her health or love life. Without discreteness, human communication breaks down.

One feature unique to human speech is *displacement*, the ability to talk about something remote in time or space. You and I can discuss the language of ancient Egypt or Plato's contributions to linguistic thinking. To the best of our knowledge no creature other than man can do this. Bee dancing can tell about food that is somewhat distant, but not about something in Europe or about yesterday's headlines.

Another unique feature of human speech is *productivity*, the ability to produce new sounds, new words, and new combinations of words. In learning a foreign language a speaker of English may have to produce sounds he has never known before, such as the German gutteral in *ach* and *ich*, or the Spanish flap in *errar*. Some language students never do learn to produce new sounds. Instead they substitute a sound from their own language, resulting in speech characterized by an "accent." But others learn to produce the new sounds with skill and accuracy, showing the sound system of human speech to be productive.

There was no word for *typewriter* before the invention of this machine, but when we needed a word it was not hard to find one. Because human speech is productive, new words enter the lexicon as new things, new concepts, and new discoveries require. Likewise, you are now reading sentences you have never seen before, yet you put the words together with little difficulty and, hopefully, come up with the meaning. You can likewise *compose* new sentences you have never seen before.

Animals have a limited repertoire. Today's apes, dogs, crickets, and horses are presumably sending the same messages that their ancestors sent since their species evolved. Their language is not productive of new forms.

Somewhat allied with productivity is *traditional transmission*, which is simply our ability to learn from others. Each human being does not have to start at the beginning and learn everything, including language, by the same process it was learned centuries ago. We can learn from being told, from reading, and from cultural influences. This is the quality that Alfred Korzybski called "time binding," which is discussed in the final section of this volume.

Man creates a knowledge pool. Into that pool goes the sum total of human experience. You and I can draw from that pool. I am now drawing from a contribution made in 1960 by Charles Hockett. I do not have to discover the thirteen design features of language. It is all there in *Scientific American*, being transmitted like a double play in baseball—Hockett to Liebert to you.

The infinite variety of sentences that any language offers would not be possible without *duality of patterning*, by which we constantly reuse the same sounds and the same word-parts in different combinations with different meanings. Hockett illustrates with *tack*, *cat*, and *act*. Each of these words is composed of three sounds: *t*, *a*, and *k*. By putting them together in three different combinations, we come up with three different words. Likewise, by changing *internal* to *external* to *externalize* we reuse parts of words to produce different meanings. As far as we know, man is unique in this ability.[9]

These design features of language are as close to a "universal grammar" as anything I have seen thus far. It may be that a grammar that fits all languages can only be ascertained by comparing human speech to animal communication, not by comparing one language to another. But new developments may change this at any time.

Observation of the thirteen design features of language would lead to the conclusion that many of these features are not distinctive from animal cries and signals, but others are. The questions, then, are: how did man or his prototype develop productivity from a nonproductive system of cries, movements, or other signals? How did he learn to discuss the far-away and the long ago? By what process did he become a time-binding creature capable of sharing in the experiences of others? One theory, advanced by Hockett in this same article, is that of *blending*:

> Sometimes a speaker will hesitate between two words or phrases, both reasonably appropriate for the situation in which he is speaking, and actually say something that is neither wholly one nor wholly the other, but a combination of parts of each. Hesitating between "Don't shout so loud" and "Don't yell so loud," he might come out with "Don't shell so loud." Blending is almost always involved in slips of the tongue, but it may also be the regular mechanism by which a speaker of language says something that he has not said before.[10]

Thus a slip of the tongue might be one means by which new language is derived. Another might occur when two calls are put together in rapid succession to indicate two different situations. Again, we quote from Hockett's article:

> Let AB represent the food call and CD the danger call, each a fairly complex phonetic pattern. Suppose a protohominoid encountered food and caught sight of a predator at the same time. If the two stimuli were balanced just right, he might emit the calls ABCD or CDAB in quick sequence, or might even produce AD or CB. Any of these would be a blend. AD, for example, would mean "both food and danger." By virtue of this, AB and CD would acquire new meanings, respectively, "food without danger" and "danger without food." And all three of these calls— AB, CD and AD—would now be composite rather than unitary, built out of smaller elements with their own individual meanings: A would mean "food"; B, "no danger"; C, "no food"; and D, "danger."[11]

[9] *Ibid.*, pp. 90–92.
[10] *Ibid.*, p. 92.
[11] *Ibid.*, p. 94.

This could very well be the beginning of discreteness. But no progress could be made, of course, unless another ingredient is added. Once a blend or compound was produced, it would have to be heard, understood, and repeated soon enough for reinforcement. It is quite possible that such blends and compounds do occur occasionally in the animal world. But they are not recognized as having distinct meaning and are not repeated; hence they do not become a permanent part of the language.

Lexicography and Semantics

In addition to speculating about the nature and origins of language, we can look at another phase of linguistics, that which deals with meaning and how meaning is achieved through language. This could lead us down two possible paths. On the one hand, we could become *lexicographers*, or students of individual words. Or we could go into *semantics*, the study of the psychology of language, the emotional and intellectual effect language has on us.

The lexicographer is usually engaged in making careful surveys of individual words or idioms and publishing his findings in a dictionary. A great deal of popular mythology surrounds the function of a dictionary. Even teachers frequently behave as if dictionaries were not written by men but handed down from Mount Sinai to combat the golden calf of error. Thus they depend on a dictionary to establish the "correct" definition of a word. Originally, lexicographers such as Samuel Johnson attempted to define each word according to the way they thought it should be used, but as the science of lexicography advanced—as linguistics advanced—dictionaries began to reflect a research approach. Lexicographers went out into the field to make careful studies of how words actually *were* used in conversation and how writers used them in literature. A lexicographer is thus not a critic but a historian. This does not mean that every time a desk dictionary is published, a staff of linguists go into the field to survey the language. Obviously, smaller dictionaries are abridged from larger ones, but this is a matter of economics, not scholarship.

Probably the only prescriptive contribution of the dictionary is the spelling. After centuries of confusion, spelling has been fairly well standardized, and a dictionary is the best place to go for the "last word." Even here, however, dictionaries change to reflect changes of custom or local preference. Most American dictionaries list both *catalogue* and *catalog* because both spellings are popular. *Colour* is favored in England; *color*, in America.

The other direction toward which we can go to investigate meaning is *semantics*. As semanticists we study the many subtle shades of meaning that words and phrases are capable of expressing. Whereas the lexicographer is concerned with the denotation, or dictionary definition of a word, the semanticist is interested in implications, emotional connotations, and the effect of language on the minds and feelings of people. He wants to understand how an advertiser, a politician, a salesman, or a teacher uses language to exert influence.

For example, as lexicographers we might give a number of definitions of a word such as *democracy*. As semanticists we ask: What did Candidate X mean last night when he spoke of a return to *democratic principles*? How could Candidate Y use the same term for what seems to be a completely different way of life? Is *democracy* one thing to X and another to Y?

On the other hand, when Candidate A refers to *progress* and Candidate B calls it *socialism*, are they talking about different things or the same thing with different labels? And if they can use such vastly different words to describe the same thing, are they really telling us something about the thing itself, or are they revealing something about *themselves*—their feelings, their attitudes, their knowledge or lack of it? Or are they in reality trying to manipulate the thoughts and feelings, the attitudes and prejudices of their audience?

As semanticists we are constantly asking: what does he *really* mean by that? And we are never quite sure of our answer, for an answer must be stated in words, and these words must, in turn, be subject to semantic analysis. The semanticist's work, like the good housekeeper's, is never done.

BACK IN THE CLASSROOM

This brief look at some of the alternatives open to linguists is by no means complete, and if it were, new vistas would make it obsolete tomorrow. For the horizons of this new science are being pushed back at a rate that makes just keeping up with new developments a full-time job. Such things as *tagmemic analysis* and *stratificational grammar* may some day steal the show from transformational grammar. At the time of this writing, however, these areas of linguistics are not well developed and are not found to a great extent in school texts. *Communication theory* and *psycholinguistics* on the other hand, are fairly well developed, but have not yet played a central role in school linguistics. Neither has.the study of linguistic development of children, although studies along this line, pioneered by such people as Piaget and Vygotsky, may some day lead to a new understanding of the whole approach to the teaching of language in the schools. Linguistics, then, is not only a fast-developing scientific study but a valuable adjunct to such areas as psychology, philosophy, and anthropology, as well as education.

Some linguists whose work we shall discuss in this volume have preferred to do much of their study in one phase of the subject or another, just as doctors may specialize in heart, skin, or ocular problems. S. I. Hayakawa, for example, has done most of his linguistic writing in semantics. Charles Fries was mainly a structural linguist, whereas Noam Chomsky is obviously a transformationalist. Still others may specialize in language history or dialectology, or find a new area of their own. As a newcomer to linguistics you may wish to investigate the entire field, to become a specialist, or like your author, to remain a school teacher who investigates the linguistics movement with a pedagogue's eternal question : *What is in it for my students?*

It is in this spirit that we now step out of the role of linguist and reenter that of teacher. For if we study linguistics as linguists and not as teachers, we may fall into the trap of developing a course of study that has the preservation of a discipline, and not the welfare of students, at its center. This is already happening in some of the schools I have observed, and progress is somewhat less than sensational. But IF WE VIEW THE MOVEMENT AS TEACHERS WITH A COMMITMENT TO OUR STUDENTS, WE CAN MAKE OUR OWN DECISIONS AND ACCEPT OR REJECT THE LINGUISTIC PACKAGE OR WHATEVER PARTS WE FEEL APPROPRIATE.

section two

---

new traditions for old

introduction to section two

It is unfortunate that the teaching of English has so often been fragmented into three separate disciplines—grammar, composition, and literature. An English program should be unified around that which language instruction is intended to do—to develop the student's competence in all phases of human communication.

But communication is a highly complex and diverse process involving so many facets of human interaction that the English teacher may feel overwhelmed at the enormity, not to mention the importance, of the task. A list of the many objectives of a fully developed language arts program in an elementary and secondary school system would include activities ranging from primary instruction in reading and writing to those fine and subtle skills that enable the student to express himself in speech and writing with dynamism, wit, clarity, organization, beauty, and imagination, as well as to enjoy and appreciate those qualities in the expression of others.

Some of the specific areas with which the language program must deal are:

1. Handwriting: Clear, legible manuscript and cursive writing.
2. Expressing: Gaining sufficient familiarity with the various forms of spoken and written English to communicate with speed and precision.
3. Spelling: Ability to spell the common words of the language and the *habit of checking spelling carefully before considering written material finished.*
4. Vocabulary: Stretching the inventory of recognizable and usable words, understanding multiple meanings and emotional connotations of words and phrases.
5. Reading: Using the clues of context, structure, and phonics for the recognition of written words.
6. Receiving: The habit and the skill of retrieving information from the spoken and the written word.

7. Enjoying: Achieving personal satisfaction from the intellectual and social processes of oral discussion, recreational reading, and written self-expression.
8. Observing: Stretching the sensory and intellectual perceptions through increased awareness of the environment.
9. Responding: Developing an empathy with people and things, and reacting to the environment with the emotions as well as the intellect.
10. Structuring: Organizing ideas into major topics and subtopics, and sorting the relevant from the irrelevant, the important from the trivial.
11. Referring: Organizing written material to build a system of information retrieval.
12. Researching: Using books, dictionaries, library catalogs, bibliographies, and other reference tools.
13. Concept Forming: Capacity to visualize and internalize new concepts as the result of verbal experiences.
14. Inferring: Seeing implications in the spoken and written word.
15. Synthesizing: Putting facts or concepts into a unified whole.
16. Evaluating: Seeing values and limitations, searching for truth and beauty, respecting achievement.
17. Evolving: Recognizing that the universe is in a constant state of change, that today's axioms will be tomorrow's mythology, that good and bad, truth and error are not absolutes, but are dependent upon the situation, the era, and the individual.
18. Creating: Using the imagination to learn intuitively and to create new structures.

This is a formidable list of objectives for any language program. It is small wonder that English teachers have sought to reduce the whole complicated affair to three easily managed phases. And the process is not without merit, for it is in reading, writing, and the study of language that one finds keys to unlock such difficult goals as *structuring*, *concept forming*, and *responding to the environment*. But the danger in this trivium lies in the tendency of English teachers to consider each of these three facets an end in itself rather than a method of enabling the student to see his environment with deeper understanding and to communicate his understanding with the highest possible degree of speed, accuracy, ease and effectiveness.

This volume deals with *one* approach to language instruction, an examination of the structure of English. Although literature and composition are major phases of any good language program, they are not the subject of this book.

The teacher must read this and similar volumes with one major question constantly pricking his intellect: How? How does one achieve this many-faceted goal? Will it be done most effectively by focusing the bulk of class time on literature? On writing compositions? On examining language? By some other means as yet undiscovered? It would seem fair to assume that some combination of the above must be achieved, but the details of scope, sequence, and proportion have yet to be filled in.

One vital phase of curriculum planning that is too often unplugged from the system is the student himself. Too many courses of study are written as if the purpose of education were to perpetuate an intellectual pursuit rather than to help young people grow.

We must also keep in mind the great *diversity* of interests and abilities of any student body. It is true that our goal is somewhat similar for all students—to produce educated functioning, happy human beings. It is part of our democratic heritage to give everyone an equal opportunity, including an opportunity to enjoy the pleasures of great literature and the intricacies of human language. But it is neither democratic nor good educational practice to run everyone through the same production line. Real democratic education allows each individual to develop his own potential, to follow his own interests. As Walter Loban recently remarked, "Equal educational opportunity does not necessarily mean identical experience."

This implies that the teacher must meet each student where he is and take him from there. If a young person has not yet learned the story of the three *there's* (*there*, *their, they're*), it is vital that such basic skills as spelling and reading be a large part of his language instruction. There is no point in giving him the "opportunity" to engage in pursuits that for him are useless, boring, and beyond his present capacity.

On the other hand, neither should a student with a sincere interest in literature or linguistics be denied the opportunity to develop these areas. Forward-looking English departments are beginning to offer elective courses such as *history of the drama, creative writing, phonology, introduction to poetry, contemporary American literature, and transformational grammar.* Some of these options could challenge the academically advanced, others might be built around less esoteric matter, with the development of the fundamental skills of reading, composition, spelling, and vocabulary the chief aims. Students could be counseled to elect courses appropriate for their interests, removing the stigma of "track" classes, and enabling the department to build the appropriate amount of linguistics, literature, composition, and oral English into each course.

Of one thing, however, I am certain. Only educators are qualified to design the course contents. They must not abrogate the responsibility to linguists, literary critics, or book salesmen. Teachers would do well to look to these specialists for advice and information, but must make their own decisions concerning what to teach on the basis of their unique professional training and experience. Both as individuals in their own classrooms and as members of departmental, school, and district curriculum committees, they must be constantly deciding whether a precious class period would be more valuably spent reading *The Prince and the Pauper* or how to make branching tree diagrams; writing a poem, a short story, or directions for making divinity fudge; outlining an article on *How to Make a Picket Fence* or the phonological system of the English language; discussing the theme of *Macbeth* or the problem of narcotics addiction.

These remarks were not intended to be facetious or sarcastic. The choices form a background against which any work on the teaching of English must be read. As long as it is understood that reading, writing, and oral English offer supporting routes to the same objective, we can proceed with a more detailed look at the structure of our language.

The next four chapters deal with those phases of linguistics that are currently in wide use as subject matter in many of the new school textbooks. These descriptive approaches to the study of language break language into constituent elements and examine their forms. The popularity of these disciplines over other possible areas of linguistics is probably the result of the tradition in teaching, a tradition viewing syntax as an essential part of language instruction.

Because of the complexity of language, these four chapters are the most technical parts of this volume. In presenting this introduction to phonology, morphology, and structural and transformational grammar, it is not my intention either to advocate or discourage their use in the public schools, but to present the findings of modern linguistics so that the teacher may consider which phases of linguistics, if any, have meaning and relevance in a school English program. The amount of technical information presented in this section goes beyond what is generally presented by the new textbooks, despite the fact that it barely scratches the surface of the work being done in linguistic science.

If the material in these chapters is new to you, I suggest that you do not try to absorb every detail as you read, but READ QUICKLY OVER THE ENTIRE SECTION TO GET A BROAD VIEW OF DESCRIPTIVE LINGUISTICS. Then, as time and inclination permit, return for a more detailed study of those areas that seem interesting and important. As you read, you might keep in mind a number of attitudes that are beginning to emerge within the ranks of educators. At one extreme we find those who advocate, with what seems to be complete and unquestioning devotion, the teaching of linguistic grammar in the public schools. At two other extremes are those who either cling tenaciously to the traditional approach or who advocate that if we have failed to demonstrate that the teaching of grammar is a significant step in the improvement of communication skills, we may as well throw out all grammar teaching, new and old, and concentrate on either literature or composition or a combination of both. Still another attitude is that the English teacher, as a professional, needs this type of technical knowledge, whereas the student is no more in need of grammatical analysis to read or write than you and I need a knowledge of mechanics to drive an automobile or need a course in physiology to digest our food.

Some things, however, seem exceedingly clear: The traditional method of teaching grammar, with its dependence on prescriptivism, ignoring of speech, and indiscriminate and unscientific definitions of language phenomena, is doomed. It may die slowly; traditions usually do, but the case against it is too strong.

What will take its place is anybody's guess. But the new grammar, whether it represents a lasting contribution to the teaching of English or a transitory stage in the development of something that has not yet emerged, must not be taught like Edmund Hillary's Mount Everest—"because it's there."

But for that very reason, it cannot be ignored. It is most definitely there, and no language teacher can call himself an informed professional without a fairly extensive knowledge of it. But once the knowledge has been obtained, the decision remains.

4

---

the atom
phonology

Phonology is the branch of linguistics that deals with speech sounds. It consists of the related studies of *phonetics* and *phonemics*. These terms are often confused, although the distinctions are fairly well-established. This chapter explores these studies for possible classroom applications.

Phonics is a method of teaching reading by studying the relationship between the letter symbols (graphemes) of a written language and the sounds (phonemes) they represent. Phonetics and phonemics are branches of linguistic studies; phonics more properly belongs to pedagogy. Phonology is concerned less with pedagogy than with analysis of the sound system of language *per se*.

PHONETICS

Phonetics is the study of the *nature* of speech sounds, including two major areas of investigation. The first approach, *acoustic phonetics*, deals with the physics of the sound wave patterns, which is usually studied by the use of special machinery for making *oscillograms* or *spectrograms*, graphic representations of the sound patterns. Since the mechanical reproduction of vocal patterns produces very complex pictures that are difficult to classify, the science of acoustic phonetics has not as yet produced data of far-reaching implications for education.

The second approach, *articulatory phonetics*, is the study of how the various phonemes are produced by the human vocal mechanism. Because phonetics is concerned with speech *sounds*, it can most effectively be discussed orally. To try to write the sounds of a language is a little like trying to describe what it is like to be kissed. Words and symbols are only substitutes. Nevertheless, poets and philosophers have been talking about kissing since the dawn of literature, and linguists have developed a system, known as the *phonetic alphabet*, to make it possible for you and me to discuss speech sounds without hearing each other's voices.

The principle of the phonetic alphabet is that each speech sound, or phoneme, is represented by a different symbol. The alphabet we use for writing English is partially phonetic, for many of the letters do represent particular phonemes, but, as any schoolboy struggling with his spelling lesson can tell you, English sound-letter relationship is beset with traps.

The International Phonetic Alphabet, illustrated in Figure 4-1, uses sixteen letters from our alphabet to indicate the consonant sounds normally associated with them. But linguists cannot use the letters *c*, *x*, *y*, or *q* because these letters either have more than one possible pronunciation or repeat sounds already accounted for by other letters. The letter *j* is also used, although not for the phoneme we generally give it, but for the sound we spell with the letter *y* in *young* and *yet*. And for phonemes that are usually spelled *ng*, *sh*, *ch*, *th*, *ge*, or *j*, I.P.A. employs symbols that are not part of our alphabet.

Figures 4-1 and 4-2 can be interpreted as follows: First note that those symbols that stand for English phonemes are printed in bold face type. Hockett places voiced and unvoiced consonants (See page 74) on separate lines; I.P.A. places them on the same line. To find the pronunciation of any English symbol on the chart, refer to the first two columns of Figures 4-4 and 4-5 with key words listed under "common spellings." The *th* in *thin* and the *th* in *then*, although spelled the same in English, require two different symbols, [θ] and [ð], because they are actually two different sounds. The word *judge*, in conventional spelling, first uses *j* then *ge* to spell the same sound. In phonetics, however, the symbol [ǰ] would be used in both places.

Not all linguists use I.P.A. Comparing I.P.A. with the phonetic system of Charles Hockett (Figure 4-2), reveals that although the two systems have much in common, they also have differences, both in the names used for classification and in the symbols representing some of the phonemes.

For example, the *sh* in *she* is represented by [ʃ] in I.P.A., but [š] by Hockett. Hockett refers to this sound as "lamino-alveolar spirant," whereas I.P.A. classifies it as "palato-alveolar fricative." (These terms are explained later.) This is more a difference in expression than a disagreement in fact. *Spirant* and *fricative* are roughly

CONSONANTS	Bilabial	Labio-dental	Dental and Alveolar	Retroflex	Palato-alveolar	Alveolo-palatal	Palatal	Velar	Uvular	Pharyngal	Glottal
Plosive	**p b**		**t d**	ʈ ɖ			c ɟ	**k g**	G q		ʔ
Nasal	**m**	ɱ	**n**	ɳ			ɲ	**ŋ**	N		
Lateral Fricative			ɬ ɮ								
Lateral Non-Fricative			**l**	ɭ			ʎ				
Rolled			**r**						ʀ		
Flapped			ɾ	ɽ					ʀ		
Fricative	Φ β	**f v**	θ ð ɹ s z	ʂ ʐ	ʃ ʒ	ɕ ʑ	ç j	x ɣ	χ ʁ	ħ ʕ	**h** ɦ
Frictionless Continuants and Semi-Vowels	w ɥ	ʋ	ɹ				**j**		ʁ		

Vowel Area

KEY: English phonemes are represented in bold face type. They are not written that way in transcription.

Figure 4-1. THE INTERNATIONAL PHONETIC ALPHABET: CONSONANT CHART. Revised to 1947.*

* Source: Robert W. Albright. *The International Phonetic Alphabet: Its Background and Development.* Indiana University. Research Center in Anthropology, Folklore, and Linguistics, Publication 57 (January 1958). Also Part III. *International Journal of American Linguistics,* Vol. 124, No. 1 (1958), Bloomington: Indiana University.

	Bilabial	Labio-dental	Apico-labial	Apico-inter-dental	Apico-dental, Apico-alveolar	Apico-domal	Lamino-alveolar	Lamino-domal	Centro-domal, fronted dorso-velar	Dorso-velar	Back dorso-velar
Stops vls.	p	ṗ		t̯(	t	ṭ	tʲ	ṭʲ	k̯	k	q k̇
Stops vd.	b	ḅ		d̯(	d	ḍ	dʲ	ḍʲ	ĝ	g	g̣
Nasals vd.	m	ɱ ɱ		n̯(	n	ṇ	nʲ ɲ ñ	ṇʲ	ĝ̃	ŋ	ŋ̣
Spirants vls.	ø	f		s̯(	s	ṣ	ş	ṣ̌	ʒ̂χ̂	x	χ ẋ
Spirants vd.	β	v	Rill	z̯(	z	ẓ	ž	ž̧	γ̂	γ	γ̇
Slit vls.				θ̯(	θ	θ̣					
Slit vd.				ð̯(	ð	ð̣					
Lateral vls.				ł̯(	ł	ł̣					
Lateral vd.				l̯(	l	l̬	ɣ lʲ	ɫ ľ			

Figure 4-2. PHONETIC CONSONANT CHART.*

* Source: Charles F. Hockett, *A Course in Modern Linguistics* (New York: The Macmillan Company, 1958), p. 71.

synonymous, as shall be seen in the forthcoming discussion. As part of his classification, Hockett includes the area of the tongue that makes the articulation, the lamina (see Figure 4-3), whereas I.P.A. notes that articulation is made in the back part of the alveolar ridge, near the hard palate.

Since this difference in terminology and symbolization can be very confusing to the beginning student of linguistics, this text adopts one popular system, that of Hockett, and uses it throughout.

Because many of the phonemes of the language are written with letters of the alphabet, it is important to be able to differentiate when a text such as this one is writing a letter and when it is using that letter to stand for a sound. Therefore, linguists enclose phonetic writing in square brackets ([ ]). To clarify the fact that a word or letter is being written in conventional spelling (*orthography*), we use *italics*. Thus the symbol *t* stands for the twentieth letter of our alphabet, part of the *graphemic* (written) system of English, but the symbol [t] stands for a sound, part of the *phonetic* (spoken) system of language.

The Human Vocal System

Most of the organs of speech also fulfill another physiological function, such as breathing or food ingestion. Human speech is produced by a column of air being pushed from the *lungs* mainly by the *diaphragm*, passing up the *larynx*, which contains the *vocal cords*, continuing through the *pharynx*, and out through the *oral* and *nasal cavities*. Figure 4-3 shows the major organs involved in speech.

As the air passes through the vocal cords, a number of things can happen. If the cords are relaxed and far apart, the air flows out freely. If the vocal cords are tense and completely closed, no air can get through. Neither of these conditions will produce speech. But if the cords are brought almost together and held tense while the air stream is passing through they can be made to *vibrate* like a reed in a musical instrument. This is known as *voice*. More relaxed cords with a narrow opening produce *friction*, resulting in a whispered, or *voiceless*, quality. Some speech sounds, such as [m b z] and the vowels are produced by voiced laryngal vibration; others such as [h p s] are known as voiceless phonemes, and are produced by friction.

The vibrations of the vocal cords (plus the friction used to make the unvoiced phonemes) produce the sound we hear, but the sound is modified into separate phonemes after leaving the larynx. The only English phoneme produced by modification within the larynx itself is [h]. If we open the vocal cords suddenly when air is pressing on them, we produce a phoneme that is not part of the English language, generally known as glottal stop [ʔ]. This is the *ugh* grunt we tend to make when

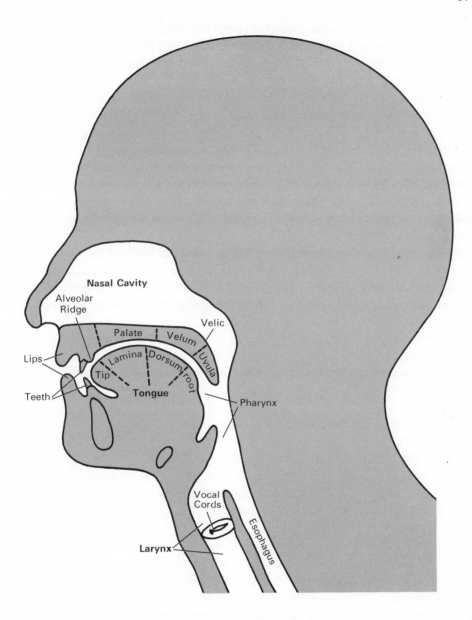

Figure 4-3.   MAJOR SPEECH ARTICULATORS.

straining to lift a heavy object. From the larynx the air continues upward through the pharynx, where it can be modified somewhat (although English involves very little pharyngal modification) and then into the nasal and oral cavities.

Separating the oral and nasal cavities is a membrane that runs from the tooth ridge at the front to the pharynx at the rear. At the upper rear of this membrane is the *velic*, which can be open, as in the illustration, or closed by movement of the *velum*, the rear part of the membrane. If the velic is open, part of the air stream enters the nasal cavity, where it is resonated, producing the phonemes [m n ŋ], the last symbol representing the *ng* in *song*. When an individual has a head cold, and the nasal membranes are swollen closed so air cannot resonate in the nasal cavity, the phonemes [m n ŋ] sound like [b d g]. Other phonemes are affected to a lesser degree because the closing of the nasal passage alters the quality of the vocal resonance, causing a condition known as *denasality*.

Most of the modification of speech sounds occurs in the oral cavity, or mouth. Here a number of things can happen. If the air passage is not highly restricted by the lips, tongue, or teeth, so that air can pass out freely, resonating in the oral cavity as it passes, a *vocoid*, or *vowel* is produced. But if the speech *articulators* restrict the passage of air at some point in the oral cavity, a *contoid*, or *consonant*, results. There is no clear-cut amount of restriction required to distinguish a vowel from a consonant. The sounds [w j h r] are sometimes classified as consonants, sometimes as vowels. In phonetics these borderline sounds are often referred to as *semivowels*.

English Phonetic Classification—Consonants

In classifying phonemes, a number of criteria are used:

First is the aforementioned classification into consonant and vowel.

The second method has also been mentioned, the division into *voiceless*, or *unvoiced*, and *voiced* sounds. All English vowels and the consonants [b d g m n ŋ v z ð ž r l j w ǰ] are voiced. Voiceless consonants are [p t k f š θ s h č].

The difference between voiced and voiceless sounds can be clearly perceived by either of the following methods: Place your hand over your larynx (Adam's apple) and say first [p], then [b]. Note that you can feel the vibrations on the voiced [b], but not on the voiceless [p]. Or place your hands over your ears and repeat voiced and voiceless phonemes from the list given. You can hear the vibrations of the voiced sounds.

Third, we classify phonemes according to the *point of articulation*, the place in the oral cavity where the speech stream is modified. Figure 4-3 shows that the membrane separating the oral and nasal cavities can be divided into a number of areas. Beginning at the front of the mouth are the *lip*, the *teeth*, the hard ridge just behind the teeth (*alveolar ridge*), the dome (*hard palate*), and the soft palate (*velum*). The tongue, likewise, can be divided into areas, although it is really a single flexible mass, and the divisions of the tongue are arbitrary and simply for convenience in the discussion. The areas of the tongue are: the tip, or *apex*; the blade, or *lamina*; the *center*; and the rear, or *dorsum*. Sometimes the blade and tip are included in the single term *apex*. The back, or *root* of the tongue, also influences speech by controlling the size of the pharyngal opening, although it is not usually considered an articulator.

Articulation is achieved by constricting the air passage in the mouth by bringing the tongue, lower tooth ridge, or lower lip in contact with or near some point along the upper wall. By naming the points of constriction we give labels to the phonemes of the language. Points of articulation are also listed in Figures 4-1 and 4-2. They may be compared with the areas drawn in Figure 4-3. Note in the following listing that the phoneme is identified by naming both the upper and lower points of contact. To interpret the sound of each phonetic symbol, turn to Figure 4-4 and match the "common spellings" with the symbol in the second column.

In English the points of contact, as listed by Charles Hockett, are:

Name (See Figure 4-2)	Articulators (See Figure 4-3)	Phonetic Symbols (See Figure 4-2 and 4-4, Column 2)
Bilabial	two lips	[p b m w]
Labio-dental	lower lip and upper teeth	[f v]
Apico-dental	tip of tongue and teeth	[θ ð]
Apico-alveolar	tip of tongue and alveolar ridge	[t d n l s z]
Lamino-alveolar	blade of tongue and alveolar ridge	[r š ž]
Lamino-palatal	blade of tongue and hard palate	[j]
Dorso-velar	rear of tongue and soft palate	[k g ŋ]
Glottal	vocal cords	[h]

Two additional phonemes, [č j̆], are really blends of their component parts, [tš] and [dž], respectively. In phonetic transcription they may be written either way, depending upon the system employed.

The fourth and last method of classification to be discussed in this text is by the *type of action* required to produce the sound. This is also shown in Figure 4-2.

English *stops*, or *plosives*, are formed by stopping the air stream to build up a pressure, then releasing it suddenly. The sounds [p b t d k g] are included in this category.

Fricatives, or *spirants*, are made by constricting a continuous passage of air in the oral cavity, producing friction by the rush of air through the constricted passage. Those are [f v θ ð s z š ž h].

The *nasals* [m n ŋ] are obtained by opening the velic to produce resonance in the nasal chamber.

The *lateral* [l] results from stopping the air with the tongue against the rear of the tooth ridge, allowing air to escape at either side. The lateral is frequently considered a type of fricative, as it is also produced by constricting a continuous air stream. In most American dialects laterals vary in placement from the frontal (apico-dental), usually at the beginnings of syllables to the velar (frequently written [x]) in such words as *full* and *fill*.

The [r] is in a class by itself. There is probably no phoneme that varies so greatly from one dialect to another. It is sometimes so pronounced, with the tongue curled high and back in the oral cavity, that it is distinctly heard as a consonant sound. Or it can be so slight, especially after vowels, that one can argue whether it is a separate phoneme or a variation of the preceding vowel. Frequently it is trilled, an effect achieved by vibration of part of the articulator by the passing air stream. The nature of [r] also depends on whether it is the initial, medial, or final sound of the word.

The *affricates* [č ǰ] are essentially combinations of stops [t d] followed by spirants [š ž]. Because these are *blends* of two consonants they are often omitted from phonemic analysis charts, and some linguists write them either as blends [tʃ dʒ] or as ligatures [ʤ]. A ligature consists of two letters written with parts connecting to show phonemic closeness or singularity.

Semi-vowels [j h w] are produced by opening the oral cavity to allow a free flow of air in a manner similar to that of vowels. Sometimes [r] is classed as a semivowel. Words such as *sly* and *shy* are evidence that [j] can be a vowel. In phonetic transcription they would be written [slaj], [šaj]. Semivowels are not included in Figure 4-2.

The Vowels

In producing vocoid, or vowel sounds, the air stream passes comparatively freely through the oral cavity, being modified mainly by the position of the tongue. Figure 4-6 shows the common tongue positions for English vowels. These positions begin at the upper part of the palatal section of the oral cavity and proceed down and back on a diagonal. The vowels formed along this line are called *front vowels*, and those formed at the velar section of the oral cavity are *back vowels*. The back vowels are formed mainly by the dorsal part of the tongue; the front vowels, by the blade. There are two central vowels in English, the low [a], and a special vowel called the *schwa*. The schwa is a common vowel sound in English, but we have no separate letter for it in the graphemic system. Therefore it is spelled with different letters in different words. Most linguists use the symbol [ə], sometimes with [ʌ] to indicate the accented form. A pronunciation guide for vowel symbols can be found in Figure 4-5.

	Common Spellings	I.P.A.	Hockett	i.t.a.	Roberts	Thorndike-Barnhart	Webster's 3rd Ed.
Stops	pie, rope, supper	p	p	p	p	p	p
	bit, robber, bribe	b	b	b	b	b	b
	tie, butter, rote	t	t	t	t	t	t
	die, paddle, rode	d	d	d	d	d	d
	kit, like, cane, lick, quit	k	k	c or k	k	k	k
	gain, beggar, rogue	g	g	g	g	g	g
Nasals	main, summer, come, dumb	m	m	m	m	m	m
	no, winner, scene, know, gnaw	n	n	n	n	n	n
	song, sink	ŋ	ŋ	ŋ	ng	ng	ŋ
Spirants	fine, cuff, wife, phone, tough	f	f	f	f	f	f
	vain, save, of	v	v	v	v	v	v
	sane, essay, rinse, cent, mice, scene	s	s	s	s	s	s
	zoo, muzzle, size, boys, boy's rise, says	z	z	z or ʒ	z	z	z
	thin	θ	θ	th	th	th	th
	then, bathe	ð	ð	th	th	TH	th
	sure, shy, attention, permission	ʃ	š	ʃ	sh	sh	sh
	loge, seizure, Jaques	ʒ	ž	ʒ	zh	zh	zh
Semi-Vowels	hail, whose	h	h	h	h	h	h
	yet; as vowel: see, Etc.	j	j	j	y	y	y
	wail, what; as vowel: rule. Etc.	w	w	w	w	w	w
Lateral	lie, roll, role	l	l	l	l	l	l
Flap	rain, hurry, rare, rhythm, wreck	r	r	r	r	r	r
Blends	jig, gentle, ridge, gorge	dʒ	ǰ	ǰ	ǰ	j	j
	chick, itch	tʃ	č	č	ch	ch	ch

Figure 4-4.　ENGLISH PHONEMIC SYSTEMS: CONSONANTS*.

* Figures 4-4 and 4-5 compare six methods of writing the English phonemic system. Two are composed for linguistic study (International Phonetic Alphabet and Charles Hockett), two are devised for teaching purposes (Initial Teaching Alphabet and Paul Roberts), and two are from dictionaries.

Category	Common Spellings	I.P.A.	Hockett	i.t.a.	Roberts	Thorndike-Barnhart	Webster's 3rd Ed.
Front Vowels	bee, be, beat, field, receive	iː	ij	ee	ē	ē	ē·ē
	bit, myth	ɪ	i	i	i	i	i
	cave, chaotic, bait, way, weigh	ɛ or eɪ	ej	æ	ā	ā	ā
	set, head, said, friend	e	e	e	e	e	e
	sat, laugh	æ	æ	a	a	a	a
Back Vowels	rule, true, few, to, too, two	uː	uw	w or ω	ū	ü	ü
	took, pull, wolf, could	u	u	ω	∞	u̇	u̇
	rope, boat, no, know, hoe, sew	o or ou	ow	œ	ō	ō	ō
	boy, join	ɔɪ	oj	oi	ơ	oi	oi
	hall, bore, haunt, awful, fought, awe, board, caught	ɔ	ɔ	au	au	ô	ô
Middle Vowels	the, sun, sir, final, mountain	ʌ or ə	ə	u	u	e	ə
	by, buy, bite, high, pie	aɪ	aj	ie	ī	ī	ī
	house, brown, howl, bough	au	aw	ou	au	ou	au
	father, got	ɑ	a	a	o	ä	ä
Blends and Finer Distinctions	hot, sorry (between ɑ and ɔ)	ɒ		o		o	e
	ask (between ɑ and æ)	a					e,
	sun (stressed form of ə)	ʌ				u	
	bird (British pronunciation)	ɜ				ėr	
	better (American pronunciation)	ɚ r.				ėr	
	due	ɪU or ju		ue		ü	yü
	when			wh		hw	
	care, air	ɛ				ã	

Figure 4-5. ENGLISH PHONEMIC SYSTEMS: VOWELS.

When the tongue is forward in the mouth to produce [ij i ej e æ], the jaws are somewhat closed and the lips comparatively *spread*. The lips are also spread on the central vowels [ə a aj]. But the tongue recedes farther back to produce [uw u ow ɔ], and the lips assume a *rounded* position. With the lips exposed to view it is easy to observe their positions, so in addition to high or low and front or back, the spread or rounded lip is sometimes used as a method of classification. The diphthong [oj] begins with rounded lips then changes to spread. In [aw] the opposite happens.

Thus [ij] might be described as *high, forward, spread*; [ow] as *back, middle, rounded,* The term *middle* is usually used to indicate neither high nor low, whereas *central* generally implies between front and back.

The phonetic alphabet constitutes another system of writing, in which spelling and pronunciation are in correspondence. For example, this sentence would be written in phonetics:

[fɔr igzæmpl ði sentins wud bij ritn in fənetiks]

Other phonetic symbols, to be discussed later in this chapter, can be added to express such important vocal qualities as pitch, stress, and timing. Any language can be read or written phonetically by a person who knows the symbols for all the sounds of that language. Much finer shades of pronunciation can be expressed by learning or

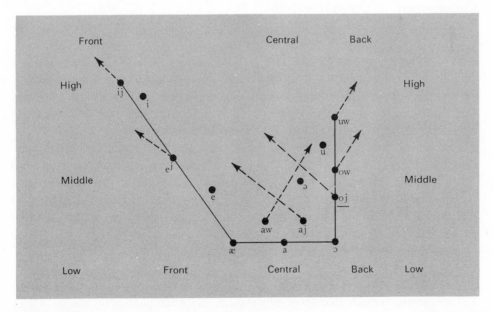

Figure 4-6. ENGLISH VOWEL CHART.

devising a system of diacritical markings. With sufficient skill in the use of phonetics a linguist can produce in writing any human vocal sound his ear can distinguish.

Conventional Spelling	Thorndike-Barnhart	Webster's 3rd Edition	Paul Roberts	Charles Hockett
au thor i za tion	ô′ thər ə zā′ shən	ˌȯthər ə′zāshən	aûth ur u zá́ shun	ɔ́θərəzejšən
ref er en dum	ref′ ər en′ dəm	ˌref ə′ rendəm	rêf u rénd um	r̀efəréndəm
cham pi on ship	cham′ pi ən ship′	′champē ən ˌship	chám pe un ship̂	čǽmpijnšip
there a bouts	ᴛнǎr′ ə bouts′	′thar ə ˌbaûts	thér u baûts	ðérəbàwts
vis u al i za tion	vizh′ ü əl ə zā′ shən	ˌvizhəl ə′ zāshən	vîzh ū ul u zá́ shun	vížələzejšən
ques tion ing	kwes′ chən ing	′kwes(h) chəniŋ	kwés chun iᵳg	kwésčəniŋ

Figure 4-7.   SAMPLE PHONETIC SPELLINGS.

PHONEMICS

Phonemics deals with the problems of discovering which phonemes are part of the conscious repertoire of sounds made by speakers of a language or dialect. Suppose, for example, that an anthropologist from another country, who speaks not a word of English, has just arrived in the United States to study Americans of the twentieth century. Suppose also that English is one of those little-known languages for which there are no textbooks and no teachers, as is typical of the situations faced regularly by anthropologists who do research in remote areas of the earth.

The first task would be to ferret out the language, so that communication could be established. Essential to this task would be an understanding of the *phonemic structure* of the language. Our man would begin by finding an *informant*—some cooperative native speaker of the language who would help by answering questions. Imagine that the scientist and the informant are working together, when into the room walks a household pet, a small furry beast. By sign language the anthropologist asks, "What is that animal called?" and the informant speaks the word:

cat.

The scientist records this bit of information, using the phonetic notation [k æ t], then asks the same question concerning another animal—this one a small, grayish rodent. The answer is:

>　*rat.*

At this point the researcher, if he is a trained linguist (and he certainly ought to be in such a situation), knows something much more significant than how to say two English words. He studies the sound structure of

$$[\text{kæt}] \quad [\text{ræt}]$$

and finds them *identical except for one phoneme*. If *cat* is one word and *rat* another, obviously the speaker is distinguishing between these words on the basis of the initial sounds. Therefore, in the sound system of this language, they are *different* sounds in the mind of the speaker—otherwise he could not use them to distinguish between the two words. The linguist notes that [kæt] and [ræt] are *minimal pairs*—words that are distinguished on the basis of only one phoneme.

Now the researcher goes a step further. He asks the name of the thing the informant is wearing on his head, and the reply is:

>　*cap.*

This gives another valuable bit of information: the final sounds of [kæt] and [kæp] are also distinguished by the speaker. He now knows four separate phonemes of the English language, represented in the sample words by the letters *c*, *r*, *t*, and *p*, and in phonetics by [k, r, t, p]. He has also detected the vowel [æ], but is not sure how to classify it yet because he has nothing to *contrast* it with.

But he can add two more phonemes to his growing list when the informant tells him that this undersized bed he sometimes uses for sleeping is called a

>　*cot.*

By contrasting the middle sounds of [kæt] and [kat] it can be determined that the speaker is able to distinguish one from the other. Now, in addition to knowing six different English sounds, our field researcher has other interesting data: The word *cat* cannot be analyzed any further. There are no other parts that contrast with parts of other words. Thus he assumes that the word *cat* is composed of three phonemes.

A phoneme is the smallest unit of sound that the speaker uses to distinguish one utterance from another. A sound can be classified as a phoneme of a particular language when it has been determined that the speaker of that language can use it to distinguish one expression from another, as the informant above distinguished [kæt] from [kat] on the basis of the contrast between middle sounds.

If the wandering linguist continued to ask for more words, building his vocabulary of English, he could eventually learn the complete sound system. Whenever he found additional pairs of words that were alike except for one phoneme he could, by contrast, isolate additional English phonemes. Although this "minimal pair" technique is not the only method of phonemic analysis, it is the most reliable. Other methods may be used when minimal pairs cannot be found. Eventually, by painstakingly breaking the language into its constituent phonemes, he would arrive at the *phonemic system* of the language.

The phonemic system is that group of phonemes used by speakers of a language to put their utterances together. The English language can be classified into thirty-eight phonemes (as in Figures 4-4 and 4-5), plus twelve *suprasegmental phonemes*, a special group to be discussed later.

Once a linguist classifies a phoneme as belonging to the sound system of a particular language, he indicates that his transcription is phonemic by writing it between slashes (/ /) instead of brackets. Thus phonemic writing can be distinguished from phonetic writing by the type of enclosure.

Not all languages use the same phonemes, or even the same number of phonemes. The English /r/ and /l/ are not present in Japanese, but Japanese speakers have a phoneme that is somewhat between these two and is not found in English. The French vowel in *père* and the German *ich* are examples of non-English phonemes. Hawaiian has the smallest recorded number of phonemes, thirteen; while Chipewyan, the language of an American Indian tribe, has the largest verified number, forty-five. One language of the Northern Caucasus has been reported to have seventy-five.

Phonemic Classification

A methodical search for contrasting utterances can be used to analyze the phonemic system of our own as well as a foreign language. For example, by looking at the words in the "at family," we see:

bat	fat	hat	gnat	rat	vat	chat
cat	gat	mat	pat	sat	that	

This one minimal set has isolated thirteen different English phonemes because the first sound of each of these words can, by contrast, be used to distinguish it from all the others.

But why should it be necessary to find minimal pairs to determine whether a sound is a phoneme? Why not simply examine the language and analyze it into its constituent parts? Phonemic analysis is concerned with the orientation of the speaker of that language. Observe, for example, the English phoneme /k/. In the word *kit* the tongue is forward in the mouth. The passage of air is restricted near the hard palate.

When you say /k/ in *coat*, your tongue is farther back, near the velum. This is because in both cases the tongue gets in position to glide into the next phoneme, either /i/, which is made in the forward part of the oral cavity, or /ow/, which is farther back. This is called *conditioning*. In English /k/ is conditioned by the succeeding vowel.

If you say *kit-coat* aloud several times, listening carefully, you will realize that the two /k/ phonemes are not only *made* differently, they *sound* different. They are, in reality, two distinct sounds. But ask a native speaker of English if they are the same and (unless he is trained in phonemics) he is fairly sure to say they are. In other words, in the English phonemic system, there is only one /k/ phoneme, and native speakers of English do not distinguish its various forms. In a complete phonetic alphabet, however, several variations of [k] would be noted. Also, in the phonemic system of certain other languages, front and back [k] are as much separate phonemes as /s/ and /z/ are in English. This is why we define phonemics as the study of the sound system of the language *as it functions in the speech of a native speaker of that language*. The linguist may see differences *within the phoneme* that the native speaker does not see—just as a physician may know more about his patient's physical condition than the patient— but phonemic analysis concerns itself not with narrow differences but with *functional contrasts*. For example, /θ/ and /ð/ are *phonemic* (two separate phonemes) in American English because we can show contrast in such words as *ether* /ijθər/ and *either* /ijðər/.

Once we realize that there are a number of ways to produce the phoneme /k/, we encounter one of the fundamentals of phonology: a phoneme is not a separate and distinct sound but a *class of sounds*. Any phoneme can have a great number of variations, but it is thought of as a single sound only by those who, in speaking their native language, are not conscious of these variations.

Each variation of sound within the phoneme is called an *allophone*. Front and back /k/, for example, are allophones of the same phoneme to a speaker of English. If we could find even one minimal pair of English words that are differentiated on the basis of front and back /k/, we would classify them as two separate English phonemes. But until such minimal pairs are located (and the language has been carefully combed by linguists), or until we see this differentiation by some other method, we will classify all allophones of /k/ as a single English phoneme. But to one who speaks Nootka or Kwakiutl—languages of Vancouver Island Indians—or Eskimo, they are two separate phonemes. In these languages speakers differentiate between front and back [k].

A number of factors operate to cause allophonic variation in a language. Vocal mechanisms of individuals vary, causing some voices to have higher pitch or greater volume. Cultural differences result in the speaker's learning to speak the language in the manner characteristic of his social milieu.

Groups of people, who, because of continued association, have certain language characteristics in common, are known as a *language community*. Language communities are not only geographical but are also social and cultural. People in a particular occupation, economic level, or social set may develop language characteristics that differentiate them from others living in the same area.

Time is another cause. Language is constantly changing. Shakespeare's contemporaries heard a different language from that of you and me, and the English of Chaucer's time is hardly recognizable to us as English. Even in a single generation new words, new slang, new customs can cause the older generation to wonder what has happened to "good old English." Within each language, all of these factors conspire to bring about a host of language communities, each with allophonic variations, and sometimes even a different phonemic system.

The brown house /brawn haws/ of the Northern Atlantic states becomes /bræwn hæws/ to the South and West. Americans usually take a bath /bæθ/, while many Englishmen take a /baθ/. These are major dialectal differences that result in different phonemic patterns. But more subtle variations can also occur, such as the placement of the point of articulation a little forward or back in the oral cavity, a tongue slightly higher or lower, or slight differences in pitch, volume, or stress. These allophonic differences are frequently not perceived by the speakers of a language, although a linguist trains his ear to hear them. He also learns a system of "close" phonetic transcription by which these minor variations can be noted.

Another important factor in allophonic variation is *conditioning*. Conditioning causes us to pronounce many of the phonemes of our language differently in different situations. For example, hold a sheet of paper by the top edge so that the bottom edge hangs an inch away from your mouth. Now say the words *tall* and *stall*. Note how a little puff of air causes the paper to jump on *tall* but not on *stall*. Take the paper away and see if you can hear the difference. This puff of air is called *aspiration*, and in close phonetic transcription we differentiate aspirated from unaspirated sounds by means of diacritical markings. Henry Gleason, for example, uses the superscript [ʰ]. In English only linguists are conscious of the difference between [t] and [tʰ], so /t/ is considered a single phoneme. In phonetic transcription, however, we would write: *tall*: [tʰɔl]; *stall*: [stɔl].

PATTERNS OF INTONATION

The discussion thus far has involved only one type of phoneme, the type that can be derived by dividing language into *segments* and giving each segment a symbol. These are commonly known as *segmental phonemes*. There is, in addition, another group of phonemes to identify not the sounds themselves but the vocal qualities imposed on the speech patterns. These phonemes concern the degree of *stress* placed on each syllable; the sound frequencies, or *pitch* of the voice; and *juncture*, or time intervals in the transition from one portion of the utterance to the other.

Examine the following words and try to decide whether they are nouns or verbs:

pervert: [pərvərt]   *permit*: [pərmit]

Although for most speakers there are some differences in the vowels of the noun and verb forms of these words, the major difference, and the one most likely to be noticed by English speakers other than linguists, is the location of the *stress*. We distinguish between *cat-rat* and *cat-cot* on the basis of a single phoneme, and we also distinguish between the noun *per'mit* and the verb *per mit'* on the basis of stress. Because native speakers of the language differentiate these two words principally by one phoneme, the words are minimal pairs, and the difference must be accounted for in the phonemic system.

Stress is the amount of emphasis accorded to a syllable in relation to the surrounding syllables. Pitch is achieved by regulating the amount of tension on the vocal cords. The greater the tension the higher the pitch. Juncture involves two aspects: (1) whether the pitch is rising or falling, and (2) whether the speech sounds flow into each other uninterrupted or a time interval occurs.

The phonemes that identify these vocal qualities are known as *suprasegmental phonemes*, and the qualities of pitch, stress, and juncture are sometimes collectively called the *intonation pattern*, or *intonation contour*.

These intonation patterns are extremely important in phonetic analysis. Not only do we distinguish between words, but whole utterances can take on different meanings when spoken with different intonations. Examine, for example:

Do I like spaghetti

If the pitch at the end of this utterance rises, it generally would be understood to signal a question, either by repeating the question: *Do you like spaghetti?* (*Let me think,*) *Do I like spaghetti?*↑ On the other hand, if spoken with unusually strong accent on the syllables *I* and *ghet*, it is more likely to indicate emphatic affirmation; *Do Í like spaghétti!* Still another meaning, sarcasm, can be derived by accenting in three places and dropping the pitch on the final word: *Do Í líke spaghétti.*↓

Actors and public speakers cultivate the art of using intonation with fine degrees of shading to stir the thoughts and emotions of their audiences. But the histrionic art is generally practiced on the intuitive level, with the performing artist depending on the "feel" of the part more than on conscious analysis of intonation. The linguist, on the other hand, uses phonetic symbols to represent these suprasegmentals on paper, just as symbols such as [p s θ] segment the language into parts.

Pitch

Most linguists use four degrees of pitch in phonetic analysis: pitches [1 2 3 4]. As with segmental phonemes, however, standardization of symbols has not been achieved. Charles Fries uses [1] to represent the highest pitch, with [2 3 4] standing for high, normal, and low, respectively.[1] Charles Hockett[2] and Henry Gleason[3] use [4] for the highest pitch with [3 2 1] going down the scale.

Another method of representing pitch seems to be in more general agreement. This is by means of horizontal lines above and below the transcription: [‾‾ — — _] representing, respectively, very high, high, normal, and low pitches. Phonetic transcription can represent pitch as follows: Close the door: [klowz\ðə/dɔr] or [klowz² ðə dɔr³].

Stress

Speakers of English are more likely to be aware of stress than pitch because only longer utterances can be distinguished on the basis of pitch, but the language contains minimal pairs of words differentiated more by stress than by segmental phonemes. English also contains pairs of words that are spelled alike in the graphemic system but differentiated in speaking largely by stress:

> *invalid*   *record*

The terms *stress* and *accent* are often used interchangeably, but accent is more frequently an over-all term for any system of obtaining emphasis on particular syllables, whereas stress is one type of accent. In a *stress language*, such as English, accent is achieved by "relative loudness or prominence,"[4] but a *tonal language*, such as Chinese, achieves this by varying the pitch or duration of syllables.

Most linguistics distinguish four degrees of stress:

Primary stress (/ ′ /) is present in one-syllable utterances, which can be demonstrated by speaking aloud a list of words containing both one and two syllable words:

> *forward, fore, ward*   *doorknob, door, knob*
> *spy, spyglass, glass*   *come, comfort, fort*
> *book, case, bookcase*   *house, hold, household*

---

[1] Charles Carpenter Fries, *The Structure of English* (New York: Harcourt, Brace and World, Inc., 1952), p. 27.

[2] Charles F. Hockett, *A Course in Modern Linguistics* (New York: The Macmillan Company, 1958), p. 34.

[3] Henry Allan Gleason, Jr., *An Introduction to Descriptive Linguistics* (New York: Holt, Rinehart and Winston, Inc., Rev. Ed., 1961), p. 46.

[4] Hockett, *A Course in Modern Linguistics*, p. 47.

As you say the sequences aloud, notice that the one-syllable words contain a stress similar to that of the first, accented syllable of the longer word. Primary stress, the strongest of the English stresses, is present in at least one syllable of every utterance. At the opposite end of the scale is the *unstressed* syllable. This is sometimes written / ˘ /, but more frequently the symbol for zero stress is omitted. Utterances of two or more syllables contain at least one zero stress. One-syllable words that receive primary stress when spoken alone may have less stress in a sequence:

Fort Knóx	*cómic book*
Book Thrée	*cócktail glass*

Or they may retain their stress in other sequences:

óld fórt	*fúnny bóok*
thírd bóok	*plástic gláss*

Between the two extremes of stress are two more degrees:
Secondary stress (/ ˆ /) may be present in utterances of three or more syllables:

rèpresentátion
dêsignátion
pénmanshîp

Tertiary stress (/ ˋ /) is the smallest degree of stress possible in English, outside of zero. Not all accentual systems of English recognize tertiary stress. Gleason, however, claims it is found in such words as *díctionàry* and *ànimátion.*[5] W. Nelson Francis illustrates the use of a four stress system with the utterance:

Têll mè the trúth.[6]

As in the case of segmental phonemes, pronouncements about how a particular utterance should be transcribed phonetically are difficult to make. Because of the great number of dialects of English and most other languages, individuals saying the same thing do not say it the same way. Even the same person may vary the way he pronounces an utterance from one time to another. Phoneticians do not attempt to establish correctness of pronunciation, as many grammarians attempted to do for usage. In transcribing an utterance a linguist makes the notation as he actually hears it. If, on some future occasion, he hears the same utterance pronounced differently, he transcribes it as he hears it this time. There is, in other words, no correct way to

[5] Gleason, *An Introduction to Descriptive Linguistics*, p. 42.
[6] W. Nelson Francis, *The Structure of American English* (New York: The Ronald Press Company, 1958), p. 153.

transcribe a language into phonetics. Only a particular spoken utterance can be said to have a proper phonetic notation.

If we add to the problem of dialects the fact that intonation patterns are frequently used as a device to indicate meaning, the difficulty of prescribing rules of transcription becomes even more complex. A rising inflection, a greater degree of accent, an unusual pitch pattern—all these are devices, sometimes quite overt, but frequently so subtle they are almost subconscious, by which we communicate shades of meaning beyond that of the words themselves.

Leo Rosten playfully tells how speakers of a certain dialect use stress to create a host of meanings for a single sentence:

> Problem: Whether to attend a concert by your neighbor, niece, or wife's friend. The same sentence may be put through maneuvers of matchless versatility:
> 1. "*Two* tickets for her concert I should buy?"
>   (Meaning: "I'm having enough trouble deciding if it's worth one.")
> 2. "Two *tickets* for her concert I should buy?"
>   ("You mean to say she isn't distributing free passes? The hall will be empty!")
> 3. "Two tickets for *her* concert I should buy?"
>   ("Did she buy tickets to *my* daughter's recital?")
> 4. "Two tickets for her *concert* I should buy?"
>   ("You mean to say they call what she does a 'concert'?!")
> 5. "Two tickets for her concert *I* should buy?"
>   ("After what she did to me?")
> 6. "Two tickets for her concert I *should* buy?"
>   ("Are you giving me lessons in ethics?")
> 7. "Two tickets for her concert I should *buy*?"
>   ("I wouldn't go even if she gave me a complimentary!")[7]

As with pitch, phonemic symbols for stress have not been standardized. Gleason[8] and Hockett[9] place their stress designations directly *over* the stressed syllable; *Webster's Dictionary*[10] places them *before* the stressed syllable; *Thorndike-Barnhart Dictionary*[11] places them *after* the stressed syllable. Although most linguists use four degrees of stress to analyze utterances, dictionaries use only three for individual

[7] Leo Rosten, *The Joys of Yiddish* (New York: McGraw-Hill Book Company, 1968). Also in *Harpers Magazine*, **237** (October 1968), pp. 83–87.

[8] Gleason, *An Introduction to Descriptive Linguistics*, Chap. 4.

[9] Hockett, *A Course in Modern Linguistics*, Chap. 5.

[10] *Webster's New International Dictionary of the English Language*, Third Ed. (Springfield: G. and C. Merriam Company, 1960).

[11] Edward L. Thorndike and Clarence L. Barnhart, *Thorndike-Barnhart High School Dictionary*, (Chicago: Scott, Foresman and Company, 1957), Frontispiece.

words. The marks themselves differ from one system to another. Webster places ['] before the syllable for primary stress, [ˌ] for secondary stress, and no symbol for unstressed. Thorndike-Barnhart places ['] after the syllable of primary stress and [´] after the syllable of secondary stress. Gleason uses [´ ˆ ` ] respectively, for primary, secondary, and tertiary stress and [ ˇ ] for unstressed.[12] Hockett uses [ ´ ] for primary stress, [ `] for secondary, and no symbol for unstressed. He further subdivides primary stress as being stronger when it occurs at the center of a speech phrase than when it is found elsewhere.[13]

To summarize briefly the discussion of stress: Stress is never considered in the absolute, but in contrast with other syllables in the utterance. Each word has one syllable with primary stress. Utterances of more than one word may have more than one primary stress. Generally:

Utterances of one syllable have primary stress:

> Go. Hi. Stop. Why? (*Does not need written stress symbol*)

Utterances of two syllables have one primary stress and usually one unstressed syllable:

> Go hóme. Hí, Joe. Stóp that. Why gó? pérmit (N) permít (V)

Utterances of three or more syllables have at least one stressed and one unstressed syllable, and possibly secondary or tertiary stress:

> Lêt's go hóme. Hí, Sâlly. Stóp that, you búlly. an întelléctual mind

Juncture

There is also contrast in the minimal pairs of utterances:

> I saw the black board. I saw the blackboard.

When *black* and *board* are separate words, there is a break in the speech flow that is not found between syllables of the compound word. It is usually a clean break, that is, [k] of *black* does not flow smoothly into [b] of *board*. This clean break is called *open transition* by Gleason,[14] and *sharp transition* by Hockett.[15] In phonetic transcription

---

[12] Gleason (1965), p. 41.

[13] Hockett, *A Course in Modern Linguistics*, p. 50.

[14] Gleason, *An Introduction to Descriptive Linguistics*, p. 42.

[15] Hockett, *A Course in Modern Linguistics*, pp. 54–55.

it is expressed by [+], so *blackboard* would be written [blǽkbɔrd] and *black board* [blǽk + bɔ́rd].

Sharp transition occurs between primary stresses in the phonetic systems of most linguists and divides utterances into phrases. Sharp transition does not occur between all words, particularly when both the last syllable of a word and the first syllable of the following word are unstressed: *Going away*: /gowiŋ əwej/ would usually be pronounced as if it were a single word.

At the end of each phrase it is appropriate to indicate whether pitch level is rising or falling. This is done with arrows. Hockett uses vertical; Gleason, diagonal lines:

Hockett: *Where are you going*↑ *I am going home*↓[16]
Gleason: *Where are you going*↗ *I am going home*→ [17]

For phrases ending in a sustained, or level tone, Hockett uses a vertical line; Gleason, a horizontal arrow:

Hockett: *Let's go* | Gleason: *Let's go*→

SUMMARY OF THE PHONEMIC SYSTEM OF THE ENGLISH LANGUAGE

The English language is usually classified into phonemes as follows:

1. 24 consonants: /p b t d k g m n ŋ l r f v θ ð s z š ž h w j č ǰ/
2. 14 vowels, some of which may be considered diphthongs: /ij i ej e æ aw ə a uw u ow oj ɔ aj/
3. 12 suprasegmentals, including:
   - 4 degrees of stress:
     - primary / ´ /
     - secondary / ˆ /
     - tertiary / ` /
     - unstressed / ˘ /
   - 3 types of juncture
     - rising / ↑ /
     - falling / ↓ /
     - sustained / | /
   - 4 levels of pitch:
     - very high /4/
     - high /3/
     - normal /2/
     - low /1/
   - 1 open transition: / + /

[16] Hockett, *A Course in Modern Linguistics*, p. 54.
[17] Gleason, *An Introduction to Descriptive Linguistics*, p. 46.

WHY PHONOLOGY?

At this point the reader would be quite justified in having serious reservations about the subject of phonology in the public schools. The question of why the entire complicated phonological structure should be included in a school course of study is a highly valid one. While the answer is far from clear-cut, some interesting facts should be observed. Phonology has already had a far-reaching effect on certain phases of language study in the schools. Most of our newer "linguistic" readers are based on the research reflected in Leonard Bloomfield's *Let's Read*,[18] while Paul Hanna's *Phoneme-Grapheme Correspondences as Clues to Spelling Improvement*[19] is paving the way for more effective methods of teaching spelling. These volumes, as well as some of their successors, are described more fully in the annotated bibliography.

Both works are based on careful study of the English language to determine the relationship between the written and the spoken systems. There seems to be some indication that helping students visualize language in terms of these two systems, with a realistic appraisal of the areas of correspondence and the areas of inconsistency, may be of considerable help in the teaching of reading and spelling.

But just how much phonology is needed for this purpose has yet to be determined. The problem that confronts the teacher is how to teach enough structure to be effective, without making it hopelessly complicated. Instead of simplifying the study of English, as some linguists believed it should, linguistics has revealed that language contains such a variety of forms that the old grammar accounts for only a portion of our utterances. English teachers who blanch at the thought of sentence fragments ignore their own speech:

When does the bell ring?   At ten o'clock.

With fifty phonemes in the English language, each with an allophonic structure of its own; with three thousand to four thousand languages estimated to exist on this earth, each with its own phonemic pattern; with an infinite variety of sounds of which the human voice is capable, it should be obvious that a public school course in linguistics can no more discuss all possible linguistic structures than a public school course in physics can teach all there is to know about the physical world.

The problem, then, becomes one of *deciding what to teach*, of finding if there is

[18] Leonard Bloomfield and Clarence L. Barnhart, *Let's Read: A Linguistic Approach* (Detroit: Wayne State University Press, 1961).

[19] Paul R. Hanna, Jean S. Hanna, Richard E. Hodges, and Edwin H. Rudorf, Jr., *Phoneme-Grapheme Correspondences as Clues to Spelling Improvement* (Washington: U.S. Department of Health, Education and Welfare, Office of Education, 1966).

anything in phonology that is important and interesting to the classroom clientele. To do this, the teacher must acquaint himself with the data brought to light by linguistic research. But these data must be considered in relation to what is known about the process of education. Finally, the teacher can build a language curriculum that uses subject matter from whatever disciplines—including linguistics—will help him achieve his purpose.

A study of phonology should, among other things, call the student's attention to the narrowness of his own culture. In Figure 4-2, seventy-two symbols are used to express in writing the consonant system of some well-known human languages. Note that only eighteen of these are part of the English phonemic system.

At birth the human being has the capacity to develop an infinite variety of speech sounds and patterns. But because his particular language uses only certain sounds, his phonemic pattern becomes limited. The vast majority of possible sounds are either blotted out of his knowledge or compressed into clusters (phonemes), the variations of which (allophones) are undifferentiated and unheard.

Hopefully, a peek at the phonemic systems of other societies might free the individual from the cultural blinders imposed upon him through language and help him realize that just as we develop only a small portion of our language faculties, we develop only a small portion of the total human capacity to understand, to visualize, and to communicate. Cultural limitations persist, despite the greatness of our technological and educational systems. There are Indians on the frozen wastes of the Arctic and in the forests of British Columbia who can differentiate between front and back [k]. What other insights may be hidden in the minds of those whom we, in our ignorance, call "primitive!"

In today's shrinking world, with the farthest points of the globe now closer than New York once was to Philadelphia, with new nations emerging and growing in strength and independence, and with all nations dependent on world trade, it becomes increasingly important for Americans to bridge the cultural barriers that now separate us from the Latin American, the Chinese, and the African. A study of phonemic systems may be a starting point.

One source of difficulty for the beginner in linguistics may be the conflicting systems and symbols discussed in this chapter. Why, for example, should the same phoneme be written /ʃ/ in I.P.A., /š/ by Hockett, /ʃh/ in i.t.a., /sh/ by Paul Roberts, and /sh/ in the dictionaries?

Studying phonology is a bit like buying commercial brands of paint. Each company (linguist) has its own system of colors (phonemes). You cannot tell what the names on the can (phonetic symbols) mean without a chart (Figures 4-4 and 4-5). Even with a chart the system is only approximate, because printer's ink (phonetic writing) is a different medium from paint (speech), and one can only roughly indicate the other. Of course, with colors of paint chosen for salesmanship and phonetic symbols for scholarship, the linguists have come closer to achieving a uniform system than commercial paint manufacturers.

One major reason for these inconsistencies is that many linguists have conducted research in a particular area and have developed systems that suit their diverse purposes. A student of Oriental languages may develop phonetic symbols that best express those languages, and these may not be the best for an Indo-European language. An anthropologist, a speech therapist, an English teacher, and a historian may find that their needs require different emphasis.

Paul Roberts, for example, has developed a system that was linguistic in approach but not too great a change from the dictionaries that were used by the students. i.t.a. is designed to facilitate the transfer from phonetic to conventional spelling, and hence retains such devices as both sh and ch, using them as the students will eventually have to recognize them.

The linguistics student should not consider these apparent inconsistencies as difficulties so much as sources for understanding the many ways in which the complex phenomena of language can be examined, conceptualized, and discussed. Gleason, for example, points out that although his vowel system includes only nine phonemes, a total of thirty-six vowels are possible because each of his phonemes can be diphthongized with $/y/$, $/w/$, and $/h/$.[20] If every dialect of English is examined, he contends, every one of these thirty-six vowel sounds will be found. Hockett, on the other hand, takes those diphthongs he considers most frequently used and includes them in a basic system that can be expanded by using additional symbols or diacritics.

Actually, is there any reason why linguists should agree on every point? Do behavioral psychologists always agree with Freudian psychologists—or even among themselves? Do historians agree concerning the causes of the Civil War? Do political scientists agree about national policy? In how many areas do human beings enjoy universal agreement?

Granted, a certain amount of uniformity in the use of symbols would be helpful. Some day this may come, but it will be difficult to achieve. Each of the major linguists seems committed to his particular system, and is as reluctant to give it up as most Americans would be to give up the familiar feet and inches in favor of the more scientific metric system. Such mechanical conveniences as the typewriter and the printing press, for example, have caused some linguists to shift from $/\int/$ to $/š/$, which can be reproduced with less hand work or special movable type.

But this difficulty of linguistics is also its strength, for we can use it to help our

[20] Gleason, *An Introduction to Descriptive Linguistics*, pp. 34–35.

students realize that there is no one, final, and ultimate phonemic system of the English language, just as there are no single, final, and ultimate answers to most complex questions concerning human activity. If we, as teachers, can approach the teaching of the English language with the same objectivity with which linguists have approached their investigations, we can substitute science for dogma. If we can recognize the complexity of language, we can help stamp out pat little clichés about what language is or ought to be.

If, for example, we approach our students with, "There are thirty-eight segmental phonemes in the English sound system," what have we really gained? Possibly a modicum of accuracy after, "We always use the nominative form of the personal pronoun after the verb of being." But have we helped anyone speak, read, listen, write, or think with greater skill? Have we excited our students with the quest for learning?

On the other hand, if we approach the study of language with a mouthful of questions instead of a bookful of answers, somebody may get curious. If we set each of our charges to the task of *ferreting out for himself* the principles upon which the English language is based, someone may begin to understand the process of scientific investigation.

Such an approach could not only help the students come to grips with the structure of language but possibly even to understand a more important point: that it is quite possible for intelligent, educated, and methodological researchers to investigate the same body of data and come up with somewhat different conclusions, or at least different methods of systematizing their conclusions. For if prominent linguists can use different vowel systems, why can't students?

By looking at language as linguists, students can learn to *listen to language and build their own taxonomies of phonemic classification.* Placing their own, individually derived phonemic systems side by side, they can see that they may have used different symbols, they may even disagree on certain points, but despite their differences there are points of agreement, and each can learn something from the other. They may begin to see that it is quite possible for individuals to have divergent points of view without anybody necessarily being wrong. Some of our most important questions have no one correct answer but rather have myriad possibilities and viewpoints. It is time for the schools to kick the memorization habit and get on with the business of education. He who can live without pat little answers to complex questions is prepared to face life in a democracy.

But this brand of teaching cannot be achieved by keeping a page ahead of the students or by reusing notes made the year the textbook was adopted. Nor can it be achieved by a teacher who is too rigid to see the merits of a fresh point of view. That is why the New English alone will not suffice. We must also plug the New English Teacher into the system.

5

atom to molecule
morphology

If language had no other purpose than to make a series of unintelligible sounds, phonological analysis would be sufficient. It is true that sound for its own sake does figure in human activity. Poets, singers, and actors are among those for whom the sound of the human voice is in itself an instrument of beauty and drama. Babies babble, apparently for the sheer pleasure of discovery, and some of our less popular acquaintances seem no less taken by the sound of their own voices. Even you and I, in our more poetic or musical moments, can find our voices a source of aesthetic pleasure.

But although the aesthetics of language is a very important part of our culture and should figure prominently in our school program, it is ancillary to the real purpose of language—that of communication. Therefore, if the wandering scholar of the previous chapter—or any student of language—really wishes to understand the nature of his medium, he must go beyond the sound system and look at the meaning the sounds are intended to convey. The ultimate purpose of linguistic study, therefore, particularly as a public school subject, is to use analysis of form primarily as a tool for arriving at meaning. Teachers who merely forsake subject-predicate agreement in favor of phonology are neither modern nor progressive. Only when linguistic analysis leads to significant new understanding can the process be justified.

To the language novice and to most traditional grammarians, the basic unit of meaning is the *word*. But if we peek once more over the shoulder of the language student of Chapter 4, we can see a number of difficulties. As his informants help him build his vocabulary of English terminology, he comes across the following "words":

dog: a four-footed carnivorous mammal

So far no difficulty. If all "words" were like this one, the word would be a satisfactory unit of language. But further down the list he finds:

dogs: more than one dog

By contrasting *dog* [dɔg] (one) with *dogs* [dɔgz] (more than one), he theorizes that the *s* [z] is itself a unit of meaning carrying the concept of plural. He uncovers substantial evidence for this theory by finding the same phoneme used in other words to carry the same meaning:

pear	a type of fruit	*pears*	more than one
boy	a young male	*boys*	more than one
girl	a young female	*girls*	more than one
table	a piece of furniture	*tables*	more than one

The data given show that some words are divisible into smaller units, and that these subunits *recur* in other words, just as the same phonemes of a language recur in a variety of combinations. Thus we must distinguish between words such as *dogs*, which can be divided into meaningful units *dog* and *s*, and words such as *dog*, which cannot be subdivided.

The use of words as the basic units of meaning becomes more complicated when we observe that the internal unity (singleness) of the structures of words decreases as we progress through the series: *dogs* [dɔgz] *dogged* [dɔgid] *dogbite* [dɔgbajt] *dog-bitten* [dɔgbîtən] *dog lover* [dɔg lǝvǝr] (one who loves dogs) *dog lover* [dɔg + lǝvǝr] (a dog with amorous intentions). In other words, as we go through the preceding progression it is difficult in some cases to tell which are one word and which are two words. We also have to account for contractions such as *don't* [downt] and *it's* [its], which combine not only two words but two parts of speech. There seems to be no clear-cut division between one word and two. However, it can be demonstrated that certain forms from the exercise can recur in other environments:

dog	[dɔg]	I have a *dog*. The *dog* went home. This is the *dog* I told you about. Joe's *dog* bit Sally's *dog*.
s	[z]	see corpus above (pears, boys, etc.)
ed	[id]	dogg*ed*: like a dog (determined)
		wood*ed* hillside: hillside like the woods
bite	[bajt]	cat *bite*: bite of a cat
		mosquito *bite*: bite of a mosquito
		frost*bite*: bite of the frost
		ant *bite*: bite of an ant

bitten [bítin]	cat-*bitten*: bitten by a cat
	mosquito-*bitten*: bitten by a mosquito
	frost*bitten*: bitten by the frost
	ant-*bitten*: bitten by an ant
lover [lôvər]	animal *lover*: one who loves animals
	bird *lover*: one who loves birds
	nature *lover*: one who loves nature
	art *lover*: one who loves art
lover [lôvər]	male *lover*: male who loves
	female *lover*: female who loves
	movie *lover*: one who makes love in the movies
	cow *lover*: amorous cow

Note that *lover* can be further subdivided into *love* (a feeling of affection) and *er* (one who _____); *bitten* consists of *bite* + the past participle *en*.

Some linguists use the term *word* only as a unit of writing rather than as a unit of speech. Because of the difficulties illustrated, the word is considered *the unit written with a space before and a space or mark of punctuation after it.* In terms of speech, words may be described as units that *may* be spoken with sharp transition before and after. This simply means that if you look at a corpus of writing you can *see* the spaces between words, but if you listen to speech the pauses are so varied in length and often so minute in duration that you cannot always tell where one word ends and the next begins.

In analyzing a single language, the word is frequently used, inasmuch as native speakers of that language have a fairly general idea of what they mean by a word. Linguists, however, are looking for terminology that is applicable to the study of *any* language, and because the structure of the word may vary from one language to another, a more precise term is needed.

For breaking language into its smallest meaningful units, as we shall attempt in this chapter, the word is too vague and not sufficiently analytical. Some linguists have proposed the term *lexeme*, the unit of lexical meaning as entered in a dictionary. A lexeme, as defined by Hockett, cannot be subdivided. *Eat* in *We eat dinner* is a lexeme, but not *eats* (can be subdivided into *eat* + *s*), *eaten* or *eating*. Corresponding somewhat to lexeme (as one of the entries in a dictionary) is the term *idiom*. An idiom is a unit whose meaning cannot be determined by an analysis of its parts. *Dog*, for example, is an idiom because a non-English speaker unfamiliar with the word would have no way of determining its meaning except by being told. *Dogs*, on the other hand, is not an idiom. One who knows the meaning of *dog* and the significance of the phoneme /z/ added to words, can figure out that *dogs* means more than one dog. There are also longer idioms. *How do you do?* is not really an inquiry into how anyone "does," and unless an individual has learned this idiom *as a whole unit* he would have no way of knowing that it acknowledges an introduction.

The American linguist Leonard Bloomfield introduced the concept of *freedom* and *bondage* into linguistic analysis.[1] Using the term *form* for a unit of lexical meaning, he described forms such as *dog, house, jump, grow*, and *good* as *free forms*, meaning they could recur in a variety of language situations (*environments*) without having to be attached to other forms. But *books, goes, heated*, and *larger* each contain one free form: *book, go, heat*, and *large*, plus one *bound* form *s, es, ed*, and *er*. Bound forms can only be used when attached to another form, as in the words above. *Contact* and *survive* are free forms each consisting of two bound forms: *con* and *tact* (*with* and *touch*); *sur* and *vive* (on and live). But none of these four parts can be used without attaching to some other form; therefore they are *bound forms*.

Any free form that cannot be divided into more than one free form is a *minimum free form*. This term probably comes closest to the popular conception of *words*. Most minimum free forms are words, and vice versa. All of the examples given (*dog, house, jump, grow, good, books, goes, heated, larger*) are minimum free forms because they contain either one free form or none. *Reject* and *eject, remit* and *emit, repel* and *expel* are also minimum free forms, each consisting of two bound forms. Minimum free forms may or may not have bound forms added.

The branch of linguistics dealing with these minimum units of meaning is generally referred to as *morphology*. Some of the vocabulary of phonology has a parallel in morphology. As the phoneme is the basic unit of sound, so is the morpheme the basic unit of meaning. /d/, /ɔ/, /g/, and /z/ are phonemes of many languages, but {dɔg} and {z} are morphemes of English, although there are other languages that use /z/ as a plural morpheme.

An exercise given earlier in the chapter indicated that the words *pear, boy, girl*, and *table* have meaning in English. Because they have meaning and cannot be divided into two or more meaningful units, they are classified as morphemes. They are *free morphemes* because they can form words without being attached to any other form. The plural {Z} was also shown to have meaning and be indivisible; hence it is also a morpheme. But because it can only be used when attached to another form, it is a bound morpheme. Thus we can list *pear* as a word of one morpheme, *pears* as a word of two. Both are minimum free forms, containing not more than one free morpheme. Another exercise contained the morphemes {dog}, {Z}, {ed}, {bite}, {en}, {love}, and {er}. (The capital letter {Z} is used to indicate a common English morpheme.)

Just as variant forms of phonemes are allophones, some morphemes have variant forms, known as *allomorphs*. Allomorphs of a morpheme, like allophones of a phoneme, are variations that do not occur as contrasts to each other but are in *complementary*

[1] Leonard Bloomfield, *Language* (New York: Henry Holt and Company, 1933), p. 160.

distribution. This means that each is found in language situations (environments) in which the other is never found. For example, the English articles *a* and *an* are in complementary distribution because *a* is never found before a vowel sound (*an apple, an elephant, an earnest effort, an only child*); *an* is never found before a consonant sound (*a book, a clock, a vowel, a big apple*). Each language has only a limited number of phonemes, each with a great variety of possible allophones, but languages usually have thousands of morphemes, only some of which have allomorphs.

Like the phoneme, the morpheme is difficult to define. We can, however, describe it in terms of some of its properties. Gleason calls morphemes the "smallest meaningful units in the structure of the language . . . which cannot be divided without destroying or drastically altering the meaning . . . ." [2] Hockett refers to them as "the smallest individually meaningful elements in the utterances of a language." [3] Morphemes *recur* in the language, so the same morpheme is used over and over in many environments, as is the case with phonemes. In order for two linguistic forms to be considered recurrences of the *same* morpheme, they must share two qualities: they must have the same phonemic structure and the same lexical meaning. In *I saw the boy* and *The boys are away*, *boy* can be shown to be a recurring morpheme. *Dog* and *hound* are two separate morphemes (*synonyms*) because they have similar lexical meaning but differing phonemic structure.

The present tense verb *lead* and the noun *lead* are separate morphemes in spite of their identical spelling because they have neither the same phonemic shape (/lijd, led/) nor the same lexical meaning. The past tense verb *led* has the same phonemic shape as *lead*, the metal, but not the same meaning. As will be explained later in this chapter, *led* contains two morphemes, the verb *lead* and the past tense morpheme, which replaces /iy/ with /e/. Thus *lead, lead,* and *led* are three separate minimum free forms, each of the first two containing one and the third containing two morphemes.

Care must be taken not to classify phonemically identical morphemes as the same until their meaning has been ascertained. For example, the word /barks/ consists of /bark/ and /s/. But examine the following utterances:

The dog barks.
That dog's bark's worse than his bite.
The dog let out three barks.

[2] Henry Allan Gleason, Jr., *An Introduction to Descriptive Linguistics*, Rev. ed. (New York: Holt, Rinehart and Winston, Inc., 1961), p. 53.

[3] Charles F. Hockett, *A Course in Modern Linguistics* (New York: The Macmillan Company, 1958), p. 123.

In the sentences shown, the phoneme /s/ forms three different morphemes, meaning *agreement with third person singular, possessive case,* and *plural* respectively. /ər/ in *waiter* and *greater* forms two different morphemes, meaning "one who" and "comparative form of adjective."

Because of these sources of possible confusion, all "conclusions" in morphemic analysis are considered tentative. Further analysis of the language may at any time upset some well-established hypothesis. For example, if one looked at such words as *dancer, sweeper, farmer,* and *banker,* it would be easy to hypothesize that the /ər/ always means "one who." This could be firmly established with dozens of words. But then if one comes across *greater, taller, meaner, nicer, hotter,* and *fatter,* it would be necessary to amend this theory to include two separate morphemes, the second meaning "adjective of comparison." Morphemes that are alike phonemically but different in meaning are usually referred to as *homophones.* When one uncovers the words *father, sister, brother,* and *mother* and tentatively concludes that /ər/ can also mean "a member of a family" this leaves the fragments *fath, sist, broth,* and *moth.* But until recurrences of these forms can be found in the language, we must tentatively theorize that *father, sister, brother,* and *mother* are single morphemes. Other occurrences of /ər/ as part of single morphemes are found in *finger, either, banner,* and *former.*

Another example of a hasty conclusion would be the classification of *big* and *large* as synonymous. It is true that they are semantically interchangeable in many environments, but *by and large* cannot be replaced by **by and big.* (The asterisk is frequently used by linguists to indicate a form that would not ordinarily be used by native speakers of the language.) Therefore these words are only partially synonymous. On the other hand, the argument could be advanced that *by and large* is a single indivisible idiom; therefore its parts do not conform to their usual morphemic classification. In this case, *big* and *large* would be synonymous, with *by and large* being considered as an exceptional usage that does not affect the usual distribution of *large.*

In some cases even linguists are not too sure how to classify certain forms. In *remote, promote, demote, reduce, produce, deduce,* we seem to have some interesting phonemic recurrences, but in current usage the semantic relationships are so nebulous that Hockett suggests that we simply refer to them as idioms.[4]

Beginners in linguistics must be careful not to confuse the *syllable* with the morpheme. The former is a phonetic unit, consisting of a vowel phoneme with or without one or more consonants clustered around it. The morpheme is a semantic

---

[4] Hockett, *A Course in Modern Linguistics,* p. 173.

(meaning) unit, and may consist of a syllable, part of a syllable, or more than one syllable. *Goes* contains two morphemes (*go* + the third person singular morpheme *es*) and one syllable. *Mississippi* contains only one morpheme and four syllables.

TYPES OF MORPHEMES

Morphemes may be classified in a number of ways. The characteristics of free and bound morphemes discussed are not absolutes, for morphemes can have a greater or lesser *degree* of freedom. *Dog* is a completely free morpheme and can occur in many environments without being attached to any other form. /-s/ plural is completely bound and can only occur as part of a noun such as *cakes* /kejks/. Some morphemes are *unique* in that they can only occur in very restricted environments. The classic example is the word *cranberry*. /bérij/ is easy to establish as a morpheme, for it recurs with the same meaning in *loganberry, blueberry, boysenberry, gooseberry*, and *strawberry*. But what of /kræn/? If we cannot find a recurrence of it, how can we classify it as a morpheme? Therefore, does *cranberry* consist of one morpheme or two? One solution is to classify /kræn/ as a *unique* morpheme, one that occurs only in one type of environment. This may change, however, for I have recently seen a commercial product in the grocery store labeled *Cranapple*. (Cranberry and apple juice mixture.) Although such occurrence in a brand name is not the same as in general usage, it shows that *cran* has at least the potential of becoming a morpheme. Even here, however, we have problems accounting for the fact that in the example shown, *cran* and *cranberry* have the same meaning.

Morphemes may range from entirely free, through various stages of uniqueness, to completely bound. For example, in addition to *cran* we have such unique morphemes as *tock*, which must be preceded by *tick*; *kith*, which only occurs in *kith and kin*; and *sake*, which is almost always accompanied by *for*. (*Do it for my sake.*)[5] Morphemes that consist entirely of segmental phonemes are *segmental morphemes*. But because intonation patterns are also morphemic, we must account for *suprasegmental morphemes*. The form *rain clouds* /réjnklàwdz/ (*Look at the rain clouds gathering.*) and the form *Rain, clouds* /réjn + klâwdz/ can be distinguished only by the suprasegmental morphemes /³´ ˋ¹/ and /³´ + ˋ²/.

Morphemes may be classified according to the way in which they function in the "word." Those thousands of morphemes that usually form the nucleus of a word

[5] An interesting discussion of unique morphemes is found in Hockett, *A Course in Modern Linguistics*, pp. 126–127.

are *roots*, while morphemes added to these roots are *affixes*. In *walks, walked,* and *walking, walk* is the root and *s, ed,* and *ing,* are affixes. Affixes added to the ends of roots, as in the examples given, are *suffixes,* whereas those placed *before* the root, as *in* and *ex* in *inhale* and *exhale* are *prefixes.* Affixes injected in the middle of another morpheme are *infixes.* English does not contain infixes, unless one chooses to consider such uncommon constructions as the past tense of certain verbs: *grind, ground,* with /gr—nd/ considered a *discontinuous* morpheme, the root, and /aj/ and /aw/ the present and past tense infixes. But this analysis would complicate English morphemics by violating the general principle that the English language does not contain infixes. Also, discontinuous morphemes are quite rare in most languages, including English, and are found commonly in only a few languages, such as Hebrew. We therefore need a simpler method of accounting for past tense constructions, as will be discussed later in the chapter.

A *stem* is any construction to which an affix can be added. Roots always contain a single morpheme, but a stem may consist of a root plus an affix. For example, *learn* is a single morpheme. In *unlearn, learn* is the root to which *un* is prefixed. It is also the stem. In *unlearning, learn* is still the root, but *unlearn* is the stem with the suffix *ing.* Thus, all roots are stems, but not all stems are roots. In *blackboards, black* and *board* are roots, and *blackboard* is the stem to which the suffix *s* is attached. Stems that consist of two roots are called *compounds.*

Morphology and phonology are closely related, inasmuch as morphemes are expressed through the medium of phonemic symbols. For example, the *genitive* (possessive) English morpheme in many cases is represented phonemically by the symbol /z/. But because the pronunciation of this morpheme is *conditioned* by the preceding consonant, the same morpheme is written differently in different environments. For example, in *boy's* it is written /z/, in *cat's* it is /s/, and in *fish's* it is /iz/. Thus /z/, /s/, and /iz/ are three *allomorphs* of the genitive morpheme {Z}. Braces are used to indicate that this is a morpheme having more than one form. In other words, {Z} stands for the morpheme that includes the three allomorphs /-z/, /-s/, and /-iz/. This discussion can be simplified still further by use of the symbol /~/, which stands for allomorphic variation. /-s ~ -z ~ -iz/ thus becomes another way of writing the sequence /-s/, /-z/, or /-iz/, and a still shorter form is {Z}.

The *morphophonemic system* of a language refers to "the ways in which the morphemes of a given language are variously represented by phonemic shapes."[6] Morphophonemics is something of a bridge between phonology and morphology, inasmuch as it involves the interrelationships of the two systems. There is, in other

---

[6] Hockett, *A Course in Modern Linguistics,* p. 135.

words, no sharp dividing line between phonology and morphology, just as we shall presently see that there is no clear dividing line between morphology and syntax. Some of the material on structure at the end of this chapter could just as well have been included in Chapter 6. Likewise, some of the morphophonemic data could just as logically have been included in Chapter 4. Some linguists consider morpho-phonemics as a separate study in itself, along with phonology and morphology.

THE ENGLISH MORPHOLOGICAL SYSTEM

Basic to understanding the structure of a language is visualizing the morphemic system by means of which its words and phrases are composed. We have seen that morphemes can be classified several ways, including free and bound, with various degrees of uniqueness between. They may also be divided into roots and affixes. Root morphemes carry the central core of the meaning of the word, whereas affixes are added to roots to give them form or additional meaning. They may be prefixed, or suffixed, and in some languages infixed. Generally, affixes fall into two major classifications. *Inflectional affixes* in English are most frequently suffixed to give words such formal characteristics as tense, number, and gender. *Derivational affixes* either regulate whether a word is to be a noun, verb, adjective, or adverb (Stem *attend* + affix *tion* becomes noun *attention*; stem *man* + affix *ly* becomes adjective *manly*.) or add lexical meaning (*un* in *uncommon* or *pre* in *predict*).

The Inflectional System

Chapters 1 and 2 pointed out that English is not a highly inflected language. However, an understanding of the inflections that remain is vital to a functional use of the language. The entire English inflectional system can be classified into eight morphemes, some with a number of allomorphs, plus a few special cases.

I $\{Z_1\}$ *The plural noun*
   A. The common allomorphs /-z ~ -s ~ -iz/, which account for most words.
      1. /-z/ after the voiced phonemes /b d g m n ŋ v ð l r j w/ and all vowels: *boys* /bɔjz/; *trees* /trijz/; *songs* /sɔŋz/; *potatoes* /pətéjtowz/.
      2. /-s/ after the unvoiced phonemes /p t k f θ/: *ships* /šips/; *books* /buks/; *lengths* /lejŋθs/.
      3. /-iz/ after the sibilant phonemes /s z š ž č ǰ/: *glasses* /glǽsiz/; *buzzes* /bə́ziz/; *wishes* /wíšiz/; *judges* /ǰə́ǰiz/.

B. Replacives (replacements of one phoneme with another, indicated by the symbol /←/).
1. /ij ← u/: *foot, feet* /fut/ → /fijt/.
2. /e ← æ/: *man, men* /maen/ → /men/.
3. /i ← u/: *woman, women* /wúmən/ → /wímən/.
4. /ij ← uw/: *tooth, teeth* /tuwθ/ → /tijθ/.
5. /aj ← aw/: *mouse, mice* /maws/ → /majs/.

C. Stem changes plus /-z ~ -iz/.
1. /-v ← f/: *leaf, leaves* /lijf/ → /lijvz/; *shelf, shelves* /šelf/ → /šelvz/.
2. /-ð ← θ/: *path, paths* /pæθ/ → /paeðz/.
3. /-z ← s/: *house, houses* /haus/ → /hauziz/.

D. /-in/, sometimes with additional stem changes in three words.
ox, oxen /aks/ → /aksin/; *child, children* /čajld/→/čildrin/; *brother, brethren* /brəðr/ → /breðrin/ (A more common plural of *brother* is brothers.)

E. Words taken directly from other languages often retain the plural allomorph of the mother language, although there is a tendency to gradually *assimilate* these words into the regular English /-s ~ -z ~ -iz/ pattern.

	singular	original plural	assimilated plural
From Greek:	phenomenon /fijnámənan/	phenomena /fijnámənə/	
From Latin:	index /índeks/	indices /índəsijz/	indexes /índeksiz/
From Hebrew:	cherub /čerəb/	cherubim /čerəbim/	cherubs /čerəbz/

F. The zero (null) allomorph /ø/ indicates that a change has actually taken place, but the new form is phonemically identical with the old. Plurals of some words fall into this class: *deer*: /dijr/ singular, /dijr/ + /ø/ plural. The zero allomorph is written only when it is necessary to point out that the transcript is referring to the new form. Some speakers use /-ø/ to pluralize *fish*, others use /-iz/: /fiš ~ fišiz/.

II {Z₂} *The genitive noun.*
A. Although some linguists prefer to classify English possessives according to structural principles[7] (to be discussed in Chapter 6), the possessive case can be classified as an inflection with allomorphs /-z ~ -s ~ -iz ~ -ø/.

[7] See for example Gleason, *An Introduction to Descriptive Linguistics*, p. 97.

B.   The first two allomorphs are conditioned according to the same phonemic principles as {Z₁}.

1.   /-z/ after /b d g m n ŋ v ð l r j w/ and vowels: *bee's* /bijz/; *boy's* /bɔjz/; *Don's* /danz/; *singer's* /síŋrz/; *Sara's* /sǽrəz/.

2.   /-s/ after /p t k f θ/: *Judith's*/jǔwdiθs/; *Frank's* /fræŋks/; *week's* /wijks/.

3.   /-iz/ after /s z š ž ǰ č/: *judge's* /jǔjiz/; *Rose's* /rowziz/ except as follows.

4.   /-iz ~ ø/ sometimes after /-z/ in proper names: *Mr. Jones'* /mistər + jównz ~ mistər + jównziz/; *Charles'*/čarlz ~ čárlziz/.

5.   /-ø/ after /-s ~ -z/ allomorphs of {Z₁} commonly used when a noun contains both the plural and the genitive inflections: *books'* /buks/; *boys'* /bɔjz/; *judges'*/jǔjiz/.

III   {Z₃}   *The third person singular verb.*

A.   Third person singular verbs are used when the subject is third person singular (*he, she, it,* or any singular noun), with allomorphs /-s ~ -z ~ -iz/ conditioned phonologically according to the same principles as {Z₁}. *He, she, it: goes* /gowz/; *swims* /swimz/; *eats* /ijtz/; *puts* /puts/; *sniffs* /snifs/; *coughs*/kawfs/; *charges* /čárjiz/; *crashes* /krǽšiz/; *misses* /misiz/.

B.   Replacives are included in some verbs:

1.   /z/ + /ə ← uw/ in *do, does* /duw/ → /dəz/.

2.   /z/ + /ø ← v/ in *have, has* /haev/ → /haez/.

3.   /z/ + /e ← ej/ in *say, says* /sej/ → /sez/.

IV   {D₁}   *The past tense verb*   }   with allomorphs /-d ~ -t ~ -id ~ ø/
V   {D₂}   *The past participle verb*}   conditioned phonologically.

A.   The past participle {D₂} structures with some form of *have*:

He has locked the door.   *The boxes have been opened.*

Details of their use are discussed in Chapter 7.

B.   In many nouns the past ({D₁}) and past participle ({D₂}) forms are identical:

Pandora opened the box.   *Many of us have opened Pandora's boxes.*

C.   In other verbs the past and past participle are different:

Hamlet drank the wine.   *He did not know he had drunk his last cup.*

1.   /-d/ usually after voiced phonemes /b g m n ŋ v z ð ž j w l r ǰ/ and vowels: *play, played* /plej/ → /plejd/; *occur, occurred* /əkər/ → /əkərd/.

2.   /-t/ usually after unvoiced phonemes /p k f s θ š č/: *lock, locked* /lak/ → /lakt/; *drop, dropped* /drap/ → /drapt/.

3.   /-id/ usually after /t d/: *plead, pleaded* /plijd/ → /plíjdid/; *seat, seated* /sijt/ → /síjtid/.

4. /-ø/ in several verbs including: *bet, bid, burst, cut, hit, let, put, rid, set, shut, spread.*

(They can bet at the races.   I bet my money yesterday.
I have bet on this horse before.)

5. /ə ← i/ in: *dig, sling, sting, swing, win,* and others: /dig/ /dəg/; /win/ /wən/.

6. /-t/ + /-e ← ij/ in: *creep*: /krijp/ → /krept/; *keep*: /kijp/ → /kept/; *sleep*: /slijp/ → /slept/ and others.

7. /-e ← (ij)/ in: *bleed*: /blijd/ → /bled/; *feed*: /fijd/ → /fed/; *meet*: /mijt/ → /met/.

D.   The list includes only the most numerous classes of verbs. Many of our commonest verbs have the most irregular morphemic construction: *go, went, gone; bring, brought, brought; choose, chose, chosen; draw, drew, drawn; eat, ate, eaten; shrink, shrank, shrunk; slay, slew, slain;* and others. The verb *be* is a classic example, having eight forms: *am, is, are, was, were, be, being, been.*

VI   {iŋ}   *The present participle.*
     The gerund.
     The progressive tenses.

This morpheme has only two allomorphs, but pronunciation varies. /in/ is common for informal speech: (*I'm coming.* /âjmkámin/); /iŋ/ for more precise usage: /âjmkámiŋ/. This inflectional morpheme is used for three constructions that are spelled and sounded alike but have different uses in the sentence.

gerund	present participle	progressive
Swimming is fun.	*I saw the swimming girl.*	*He is swimming.*
He likes riding.	*The riding party left.*	*They are riding.*

VII   {ər}   *The comparative adjective.*
VIII {ist} *The superlative adjective.*

These morphemes have only one form, with occasional irregularities.

| *fine, finer, finest:* | /fajn/, /fájnər/, /fájnist/ |
| *nice, nicer, nicest:* | /najs/, /nájsər/, /nájsist/ |

Of special interest is the highly irregular form:

| *good, better, best:* | /gud/, bétər/, /best/[8] |

One method of expressing morphemic changes that accompany change of form is

---

[8] For a comprehensive treatment of the English inflectional system, see Gleason, *An Introduction to Descriptive Linguistics*, Chap. 8.

through the *paradigm*, or table of forms. In highly inflected languages, such as Latin and Greek, paradigms are an essential part of the grammar, but in English they assume less importance. The noun paradigm, for example, consists of four forms. Note that only in irregular nouns is each change in written form accompanied by a phonemic change:

stem	child	/čajld/	book	/buk/	teacher	/tíjčər/
{Z₁} plural	children	/číldrin/	books	/buks/	teachers	/tíjčərz/
{Z₂} genitive	child's	/čajldz/	book's	/buks/	teacher's	/tíjčərz/
{Z₁} and {Z₂}	children's	/číldrinz/	books'	/buks/	teachers'	/tíjčərz/

Verbs have a 5 part paradigm:

stem	*run*	/rən/	*plead*	/plijd/	*rise*	/rajz/
{Z₃} 3rd Pers. Sing.	*runs*	/rənz/	*pleads*	/plijdz/	*rises*	/rajziz/
{D₁} past tense	*ran*	/ræn/	*pleaded*	/plíjdid/	*rose*	/rowz/
{D₂} past participle	*run*	/rən/	*pleaded*	/plíjdid/	*risen*	/rízin/
{iŋ} present participle gerund progressive tenses	*running*	/rə́niŋ/	*pleading*	/plíjdiŋ/	*rising*	/rájziŋ/

The traditional concept of the "three principal parts" (The principal parts of a verb consist of the stem, past {D₁}, and past participle {D₂} forms.) of the verb is based on the paradigm, but unfortunately ignores {Z₃} and {iŋ}.

The adjective paradigm has three simple steps:

stem	*good*	/gud/	*tall*	/tawl/	*fine*	/fajn/
{ər} comparative:	*better*	/bétər/	*taller*	/táwlər/	*finer*	/fájnər/
{ist} superlative:	*best*	/best/	*tallest*	/táwlist/	*finest*	/fájnist/

The eight *personal pronouns* pattern in five parts. Because there is such great variation in forms, description by allomorph becomes too complicated. Therefore, personal pronouns are usually expressed in tables of paradigms that show major changes in form. The process by which the phonemic construction of a morpheme is completely or almost completely changed in transformation is known as *suppletion*. Suppletion is most common in English pronouns (/mij ← aj/), but it is also present in some verbs (/went ← gow/).

THE PERSONAL PRONOUN PARADIGM

nominative		objective		possessive (determiner)[9]		possessive (Class I)[10]		reflexive	
I	/aj/	*me*	/mij/	*my*	/mai/	*mine*	/majn/	*myself*	/majsélf/
we	/wij/	*us*	/əs/	*our*	/ar/	*ours*	/arz/	*ourselves*	/arsélvz/
you	/juw/	*you*	/juw/	*your*	/yɔwr/	*yours*	/jawrz/	*yourself*	/jawrsélf/
								yourselves	/jawrsélvz/
he	/hij/	*him*	/him/	*his*	/hiz/	*his*	/hiz/	*himself*	/himsélf/
she	/šij/	*her*	/hər/	*her*	/hər/	*hers*	/hərz/	*herself*	/hərsélf/
it	/it/	*it*	/it/	*its*	/its/	*its*	/its/	*itself*	/itsélf/
they	/ðej/	*them*	/ðem/	*their*	/ðer/	*theirs*	/ðerz/	*themselves*	/ðemsélvz/
who	/huw/	*whom*	/huwm/	*whose*	/huwz/	*whose*	/huwz/		

It should be noted that there is an arbitrary quality to many of the constructions and paradigms shown, that what goes into them is partly dependent on whose speech one observes and under what circumstances. For example, the form *our* may be pronounced /awr/, but in rapid conversation is more likely to become /ar/. And despite the protestations of traditional grammarians, *It is me* and *Who did you see?* are firmly entrenched and commonly accepted English patterns.

Verb patterns are also likely to show variation, with such alternate forms as *knitted* or *knit*, *dreamed* or *dreamt*, *leaped* or *leapt*, and *got* or *gotten*.

The Derivational System

English derivational morphemes are of two types: *Distributional morphemes* determine the distribution of the word, or what function it can perform within the sentence. A distributional morpheme is usually suffixed to a word, determining whether the word is to be a noun, verb, or adjective. It may also add lexical meaning. *Lexical*

---

[9] Determiners and Class I words are discussed more fully in the next two chapters. Temporarily, determiners may be considered words that have the same sentence position as articles:

    a hippopotamus   *the biography*
    my hippopotamus   *your biography*

[10] Class I words may be thought of as filling the sentence positions of nouns; that is, wherever a noun can be used, any Class I word is grammatically possible:

    Apples are red.   *This is Tommy.*
    Mine is red.   *This is yours.*

morphemes give the word additional meaning, and are usually prefixes. There are too many distributional morphemes in the English language for a complete listing in an introductory text, but the more common ones are given as follows:

DISTRIBUTIONAL MORPHEMES

noun suffixes	meaning	examples
-age	process or state	*leverage, passage*
-ance	act or condition	*acceptance, variance*
-ard	one who does or is	*drunkard, wizard*
-ate	rank or position	*delegate, primate*
-ation	state of	*insinuation, confrontation*
-cy	state of	*literacy, complacency*
-dom	state of	*wisdom, martyrdom*
-er	one who	*teacher, singer*
-ess	feminine	*tigress, waitress*
-form	having the form of	*uniform, multiform*
-hood	state of	*childhood, statehood*
-ion	action of	*union, differentiation*
-ism	doctrine	*communism, catholicism*
-ist	believer or doer	*socialist, moralist*
-ity	state of	*civility, brutality*
-ment	state of	*entrenchment, bewilderment*
-ness	state of	*troublesomeness, smallness*
-or	doer	*calculator, incinerator*
-th	quality	*length, warmth*
-tion	state of	*expedition, edition*
-tude	quality	*pulchritude, latitude*
-ty	state of	*joviality, activity*

verb suffixes	meaning	examples
-ate	make	*animate, educate*
-en	become, make	*lengthen, sharpen*
-esce	become, grow	*convalesce, acquiesce*
-fy	make, cause to	*justify, glorify*
-ish	do, make	*punish, finish*
-ize	make, cause to be	*mechanize, satirize*

Distributional Morphemes—*cont.*

adjective suffixes	meaning	examples
-able	able, like	*favorable, unspeakable*
-ate	having	*fortunate, compassionate*
-ed	having quality of	*fluted, windowed*
-en	made of, like	*wooden, fallen*
-esque	in the style of	*Romanesque, picturesque*
-fic	making, causing	*terrific, soporific*
-ful	full of	*zestful, grateful*
-ible	able	*possible, edible*
-ish	like	*boyish, greenish*
-less	without	*helpless, childless*
-like	similar	*childlike, dreamlike*
-ly	like	*womanly, kingly*
-ous	characterized by	*religious, marvelous*
-some	likely to, showing	*wearisome, lonesome*
-ward	in the direction of	*upward, forward*

Lexical morphemes alter the meaning of the word but usually do not affect its position in the sentence or its part of speech.

LEXICAL MORPHEMES—PREFIXES

prefix	meaning	examples
a-	against, without	*atypical, atheist*
a-	of, to	*aware, awake*
ab-	from, away	*abstract, abdicate*
ante-	before	*antedate, anteroom*
anti-	against	*antiaircraft, antibody*
apo-	from, away	*apogee, apology*
bi-	two	*bicycle, bisect*
cata-	down, away	*catastrophe, cataract*
circum-	around	*circumference, circumstance*
com-	together	*comrade, common*
contra-	against	*contraband, contradict*
di-	many	*dialogue, dichotomy*
dia-	through, across	*diameter, dialect*
dis-	apart, away, not	*distort, discourage*
ex-	out	*extrovert, extend*
for-	away, from	*forever, forget*
fore-	before	*forewarn, forefathers*
hyper-	excessive	*hypersensitive, hypertension*
hypo-	under	*hypochondria, hypodermic*
in-	not	*inflexible, incapable*
inter-	among, between	*interrupt, interdict*

Lexical Morphemes—*cont.*

prefix	meaning	examples
mis-	poorly, not	*mistake, misinform*
mono-	one	*monotone, monologue*
post-	after, following	*postmortem, postscript*
pre-	before	*predict, previous*
pro-	forward	*problem, procure*
re-	backward, again	*return, reassert, regress*
retro-	backward	*retrogress, retrorocket*
sub-	under, beneath	*submarine, subdivision*
sym-	with, together	*symptom, sympathy*
trans-	across	*transport, transcontinental*
un-	not	*unable, uninformed*
uni-	one	*unit, unicorn*

Root morphemes are derivational elements of language. In some cases they are free morphemes that form words unassisted, but they frequently function as word nuclei to which affixes are added. The difference between a root and an affix is not always clear-cut. In the word *uniform*, for example, *uni* could be considered a root onto which the suffix *form* is added, or it could be a prefix added to the root *form*. A discussion concerning how to analyze such problems seems less fruitful than learning how derivational and inflectional affixes function in English and learning the lexical meaning of as many free and bound morphemes as possible. It is this combination of knowledge of a large store of English morphemes, plus an understanding of how they fit together, that builds language fluency.

A few common English root morphemes are listed as follows:

LEXICAL MORPHEMES—ROOTS

root	meaning	examples
-ag, -act-	do	*agenda, actor*
-am, -amic-	love	*amateur, amicable*
-anthrop-	man	*anthropology, anthropoid*
-aqu-	water	*aquatic, aqueous*
-arch-	ancient, chief	*archaic, archeology*
-astr-, -aster-	star	*asteroid, astronomy*
-aud-, -audit-	hear	*auditory, audible*
-auto-	self	*automatic, automobile*
-ben-, -bene-	good	*benefit, benefactor*
-biblio-	book	*bibliophile, bibliography*
-bio-	life	*biography, biology*
-capit-	head	*caption, capital*

Lexical Morphemes—*cont.*

root	meaning	examples
-carn-	flesh	*carnal, carnivore*
-cent-	hundred	*per cent, centimeter*
-chrom-	color	*panchromatic, chromium*
-chron-	time	*chronicle, chronological*
-clud-, -clus-	close	*include, seclude*
-cogn-	know	*cognition, recognize*
-cred-	trust	*credit, credible*
-crypt-	secret	*cryptic, cryptogram*
-dem-, -demo-	people	*democratic, epidemic*
-duc-, -duct-	lead	*conduct, education*
-fer-	yield	*transfer, fertile*
-fid-	faith	*perfidy, fiduciary*
-fin-	end, limit	*infinite, final*
-frag-, -fract-	break	*fracture, fragment*
-gen-	birth	*engender, generation*
-gen-	kind, race	*genetic, genesis*
-geo-	earth	*geography, geometry*
-gram-	write, writing	*telegram, grammar*
-graph-	write, writing	*graphite, geography*
-hydr-	water	*hydraulic, dehydrate*
-junct-	join	*junction, conjunctive*
-jud-	judge	*judicial, prejudice*
-jug-	join	*conjugal, conjugate*
-loc-	place	*location, local*
-log-	word, study	*dialogue, logic*
-magn-	large	*magnificent, magnify*
-man-	hand	*manual, manipulate*
-micr-	small	*microcosm, microscope*
-mort-	die, death	*mortal, mortician*
-neo	new	*neoclassic, neophyte*
-omni-	all	*omniscient, omnibus*
-pan-	all, entire	*pancake, pan-American*
-pater-, -patr-	father	*paternal, patron*
-phil-	like, love	*philanthropist, bibliophile*
-poly-	many	*polygamy, polyglot*
-port-	carry, bear	*transport, portable*
-prim-	first, early	*primitive, primary*
-punct-	point	*punctuation, puncture*
-sci-	know, knowledge	*science, omniscient*
-scrib-, -script-	write	*scribble, manuscript*
-spec-, -spic-, -spect-	look, see	*introspective, suspicion*
-spir-	breath, breathe	*respiration, expire*
-tract-	draw, pull	*tractor, traction*
-vid-, -vis-	see	*vision, evidence*
-vit-	life	*vital, vitamin*
-zo-	animal	*zoology, protozoa*

Compounding

In addition to the *root + affix* method, English words can be constructed through the combination of two or more roots, each of which may be a free morpheme. Such a word is called a *compound*. A *coat* worn *over* everything else becomes an *overcoat*, as a *coat* to protect against *rain* is a *raincoat*.

Many compounds, such as the above, are semantically as well as morphologically compounded. That is, the meanings of the two root morphemes determine the meaning of the compound. Anyone hearing the form *blackbird* could make an intelligent guess what it means if he knew *black* and *bird*.

Other compounds are *idiomatic*. Their roots do not reveal their sum. One has to know that a *redcap* is a pullman porter. The meaning cannot be derived from analysis into *red* and *cap*. Idiomatic compounds often result from language change in which one root becomes obsolete, as in *dreadnought* and *beware*.[11]

Summary of English Morphology

In describing the changes that take place in the structure of a word, we have dealt with a number of linguistic processes:

I. *Addition* involves stringing together of morphemes to form words. Addition consists of:

  A. *Affixation*, which may be in the form of

    1. Prefixation, usually with lexical morphemes:
      fore + tell = foretell

    2. Suffixation, usually with inflectional or distributional morphemes: *rely + able = reliable*

    3. Infixation, not found in English

    4. Superfixation (change in intonation pattern, as in: reject, reject: /ríǰekt/, /rijékt/). If the phonemic shape of a word is not modified along with its lexical or inflectional change, we can refer to this as *zero affixation*, or addition of the zero morpheme /ø/: *one deer, many deer* /dijr/ → /dijr + ø/.

  B. *Reduplication* is a process not yet discussed. It consists of the repetition of a morpheme to give additional lexical meaning. It is rare in English, used mainly

---

[11] An excellent and comprehensive treatise on English compounds is by Robert B. Lees, *The Grammar of English Nominalizations* (Bloomington, Indiana: University Research Center in Anthropology, Folklore, and Linguistics, 1960), Publication 12.

for alliterative effect in such words as *choo-choo train* or *put-put boat* or in interjections as *uh-uh* or *tut tut*. *Partial reduplication* is found in *bow-wow, oh ho,* and *tick-tock*. Gleason gives an interesting example from Tagalog, a Phillipine language, in which the initial syllable of certain forms is reduplicated to give additional meaning of 'only ....': "/isá/ 'one,' /iisá/ 'only one'; /dalawá/ 'two', /dadalawá/ 'only two'; /tatló/ 'three', /tatatló/ 'only three...' Etc."[12]

II.   *Subtraction* is the reverse of addition, the taking away of morphemes. This process may simplify analysis of some languages in which the bound morpheme takes so many different forms it is simpler to begin with the longer form and describe the change as involving *loss of the bound morpheme.*

III.   *Replacement* of one morpheme by another takes place in such forms as *sing, sang* /siŋ/, /sæŋ/ (æ ← i/).

IV.   *Suppletion* is the complete replacement of one form for another, as in *go, went* /gow/, /went/ (/went ← gow/).

IMMEDIATE CONSTITUENTS

Teachers with a flair for tradition will be pleased to know that the linguists have not given up the practice of diagramming. On the contrary, diagramming takes on increased importance as linguistic analysis passes from morphology to transformational grammar.

However, the traditional method of diagramming, with its main line and modifiers, is more appropriate for Latin than for English. Observe the familiar diagram:

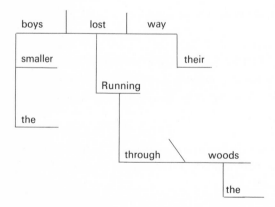

[12] Gleason, *An Introduction to Descriptive Linguistics*, p. 90.

This diagram expresses the "base and modifier" theory that dominated public school grammar at the time of its inception and is still the basis for many of our textbooks. It involves analyzing a sentence into its skeletal parts—simple subject, simple predicate, and simple complement—and attaching the other words as subordinate elements to one of these main units.

Although the theory does have considerable validity, this method of expressing it in a diagram can do as much to *obscure* the structure of the sentence as to reveal it. It is better adapted to Latin and does a fairly good job of exposing the structure of sentences in that language. The inflectional pattern of Latin reveals whether a noun is a subject or object. Therefore, in a diagram such as the one shown, the relationship of various words to each other (subject, object, etc.) in the sentence is shown by the inflection of the word itself. But in English the inflectional pattern is so brief that we depend on word order to reveal meaning. Thus any diagram of an English sentence that mixes the word order can do more to confuse than to help us understand the sentence structure. While our students are not linguistically sophisticated enough to understand all of this, they are sufficiently familiar with their own language to sense the uselessness of the whole process and resist it.

The diagram also fails to break the words themselves into their component parts. To ignore morphemic analysis is to ignore the really basic units of meaning. What is needed, then, is a system of analysis that (1) preserves word order, (2) can be conducted on a *syntactic* basis, showing the relationship of the words within the sentence, and (3) can also be *morphological*, breaking complex words into component morphemes. By analyzing language into both syntactic and morphologic units, we can arrive at a much deeper understanding of the relationships of various sentence parts. These relationships, not revealed by traditional diagramming, are sometimes referred to as the *deep structure* of a sentence.

A basic principle of linguistics is that of *immediate constituents*. A *constituent* is any linguistic form that may be included as part of a longer linguistic form. *Joe* /jow/ and *'s* /z/ are constituents of *Joe's* /jowz/. *The, smaller,* and *boys* are constituents of the phrase *the smaller boys*. But unlike *Joe* and *'s,* analysis of *the smaller boys* into constituent parts is complicated by the choice of where to make the first division.

In deciding how to divide this phrase in half we have three possibilities:

A   the boys—smaller
B   the smaller—boys
C   the—smaller boys

Analysis A violates the important word-order of the phrase and obscures the construction so completely that it must be rejected immediately. In choosing between B and C, *smaller boys* seems to have more internal unity than *the smaller.* We therefore reject **B** in favor of **C**:

Thus, *the* and *smaller boys* are immediate constituents of *the smaller boys*; that is, they are the two parts derived by making a "cut." Having gone this far, we can now subdivide *smaller boys* into immediate constituents:

the | smaller | boys

Morphemic inspection reveals that two of the words in the phrase can be subdivided into morphemes:

the | small : er | boy : s

Finally, if we add the suprasegmentals to this phrase, we can isolate the intonation pattern as a morpheme:

2′   3^   ↓

the | small : er | boy : s

Including the suprasegmental, the phrase has now been shown to include six *ultimate constituents*, or parts that cannot be further subdivided without destroying meaning.

In *The Structure of English*, Charles Fries lists rules for cutting longer constructions:[13]

First, cut off "sequence" signals that relate to the whole sentence rather than to any of its parts:

However, || *when Lolly sings all the people within hearing gingerly slip away.*

Next, cut included sentences that also relate to the entire sentence:

However, || *when Lolly sings* || *all the people within hearing gingerly slip away.*

Third, separate subject from predicate.

Then begin cutting off modifiers of the subject. Postmodifiers are cut off before

---

[13] Charles Carpenter Fries, *The Structure of English* (New York: Harcourt, Brace and World, Inc., 1952), p. 267. Fries lists a total of ten rules, six of which concern the order of cutting. These six rules are abstracted here.

premodifiers, and cutting is done from the most remote modifiers to those closest to the subject, in that order:

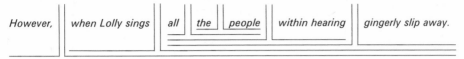

Fifth, separate modifiers of the predicate. Begin with premodifiers, then post-modifiers. Again work from the most remote to those closest to the head word:

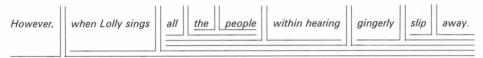

Note that up to this point, word groups, such as *when Lolly sings* and *within hearing*, are maintained as units. The sixth and final step is to separate these into constituents:

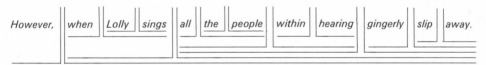

Although the sequence suggested is a good starting point, it has some limitations. Most of these can be overcome, however. For example, a morphemic breakdown can be added, separating by dashed lines such constructions as *sing ¦ ¦ s, people* ($\{$person$\}$¦ ¦$\{$-Z$_1\}$), *hear¦ ¦ing, ginger¦ ¦ly,* and *a¦ ¦way.* This, of course, does not properly differentiate between inflectional and derivational morphemes. Transformational grammar (Chapter 7) provides another framework for more detailed breakdown of the sentence into its constituents, with each constituent properly labeled.

The same type of analysis can also be applied to single words on a strictly morphological basis. The following principles are generally applied:

First "peel off" the inflectional morpheme, if there is one.

Then divide derivational morphemes from the stem.

If the stem is a *derived stem* (more than one morpheme) instead of a simple stem (one morpheme), subdivide the stem into constituents.

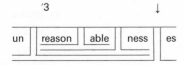

Other techniques can be used to arrive at essentially the same result. The box diagram begins with the whole word and expresses each cut on a separate line:

'3				↓
un	reason	able	ness	es
un	reasonable		ness	es
un	reasonableness			es
unreasonableness				es
unreasonablenesses				

Probably the most important diagramming technique, however, is the *branching tree*, which provides the greatest amount of flexibility and is used extensively in transformational grammar:

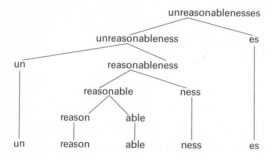

MORPHOLOGY AND THE CLASSROOM

Teachers who have wrestled with the problem of broadening their students' knowledge of the words of the English language are familiar with the difficulty and frustration generally encountered in "vocabulary drill." Students often display a high degree of skill and enthusiasm for resisting the learning of new words, particularly those students whose vocabularies are most in need of expansion. Yet one of the major obstacles to educational progress is the students' meager vocabularies—vocabularies often so inadequate that they are unable to read much of the material in the textbook with ease and comprehension or to express themselves in writing because word poverty handcuffs the mind and paralyzes the pen.

In my career as a high school English teacher I can remember trying every method I could find to expand the lexicon of my students. I used vocabulary development texts, drew word lists from the literature, and had students make "personalized" word lists. I believe I can claim moderate success with the highly motivated college-bound students, less success with the average students, and apathy on the part of the terminal students who could not read, write, or think with maturity because they lacked the words with which to operate.

In time, however, I found certain methods of word-attack that could be used effectively in the classroom, and some of these techniques can be partially explained on the basis of linguistic principles. For example, I found that a deeper understanding of language was achieved by asking students to *make an educated guess* what a word means *in the particular sentence in which it appears* than by sending students on what must seem to them an endless series of trips to the dictionary. Suppose, for instance, the class came across the following passage from *Hamlet*:

> 'Tis a consummation
> Devoutly to be wished. To die—to sleep.[14]

Obviously, this passage cannot be interpreted without understanding the word *consummation*. My desk dictionary carries the definition: "The act of consummating, or the state of being consummated; fulfillment." The first definition (which is as far as many students read) of *consummate* is: "To bring to completion or perfection; achieve." The second definition deals with the act of physically completing a marriage.

The dictionary has been of only the most tenuous help, for there is nothing either fulfilling or sexual in what Hamlet is thinking at this moment. But if one reads the entire soliloquy from the famous "To be or not to be" to the entrance of Ophelia, it becomes evident that Hamlet is wondering if life is worth living, and the *consummation* referred to here is death. A careful study of the content in this case is more helpful than the dictionary.

This is not to imply that the dictionary is not a useful tool for vocabulary building. Quite the contrary, it is the most useful single tool available for language study. As a *supplement* to the study of words in context—as a means of discovering that *consummate* has something to do with bringing to an end—the dictionary is the student's best friend. But it is only by seeing the same word over and over in many contexts that any real depth of understanding can be achieved. This, however, is more of a

---

[14] William Shakespeare, *Hamlet*, Act III, scene i.

semantic than a morphological process and is discussed in greater detail in Chapter 9.

In morphology I found another, more direct tool for word-attack. After my students had studied the structure of words, including the different types of morphemes and their various functions, they found some interesting clues to meaning in the words themselves.

It should become immediately apparent, for example, that *consummation* is a noun because it ends with the nominalizing derivational suffix *tion*. The student who has built up a vocabulary of *tion* words—*imagination, information, beautification, cogitation*—should automatically place *consummation* in this category. Often in vocabulary work I have asked students to use their new words in original sentences. I have found that linguistically unsophisticated pupils sometimes write such sentences as *That was a consummation story*, a difficulty arising from failure to recognize suffix clues as the determiners of the part of speech, as well as a problem discussed in the next chapter: how the various parts of speech are put together to form sentences. The latter difficulty seems unrelieved by years of training in traditional grammar.

Further investigation of *consummation* can lead to discovery that *consummate* is a verb because of its *ate* suffix. Thus we have learned not only *consummation*, but we have a good head start on *consummate*. Once the student understands the morphological concepts of suffixation determining the part of speech as well as the role of English prefixes and inflections, he is on the way to *consume* (*consumed, consuming*), *consumable* (*consumables*), *consumedly, consumer* (*consumers*), *consummate* (adjective), *consummately, consummative, consummator, consumptive, consumptively*, and *consumptiveness*.

A working knowledge of the derivational prefix, suffix, and root system, as outlined briefly on pages 111 through 114, should enable the student to decode hundreds of new words as he encounters them in his reading. Once the student realizes that *scribe* (from the Latin *scribere*) means *to write*, he has at his command:

describe	*inscribing*	*scribbles*
describer	*inscription*	*scribe*
describing	*manuscript*	*scribes*
description	*scribble*	*script*
inscribe	*scribbled*	

Not that there is anything new and startling about the "prefixes, suffixes, and roots" method of teaching vocabulary. Good teachers have been using it for years. Others, unfortunately, have either been ignoring vocabulary development or have been teaching a long, discouraging list of individual words. And even the best teachers of the past did not have at their command a simple, organized statement of the structure of English words. Just as a lack of knowledge of the sound structure of the language can be a major deterrent to learning language skills—particularly reading—so is a lack of knowledge of the morphological structure of the word a major deterrent to developing a vocabulary suitable for life in a technological age.

As Jerome Bruner pointed out:

> Students, perforce, have a limited exposure to the materials they are to learn. How can this exposure be made to count in their thinking for the rest of their lives? The dominant view among men who have been engaged in preparing and teaching new curricula is that the answer to this question lies in giving students an understanding of the fundamental structure of whatever subjects we choose to teach. This is a minimum requirement for using knowledge, for bringing it to bear on problems and events one encounters outside a classroom—or in classrooms one enters later in one's training. The teaching and learning of structure, rather than simply the mastery of facts and techniques, is at the center of the classic problem of transfer.[15]

Rather than memorizing long lists of Greek and Latin prefixes and roots, students should come out of the study of morphology with the following summary of the structure of the English morphological system:

1. A lexicon of roots derived from various mother tongues:
    aud (hear) becomes *auditor*;
    port (carry) becomes *porter*;
    junct (join) becomes *conjunction*.
2. Derivational prefixes added to these roots to modify the lexical meaning:
    circum (around): *circumstances*;
    hyper (beyond): *hyperbola*;
    retro (backward): *retroflex*.
3. Combinations of roots (compounds) or root plus prefix that form stems:
    air + plane = airplane   to which other affixes
    gentle + man = gentleman   can be added.
4. Derivational suffixes (plus a few derivational prefixes) added to determine part of speech:
    verb *attend + tion* = noun *attention*;
    verb *manage + able* = adjective *manageable*;
    adjective *weak + en* = verb *weaken*;
    en + noun list = verb *enlist*.
5. Inflectional suffixes added to account for such factors as number, time, and person:
    dolphin + s $(\{Z_1\})$ = plural *dolphins*;
    cook + ed $(\{D_1\})$ = past *cooked*;
    tiny + est $(\{est\})$ = superlative *tiniest*.

[15] Jerome S. Bruner, *The Process of Education* (Cambridge: Harvard University Press, 1960), p. 11.

At the same time the student is grasping the structure of English words, he is building his lexicon of derivational morphemes. The teacher should not present a long and discouraging list of prefixes, suffixes, and roots to memorize during the "unit" on vocabulary development, but should build the list one morpheme at a time. Each new word encountered in the reading is an opportunity to add something to the list. Vocabulary might develop from *junction* to *conjunction* to *conjoin* to *enjoin* to *enlist*. But at each step along the way the new morphemes—*junc*—*tion*—*con* —*en*—*list*—are classified and learned so that when encountered again they can, in combination with the context, make the learning of new words both interesting and no more complicated than necessary.

Teaching morphology *per se* is not as great a switch from traditional grammar as one might imagine. Because morphology, as does most of linguistics, goes directly to the structure of the language with principles that are observable and usable, it offers the teacher the *opportunity* to expand the students' linguistic awareness. But the opportunity does not guarantee results.

The New English becomes a significant step forward to the teacher who realizes that it is less a switch in subject matter than it is in *method*. It is not a switch from line diagrams to the branching tree as much as from giving answers to asking questions. The traditional grammarian knew all about language. He could name the eight parts of speech backwards and would never split an infinitive. The linguist is a student. He studies words, analyzes them into parts, and matches them with other words on the basis of recurring morphemes. He forms theories, tests them, and tentatively accepts or rejects them in favor of new theories that in turn must be tested. And the most exciting part is that there is still so much that we do not know about language that teacher and students have the opportunity to explore together, to join forces to push back the frontiers of their linguistic understanding.

6

the pieces come together
structural grammar

A group of words written down at random is like the pieces of a jigsaw puzzle scrambled on a table:

> *of, patterns, us, examine, the, this, of*
> *language, let, ours, intricacies of, the*

We have only a confusing mass of shape and color, with merely the vaguest hints of a pattern. It is only by placing each piece in its correct position that any sort of meaningful picture emerges:

> *Let us examine the intricacies of the*
> *patterns of this language of ours.*

Each of the three thousand to four thousand languages and dialects in the world has a system for putting words together. Although these systems overlap, with many features common to a number of languages, there are enough differences to require that a study of any particular language be based on that language and its unique features.

The ways in which speakers of a language pattern words is generally referred to as the *syntax*, or *grammar*, of that language. Some linguists include morphology as a branch of syntax. In this volume, however, we have looked at morphology as the patterns that exist *within* the word, whereas this chapter on syntax considers whole words and how they form sentences.

Traditional grammar is concerned with fitting words into appropriate part-of-speech categories and with analyzing sentences into significant units. The same is true of *structural linguistics*, but, as pointed out in earlier chapters, our present eight parts of speech are not the only or ultimate methods of classifying words, as many traditionalists believe. The parts of speech evolved slowly and are still evolving. From the simple noun-verb differentiation of Plato, grammarians have been speculating about word classification for over two thousand years. Otto Jespersen listed six parts of speech: substantives, adjectives, verbs, pronouns, particles, and numerals.[1] The participle was a firmly established part of speech for many years until Joseph Priestly, in his *Rudiments of English Grammar*, eliminated it, but added the adjective.[2] Since that date, the eight parts of speech have remained as Priestly stated them—until they were challenged by modern linguists.

Examine, for example, the *pronoun*. Traditionally we define a pronoun as a "substitute for a noun." But investigation of English sentences indicates that substitution is a bit more difficult to determine than this superficial look at language would indicate. In the sentence *Mr. Simpson said the homework would be due April 22*, observe a few of the possible words that can be used to "substitute" for *Mr. Simpson*:

> He said . . . .　　　　　　That wonderful man said . . . .
> The teacher said . . . .　　Old Sour Puss said . . . .

Each of the above—*he, teacher, Sour Puss*, and *man* is a substitute for *Mr. Simpson*. Or, if one begins with the sentence *The teacher said . . .*, *Mr. Simpson* might be considered a substitute. Yet traditional grammar contradicts its own definition by admitting only *he* as a pronoun. It would seem fairly clear at this point that *he* is set apart from the other words not because it is the only "substitute" word, but because it is structurally different, as classified morphologically. That is, *teacher, Sour Puss*, and *man* are words that have a paradigm based on the inflectional morphemes $\{Z_1\}$ and $\{Z_2\}$, while *he* operates in a five-part paradigm: *he, him, his, his, himself*.

The entire question of substitution is much more complex than traditional grammar would admit. In the example given, for *April 22* you can "substitute" forms such as *next Friday, soon, after the spring vacation*, or *sooner than you think*. In the sentence *Jim does his homework every day, but Harry doesn't*, traditional grammarians would classify *doesn't* as an "elliptical" expression, standing for *doesn't do his homework every day*. Many linguists, however, reject such speculations, claiming that a sentence element either is or is not part of the structure, and that the word does (do + $\{Z_3\}$) is

[1] Otto Jespersen, *Essentials of English Grammar* (London: S. Allen and Unwin, Ltd., 1933).

[2] Joseph Priestly, *Rudiments of English Grammar* (London: J. Johnson and F. and C. Rivington, G. G. and J. Robinson; J. Nicols, and W. Lowndes, 1798), pp. 7–8.

in reality a substitute for the antecedent form *does not do his homework every day.* Rather than become involved in such fruitless speculation, would it not be better to begin afresh and, armed with our current knowledge of language and its operations, build a new grammar that can be observed, tested, and measured?

This is precisely what the late Charles Fries did in 1952 in his classic volume, *The Structure of English.* This work was the basis for much of what we now know as structural grammar. Fries began his dissertation on the parts of speech by dividing all words of the English language into two groups, the *classes* (often called *form classes,* or *form words*) and the *function words.* A number of differences distinguish form from function words:

1.   Form class words usually have more lexical meaning. They include words such as *house* and *city, run* and *swim, good* and *black, slowly* and *dangerously.* They can be interchanged with other words of the same class without losing *structural* significance, although the *meaning* of the sentence changes if you change from *The house is large* to *The city is large.* Function words have less lexical meaning but are vital in signaling the structure of the sentence. *Book is table* is not a grammatical English sentence, but *The book is on the table* is made functional by the insertion of function words. On the other hand, if we change the sentence to *The book is under the table,* we change the meaning just as much as when we change *house* to *city,* despite the fact that *on* and *under* are function words. Thus we have not arrived at a *definition* of form words but a *description* of one common characteristic. To classify form and function words, we must look at other characteristics as well.

2.   Every form class contains thousands of words. The number of words that can be used in place of *run* and *swim* is legion, but function groups can consist of a single word. *Not,* for example, is in a function group of its own, as is *there* (according to Fries' method of classification).[3] Other function groups consist of only a few words. A count of the total number of function words in the English language will vary somewhat among linguists, for they do not all use the same system of dividing words into groups; Fries has counted a total of 154. This is subject to interpretation. Fries classifies numbers (*twenty-seven, thirty-eight, sixteen*), for example, as function words, and as there are a great many of these, it would seem reasonable to assume that he considers all numbers a single function word.

3.   Form words are structured with roots and affixes. The preceding chapter on morphology was concerned mainly with form class words, those that may contain more than one inflectional or derivational morpheme. *Run* can become *ran*; from

[3] Charles Carpenter Fries, *The Structure of English* (New York: Harcourt, Brace and World, Inc., 1952), pp. 92, 97.

beautiful we derive *beautifully*; and the verb form of *light* is *enlighten*. But what can you do with *how*, *to*, or *at*?

4.   Form classes are a *productive* class, which means that new words are being added regularly to the lexicon. The older, Second Edition of *Webster's New International Dictionary*, for example, shows no entry for *automation* or *cybernetic*. As long as new things and new concepts continue to be assimilated into our culture we will need new words to describe them. On the other hand, it is extremely unlikely that new personal pronouns will come into the lexicon within the foreseeable future.

5.   Because of their lexical meaning, form class words occur only in contexts concerning the things that the words stand for. One could imagine, for example, a lengthy novel in which such very common words as *paper*, *swim*, and *red* never appear. Unless one is talking about paper, there is no reason to use the word. But it is hard to imagine a work of any length that did not contain such function words as *the*, *of*, and *and*. Because function words are needed to fit sentences together, they appear in the text *regardless of content*.

THE ENGLISH PART-OF-SPEECH SYSTEM

Although the part-of-speech system devised by Charles Fries is by no means the only linguistically acceptable one, it serves its purpose well, and many grammarians use it as a model for structural linguistics. Instead of attempting to define each part of speech—a trap in which the traditionalists have too long been caught—we shall simply look at some of the major characteristics of each classification.

The Form Classes

Class I Words

Class I words can be substituted for *teacher* in one or more of the following sentences:

1.   *The teacher is nice.*
        The pudding is nice.
        The kitten is nice.
        The picnic is nice.
2.   *The student touched the teacher.*
3.   *Mr. Jones is a teacher.*
4.   *He gave it to the teacher.*
5.   *He gave the teacher his homework.*

Class I words can sometimes be used in a certain type of construction immediately after another Class I word:

> *My friend, the <u>teacher,</u> is nice.*
> *The student saw the mathematician, a <u>teacher.</u>*

The list of words that can take the place of *teacher* in some of these constructions—*party, tree, house, rain, experience, doctor*—runs into the thousands. This does not mean that all Class I words can be used in all sentences in which other Class I words appear. One might say *The weather is nice*, but we would not expect to hear **He gave it to the weather*. The latter sentence is *structurally* correct inasmuch as it uses the Class I word *weather* in a place where Class I words normally appear, but it is *semantically* meaningless. Therefore, we must consider meaning as part of the complete grammar of a language.

Class I words are usually preceded by such words as *a, the, this, some, my*.

> *My teacher is nice.*
> *This teacher is nice.*
> *Some teachers are nice.*

However, these introductory words are frequently omitted, particularly when the Class I word is in the $\{Z_1\}$ form:

> *Teachers are nice.*

The previously mentioned criteria describe Class I words in terms of their *function*, or position in the sentence. This is related to the discussion in Chapter 1, pages 17–18. But Class I words also have certain characteristics of *form*, described as follows:

Class I words can take $\{Z_1\}$ plural inflection, in which case *is* changes to *are* in Patterns 1 and 3:

1. *The teachers are nice.*
2. *The student touched the teachers.*
3. *Mr. Jones and Miss Bailey are teachers.*
4. *He gave it to the teachers.*
5. *He gave the teachers his homework.*
6. *My friends, the teachers, are nice.*

There are some exceptions to these examples. *Music* does not inflect $\{Z_1\}$. *Deer* and *sheep*, as pointed out in Chapter 5, use null /ø/ allomorph inflection for plural. Class I words that indicate quantity are usually not inflected, although at times they are. The rules are subject to many exceptions, and even to some disagreement:

The milk is cold.	but	**The milks are cold.* (*Milks* may, however, refer to containers of milk.)
The water is nice.	but	*The waters are nice.*

Class I words that do not inflect $\{Z_1\}$ are sometimes referred to as *noncount* words, as will be explained in the next chapter. Class I words can take $\{Z_2\}$ genitive inflection, in which case the constructions are not the same. In this case they are generally followed by another Class I word:

The teacher's room is crowded.
He joined the teachers' association.

By now it is becoming clear that because of the complexity of language, a definition of the form classes would have to be so restricted by "exceptions," that it would not be acceptable. Actually, one exception is all that is needed to invalidate a definition. We can, however, *describe* these word categories with sufficient precision to use the terms with mutual comprehension. It must be understood that we have not learned all there is to know about the various classes of words and that we are still probing for more accurate clues to classification. Perhaps with further research linguists will be able to classify all words of the language with precision and certainty, but such definitions will probably be long and complex and subject to change as language habits change.

Class I includes roughly, but not exactly, the words that have previously fallen into the traditional term *noun*. The major difference lies in the flexibility of approach. The traditional grammarian assumed that, having defined *noun* as *a person, place, or thing*, that was the end of it. Actually, there are a number of ways to look at these classifications. One could build a part-of-speech grammar entirely on form (inflectional suffixes), defining *Class I* words as those that can inflect $\{Z_1\}$ or $\{Z_2\}$. But such a grammar would fail to take into account one of the most significant factors of the English language—that the position that a word occupies in the sentence is vital to its classification:

The student saw his chance.
Let's chance it.
Our chance meeting was nice.

Although *chance* appears in all three sentences, it is a Class I word in the first sentence, a Class II word in the next, and has some characteristics of both Class I (inflection) and Class III (position—see page 133) in the third. Also, a grammar based on morphology alone would not account for the differences between the many types of function words that we shall presently encounter.

We could construct a grammar based on sentence position, but this would be subject to such confusions as:

Mr. Jones and Miss Bailey are teachers.
Mr. Jones and Miss Bailey are nice.

Although *teachers* and *nice* occupy the same position in the sentence, any native speaker of English knows intuitively that these words perform vastly different functions. This forces us to recognize that as native speakers our knowledge of language is principally imitative-intuitive, and that we know more about our language from having used it all our lives than from having studied it. Learning the grammar of our own language, then, is no more an *a priori* key to understanding how to communicate than learning psychology is a necessary step in responding to a stimulus. Both subjects, however, provide interesting material for an intellectually curious individual to gain new insights into himself and his fellow man.

As long as we remember that we are simply describing the major characteristics of the various kinds of words, we can continue our analysis.

Class II Words

Class II words are similar to the traditional classification, *verbs*, and can be used in the position of *are*:

> The teachers are nice.

This group includes such words as *feel, become, sound,* and *seem,* and are frequently called *linking verbs,* or *copulative verbs.* Class II words can be used in the position of *run*:

> They run.

There are many words in this Class II category—*jump, swim, think, sleep, help,* and *breathe.* As used in this construction, they are *intransitive verbs.* Class II words can be used in the position of *hit*:

> He hit the table.

In this position are found such words as *throw, drive, kick, beat,* and *read.* These are known as *transitive verbs.* Some Class II words can be used in either the transitive or intransitive construction.

> They run fast.   The dancers kick high.
> They run this town.   The dancers kick their partners.

Some Class II words can be used in all three positions:

> The teachers sound nice.
> The teachers sound the bell.
> The teachers sound off.

Sound is actually a different word in each sentence.

Class II words can take the $\{Z_3\}$ third person singular inflection:

> *I run away.*   *The teachers look nice.*
> *You run away.*   *The teacher <u>looks</u> nice.*
> *The dog <u>runs</u> away.*

Class II words can take $\{D_1\}$ past tense inflection:

> *The teachers seem nice.*   *The dancers kick high.*
> *The teachers <u>seemed</u> nice.*   *The dancers <u>kicked</u> high.*
>
> *The cats jump the fence.*
> *The cats <u>jumped</u> the fence.*

Class II words can inflect $\{D_2\}$ for past participle:

> *The teachers have seemed nice.*
> *We have eaten our lunch.*
> *They have run* (/ø/ allomorph) *well.*

Class II words can inflect $\{i\eta\}$ for gerund, present participle, and progressive, although these forms are used in different constructions:

> *This is a running river.*   (present participle)
> *Running the race is fun.*   (gerund)
> *He is running the race.*   (present progressive)

Some textbook writers, including Paul Roberts, do not consider *be* as a verb, but as being in a class by itself. Others, such as Conlin, Herman, and Martin, classify it with linking verbs. If students come across these apparent contradictions as they progress from one text to another there should be no problem if the teacher has oriented them properly. Essential to the New English is the concept that words are Class I or II, nouns or verbs, not because they genetically *are* certain things, but because the grammarian sets up his criteria, then classifies words according to the criteria he has set up. Before a teacher can ask his students a question concerning grammar, he must make it clear what standards are being used for classification. This is usually done by the textbook adopted for that particular class, but if the students have been exposed to other systems, some explanation may be necessary.

Roberts, for example, claims we cannot invent new forms of *be*, as we can invent new verbs (*be* is nonproductive). Therefore *be* is not in the same class as verbs.[4] He also points out that *be* has a different inflectional pattern: *am, is, are, was, were, be, been, being*, in contrast to the five-part paradigm given in the previous chapter for verbs.

---

[4] Paul Roberts, *The Roberts English Series* (New York: Harcourt, Brace and World, Inc., 1967), Vol. VI, p.129.

If these are the standards, then *be* is definitely not a verb. But Conlin, Herman, and Martin seem to base their classification of *be* as a linking verb on another standard— that is, its function in the sentence. *Be* patterns as other linking verbs:

> *I am tired.*   *She was happy in those days.*
> *I feel tired.*   *She looked happy in those days.*

The pairs of sentences given are similar in form, but when *be* patterns the same as transitive or intransitive verbs, a different sentence type is produced, as we shall see later in the discussion of kinds of sentences.

> *Mary sleeps in the house.*
> *Mary is in the house.*

Class III Words

Class III words can be used in the positions of *nice* in both:

> *Teachers are nice.*
>   and
> *The nice teachers . . . .*

Note that *both* positions must be capable of occupancy. Sentences such as *Teachers are people* include position words in Class III that are not part of the Class III lexicon. Class III words include many forms, such as *tall*, *short*, *grumpy*, *young*, *happy*, and *polite*. This class is similar to *adjectives*.

Class III words can inflect {ər} and {ist}. The {ist} inflection is usually accompanied by *the*:

> *Teachers are nicer.*
> *Teachers are the nicest . . . .*

Class III words can enter into a construction with *more* or *most* as an alternative to the inflections. The *most* form is usually accompanied by *the*.

> *This teacher is more beautiful.*
> *This teacher is the most beautiful.*

This description of Class III words excludes many words traditionally classified as adjectives, such as *this*, *my*, *the*, *some*, *all*, and *many*, since these words do not meet the Class III criteria. English does not include such expressions as:

> **The teachers are <u>this</u>.*
> **The <u>my</u> teachers are in their classrooms.*
> **Margie is the most <u>the</u> girl I know.*
> **Spaghetti is <u>aller</u> than macaroni.*

These words fall into a special classification to be discussed shortly.

Class IV Words

One linguist considers Class IV words as a subdivision of Class III: those adjectives that inflect *ly* for adverbial use,[5] but Fries places them in a class by themselves. This does not imply that all Class IV words carry *ly* inflections, but many of them do. Generally, they can be described as words that fit into the position of:

1. *There* in *The teachers are there.* (*here, somewhere, upstairs, in, near.*) These are frequently called *adverbs of place.*
2. *Early* in *The teachers come early.* (*soon, now, never, yesterday, forever.*) These may be considered *adverbs of time.*
3. *Clearly,* in *The teachers speak clearly.* (*well, beautifully, carefully, rapidly, safely, up, out.*) This last group comprises the *adverbs of manner.*

Class IV words can pattern with Class III and Class I words in some cases:

The teachers are there.	(Class IV)
The teachers are nice.	(Class III)
The teachers are people.	(Class I)

However, Class I words belong to other constructions to which Class IV words cannot be admitted (such as together with *the* and *a*):

The people came. *The there came.

Class III words must also be usable in a preposed position with the Class I word.

The nice teachers.... *The there teachers....

Class IV words have another interesting characteristic that sets them apart from all other words in the English language. They do not have a set position in the sentence but can be moved about at the discretion of the writer. This characteristic is discussed more fully later in the chapter.

The sentences used as models in this section do not make it possible for all examples of any given class to be used in all constructions. For example, one is hardly likely to hear *The teachers are green*, although this pattern is perfectly grammatical. But it is not *logical* except under unusual circumstances (green with envy, teachers from another planet, or covered with green stuff). However, as soon as the Class I word (teachers) is changed to *trees, paints,* or *books,* green becomes a meaningful Class III word.

[5] Charles F. Hockett, *A Course in Modern Linguistics* (New York: The Macmillan Company, 1958), p. 211.

Function Words

The remainder of the words in the language are differentiated from the form classes on the basis of the criteria on pages 127–128. Hockett uses the terms *functors* (function words) and *contentives* (form classes), classifying functors into three types: *substitutes*, including such words as *it* and *all*, and affixes such as *'s*; *markers*; and *inflectional affixes*.[6] Fries lists fifteen groups of function words, identifying them by letter from A to O. It is difficult to present a satisfactory complete grammar of function words. Many systems are either like Hockett's, too sketchy to serve our purpose, or so detailed, like Fries', that one wonders if it is worthwhile taking a group of students through the entire involved process. What is to be gained by studying the differences between "Function Group F": those words that can take the position of *at* in: "*The concerts at the school...*" and words in "Function Group J": those words that can take the position of *after* in "*The orchestra was good after the new director came*"?[7]

Some of the structure words, however, figure prominently in the terminology of transformational grammar. In *Patterns of English*, one of the earliest linguistics textbooks to appear for public school use, Paul Roberts listed the following members of the function groups, after first noting that listing all function words would be a complicated affair:

1. *Determiners* are preposed with nouns, including *the*, *a*, *an*, *this*, *his*, *their*, *every*, *some*, *all*, and many others. They serve as signals that the following word is a noun.
2. *Pronouns* can be used in the positions of nouns but do not have preposed determiners, including *I*, *me*, *we*, *you*, *anybody*, *everyone*. (Pronouns are among the few function words that inflect, as shown in Chapter 5, page 110. Pronoun inflections, however, do not follow the usual inflectional pattern of the form classes, but operate through suppletion in five-part paradigms.)
3. *Prepositions* form clusters with nouns, plus determiners if any, including *to school*, *up a tree*, *in time*, *after the ball*, *without eating*, and *about Harry*.
4. *Auxiliaries* pattern with verbs, including such forms as *may*, *will*, *do*; forms of the verb *be* that pattern with $\{ıŋ\}$ and $\{D_2\}$ verbs: *am running*, *are going*, *were eating*, *was watched*, *is helped*; *have*, *has*, and *had*, which pattern with the $\{D_2\}$ verbs: *have run*, *has walked*, *had taken*.
5. *Intensifiers* pattern with adjectives and adverbs, and include *very*, *most*, *quite*, *somewhat*, and *fairly*.

---

[6] Hockett, *A Course in Modern Linguistics*, p. 264.
[7] Fries, *The Structure of English*, pp. 95, 100.

6. *Conjunctions* can be used in the position of *and*, including *but, or*, and the discontinuous conjunctions *either . . . or* and *neither . . . nor*.

7. *Sentence connectors* can be used in the position of *therefore*, including *nevertheless* and *moreover*. They usually connect entire sentences rather than smaller units.

8. *Subordinators* can be used in the position of *because*, including *whenever, if, after*, and others.

9. *Question words* include *who, which, what, why, where, when, how, whom*, and *whose* when used to ask a question.[8]

Note that even in this "linguistically oriented" textbook, such standards as form, function, and meaning are indiscriminately mixed, although function is the principal standard.

Other authors of school textbooks have organized function words somewhat differently. Conlin, Herman and Martin, in their eighth-grade text discuss:

1. *Connectives*, including "coordinators, subordinators, prepositions, and conjunctive adverbs"

2. *Pronouns*, limited to personal pronouns

3. *Auxiliaries*, including *was* and *were* in the progressive

4. *Determiners*, limited to articles

5. *Particles*, including "a number of miscellaneous words (negatives, greetings, intensifiers) that are difficult to place in a definite category."[9]

The Postman English series discusses *determiners, auxiliaries, intensifiers, prepositions, conjunctions*, and *subordinators*.[10]

Note that not only does practice vary from one text to another, but there is no sharp dividing line between what is "traditional" and what is "linguistic." Traditional terminology is blended into the vocabularies of most linguists, although in many cases the terms have been given a new description. An excellent example is the use of the term *form classes* (Class I, II, III, and IV). Fries applied these new terms in an apparent effort to direct our thinking away from a vocabulary that had grown stale through the centuries, and had been defined so sloppily that it had lost its value for scientific analysis. But the words *noun, verb, adjective*, and *adverb* had become so ingrained in our language—were so much a part of our *culture*—that they crept back into linguistics and are still probably more frequently used by linguists than the newer

---

[8] Roberts uses the term *structure groups* in *Patterns of English* (New York: Harcourt, Brace and World, Inc., 1956), pp. 293–296.

[9] Conlin, Herman, and Martin, *Our Language Today* (New York: American Book Company, 1966, 1967), Vol. 8, pp. 207–208.

[10] Neil Postman, Harold Morine and Greta Morine, *Discovering Your Language* (New York: Holt, Rinehart and Winston, Inc., 1963), Vol. VII, Chaps. 9, 10, 11, 21, 22, 23.

terminology. From the teacher's point of view, traditional parts of speech must still be taught, if for no other reason than because dictionaries continue to use them. This is just one more example of how difficult it is to get people to change their language habits.

THE ENGLISH SENTENCE

Because of the great variety and complexity of English sentences, analysis of these constructions can become bogged down in detail unless some simplified method of expressing the framework of the sentence is found. We learned to do this in the previous chapter by means of a syntactic diagram. In this method the sentence is "cut" into its immediate constituents (IC), then each IC is cut, until the smallest units are derived:

| The | old | man | could | see | a | unicorn | in | the | garden. |

In the diagram shown, note the order of the cuts. This order follows the rules listed in the previous chapter on pages 118–119.

1. Separate subject from predicate. (No sentence modifiers are in this example.)
2. 3. 4. Cut sentence into constructions that have some degree of internal unity. Fries' rules do not fully account for constructions within constructions that are not modifiers. Some are modifiers of the complement (*unicorn* | *in the garden*) or stand in complementary, and not modifying relationship (*in* | *the* | *garden*).
5. 6. Now peel off modifiers, beginning with the most remote.
7. Finally, separate the parts of the remaining unified constructions.

Another method would be to begin by combining the smallest unit into the next larger units, then combining these into still larger units, and so on until the sentence consists of the two or three largest constituents. Each time a ligature (combining of two forms into one) is made, the product should be parallel in construction with the IC's from which it was derived. This means that in other sentences the combined form should be capable of being substituted for the longer form. By this analysis the same sentence would be:

The old man	could see	a unicorn	in	the garden
The man	saw	a unicorn	in	there
The man	saw	a unicorn	there	
The man	saw	a unicorn		

The sentence derived in the final frame is called the *kernel sentence*, and each kernel illustrates one possible pattern that English sentences can take. The form illustrated could be shortened still further by changing the nouns to pronouns, eliminating the determiners, but this is not necessary for our purpose.

By making certain changes in the kernel sentence, it is possible to generate an infinite variety of new sentences. One method would be to substitute other members of the same form class:

> *The man saw a unicorn.*
> *The boy saw a unicorn.*
> *The boy saw a friend.*
> *The boy hit his friend.*

As the form words are replaced the meaning changes, but the structure of the sentence remains the same.

If the Class I word (noun) is changed to plural, a pronoun, or a proper noun, the determiner may be eliminated:

> *The man likes the woman.*
> *Men like women.*
>
> *The monkey ate the banana.*
> *Monkeys eat bananas.*

> *The man read the book.*
> *He read the book.*
> *Joe Smith read the book.*
> *Joe Smith read it.*

By adding new constructions to the sentence, longer and more complex sentences can be generated:

> *The man saw a unicorn.*
>
> *The old man saw a unicorn in the garden.*
>
> *The amazed old man saw a tiny unicorn nibbling on flowers in the garden.*
>
> *The unhappy old man with a nagging wife finally saw, or thought he saw, a tiny unicorn standing in the garden calmly nibbling on his prize flowers.*

But each of the succeeding sentences is generated from the kernel *The man saw the unicorn.*

In the part-of-speech section at the beginning of this chapter, the patterns illustrating uses of the form classes were kernel sentences. They illustrate a very important principle of language study and one that is particularly important in English: The various parts of speech have certain "slots" into which they can be fitted. These slots, plus the classes of words that fill them are sometimes called *tagmemes*. Thus a "slot and filler" grammar describes ways in which various classes of words can be used in specific positions.

If all the sentences of the English language were reduced to kernels, combining compound as well as subordinate elements, most English sentences could be represented by a comparatively small number of patterns. Kernel sentences, described here with traditional terminology, are limited to simple declarative forms. Other types are described in the next chapter.

ENGLISH SENTENCE PATTERNS

With Intransitive Verbs

Pattern I: (D) Noun   Verb

The noun-verb (subject-predicate) relationship is the basis for all English favorite form sentences. Pattern I consists of this noun-verb combination with no other immediate constituents. The *D* in parentheses means that a determiner *may* be present.

> *Students study.*
> *The sun shines.*
> *Nobody knows.*
> *A child grows.*
> *John sings.*

Pattern II: (D) NOUN   VERB   ADVERB

This is the other basic major pattern that can be produced with an intransitive verb.

> *Students study here.*
> *The sun shines daily.*
> *Nobody knows yet.*
> *John sings beautifully.*

Adverbs are sometimes referred to as "movables," inasmuch as in some sentences they can be placed in a different position: *Dutifully he worked. He dutifully worked. He worked dutifully.* This does not produce new kernel sentences but *transformations* of Pattern II. Transformations will be discussed in detail in the following chapter.

With Transitive Verbs

Pattern III: (D) NOUN   VERB   (D) NOUN

The second noun in this pattern is traditionally known as the *direct object*, or the *object of the verb*.

Your students study their lessons.
The sun radiates heat.
Nobody knows it.
The child grows flowers.
John sings a song.

Pattern IV: (D)   NOUN   VERB   (D)   NOUN   (D)   NOUN

This is the *indirect object—direct object* pattern.

The students gave the teacher their homework.
The sun provides the earth energy.
Nobody tells me anything.
The child gives his flowers some water.
John sang Sally a song.

With Linking Verbs

Pattern V: (D)   NOUN   L-VERB   ADJECTIVE

This pattern is traditionally known as the *predicate adjective.*

Students seem eager.
The sun feels warm.
Nobody is unhappy.
The child looks pleased.
These children are talented.

Note that the adjectives appearing in other parts of the sentence preposed with nouns do not produce new kernel sentences but simply expansions of existing ones:

The eager students do their homework.
The warm sun shines.
The happy child plants flowers.

Pattern VI: (D)   NOUN   L-VERB   (D)   NOUN

This is the *predicate nominative* pattern.

Your students are scholars.
The sun is a sphere.
Nobody is your enemy.
The child seems a man.
John became a musician.

Pattern VII: (D)   NOUN   L-VERB   ADVERB

Those students are here.
The sun is out.

Classification of words such as *here* and *out* is not simple. They fill Class IV slots in sentences, but do not inflect as adjectives or adverbs. To make them adjectives would be especially difficult: Something cannot be **outer* or **herest*. Nor can you describe Mr. Jones as a *here* person or an *out* man, although recent common jargon includes talk about *in* groups and *out* groups. On the other hand, you cannot do something **herely* or **outly*, although these words do have the movable characteristic of adverbs:

She is here.	*Here she is.*
Out ran the heroine.	*The heroine ran out.*

They do answer the question *where*, and hence could be considered *adverbs of place*, which are discussed more fully in the next chapter.

These seven patterns are by no means the only English sentence patterns, but they are the most common. Just as different phonemic and morphemic systems can be found among various linguists, so can different systems for parts of speech and basic sentence patterns. Paul Roberts' *English Sentences* (1962)[11] lists ten basic patterns, although his earlier work, *Patterns of English* (1956) had listed seven.[12] Roberts considers the *Noun—Verb—Adverb* as a variant of the *Noun—Verb* kernel, but differentiates verbs into seven different types, including *be*, which he does not consider a verb but a separate category, and classifies sentences mainly according to the type of verb they contain. In *Our Language Today*, Conlin, Herman, and Martin discuss six basic kernel sentences.[13] Just how many sentence patterns are really "basic" is still an open question. To expand the list in this text with some of the less common patterns would not be difficult: There are *objective complement* sentences:

(D)　NOUN　L-VERB　(D)　NOUN　(D)　NOUN

> *Some students consider lessons a pleasure.*
> *The moon thought the sun a nuisance.*
> *The children believe their teacher a hero.*
> *John felt Bill an intruder.*

(In these sentences the infinitive *to be* is implied—and frequently expressed—before the final noun.)

(D)　NOUN　L-VERB　(D)　NOUN　ADJECTIVE

> *Some students consider lessons boring.*
> *The children thought the clown funny.*

---

[11] Paul Roberts, *English Sentences* (New York: Harcourt, Brace and World, Inc., 1962), pp. 30–45.
[12] Roberts, *Patterns of English*, pp. 297–299.
[13] Conlin, Herman, and Martin, *Our Language Today*, Vol. 8, pp. 306–308.

There are also *verbal complement* sentences:

(D) NOUN   VERB   (D)   NOUN   VERB

> *The teacher helps the students learn.*

There are grammatical sentences with forms other than nouns for subject:

A quotation:	*"Scram!" was his reply.*
An adverb:	*Here is where we met.*
A gerund	*Swimming is my favorite sport.*
An infinitive:	*To ride a horse was his great ambition.*
A phrase:	*Teaching the New English offers great challenges.*

Traditional grammarians may explain this group by reversing the order of the first two sentences, making *reply* and *where we met* the subjects, and by classifying gerunds and infinitives, as well as the phrase *teaching the New English* as nouns.

There are sentences with a number of verbals strung together.

> *The students wanted to try to help stop the fighting.*

Traditional grammarians would consider only *wanted* as a verb, with *try, help*, and *stop* as noun infinitives and *fighting* a noun gerund. However, these words have all the inflectional characteristics of verbs and none of those of nouns.

Obviously, this list of kernel sentences could be greatly expanded. Language is a complex phenomenon, and it takes a highly complex phenomenon to describe it completely. But such complexity is not necessary. One can learn the essentials of any subject, including linguistics, in a practical, workable school course of study.

An interesting point is raised in the sentence:

> *The children consider the lessons fun.*

Is *fun* in the above sentence a noun or adjective? Traditionally, *fun* is a noun. It is so listed in *Webster's New International Dictionary, Second Edition*. But one cannot place a determiner before it in this construction. The children cannot consider their lessons *a fun, or even *some fun. One can usually place *some* before collective or quantitative nouns: *some water, some paper, some sand*. Nor does *fun* commonly take either the $\{Z_1\}$ (*funs) or $\{Z_2\}$ (**fun's*) noun inflection. But neither will *fun* take the adjective inflections (**funner, funnest*), although it takes the alternate forms *more fun, most fun* quite frequently. Also, *fun* is being used increasingly in an adjective position: *a fun thing*. Originally a slang usage, it is now so common that billboards within a few miles of my home advertise a certain establishment as "a fun place." In every likelihood *fun* as an adjective will soon be a firmly established member of the formal lexicon, and it is catching on because it fulfills a need. No other word quite so perfectly and briefly describes a quality for a generation concerned with *fun* things. But when it comes to the classification of such sentences, the linguist realizes that not all linguistic phenomena lend themselves to neat little categories. And by the time a workable system of linguistic classification has been derived, new changes in speech habits will come along to provide linguists with a new set of *fun* problems.

In this chapter we described the parts of speech largely on the basis of the positions that they take within a sentence. We then went on to describe kernel sentences on the basis of the arrangement of the various parts of speech. This circular type of reasoning demonstrates the need for using more than one criterion for grammatical description. Because of the complexity of language, all possible clues including word order, morphologic structure, and meaning must be employed in analysis. No one method is sufficient. A linguist is like a detective who painstakingly follows up every possible lead, knowing that any one or any combination of clues may lead to a solution.

FROM KERNELS TO LANGUAGE

How is it possible that out of the few kernel sentences listed in this section an entire language with an infinite number of sentences can be created? Several processes are involved, some of which have already been mentioned. These will now be summarized.

Suppletion. Because the lexicon of form class words is so large, the speaker can indulge in an almost endless variety of combinations of nouns, verbs, adjectives, and adverbs, substituting one for another indefinitely.

Inversion. In some cases it is possible for the order of forms to be reversed. This has been noted in discussing adverbs, the forms moved about so frequently that they have been referred to at times as the English *movables*.[14] But adverbs are not the only forms subject to inversion. Particularly for emphasis or poetic effect or to ask a question, a speaker of English will invert the elements within a sentence:

I must see this.	*This I must see.*
The villainous hordes swept down the mountain.	*Down the mountain swept the villainous hordes.*
Mr. Wilson is coming.	*Is Mr. Wilson coming?*

[14] An interesting discussion of movables is contained in Walter Loban's *The Language of Elementary School Children*. In studying the language development of children, Loban considered the ability to handle movable constructions one of the indicators of verbal progress. He found that those students classified into the "high" group consistently used a more extensive repertoire of movable clauses and multiple movables (movable constructions within a movable construction).

Expansion. A major source of new sentence generation is expansion, the speaker's tendency to add more constructions to the kernel sentence.

Constructions that are incapable of expansion are referred to as *closed constructions.* Interjections are the main English closed constructions. There is little more to be said about *Ouch!* or *Gee whiz!* Pronouns and proper nouns tend to be partially closed. One can expand *men* to *the big men*; *the men in the back yard*; *or the brave men, living and dead, who struggled here*, but one seldom hears *the big Mr. Jones* (although *the late Mr. Jones* is fairly common) and never **the big he*.

The details of how *open constructions* are expanded vary from one language to another, and each language must be studied as a unit. Many languages, including English, are expanded by *layering*, that is, by the addition of *layers* of meaning attached to *head words*. Head words are generally nouns or verbs around which other words can be placed to form a *cluster*. In the preceding paragraph we saw how the noun head *men* could take on three sets of *attributes* (words that cluster around it) to form three *noun phrases*. Note that the term *phrase*, as used hereafter, is not the same as in traditional grammar. Here a phrase is any construction consisting of a head word, often with attributes clustering around it to give additional layers of meaning.

Verbs can be expanded in the same manner as nouns. *Brought* can become *brought home*; *often brought from town*; or *brought forth on this continent a new nation, conceived in liberty, and dedicated to the proposition that all men are created equal.* This latter construction is an example of how multiple expansions form a long complex sentence.

All men are created equal is the kernel to which the *passive transformation* has been added. Transformations are another major source of new English sentences and are discussed at length in the following chapter. Within the larger construction, the clause *that all men are created equal* may be considered a *dependent clause.* A clause has been defined as "the maximal unit of utterance."[15] An *independent clause* is "not included in a larger construction," whereas a *dependent clause* is so included.[16]

That all men are created equal would therefore be a dependent clause because it is included in *proposition that all men are created equal*, and the whole construction is an expansion of the head word *proposition*. In the larger context, *dedicated to the proposition that all men are created equal* is an expansion of the head word in that construction, *dedicated*. *A new nation, conceived in liberty, and dedicated to the proposition that all men are created equal* is, in turn, an expansion of the head word *nation*. By continually widening the scope of inquiry, one eventually comes to the conclusion that the entire

---

[15] Robert A. Hall, Jr., *Introductory Linguistics* (Philadelphia: Chilton Company, 1964), p. 213.
[16] *Ibid.*

construction is an expansion of the head word *brought*. If this is broadened still further to include the opening constituent: *Fourscore and seven years ago our fathers . . .* it becomes evident that *Fourscore and seven years ago* also clusters around *brought*, making a discontinuous construction with *our fathers* an infixed noun phrase. The sentence is thus reduced to a Pattern III, NOUN—VERB—**NOUN** type, with the kernel *fathers brought*.

Although the traditional grammarian would arrive at a similar conclusion about the skeleton of the sentence, the difference between calling *fathers brought* the *subject* and *predicate* and calling it a *Pattern I kernel* is more than a difference in terminology. It is a difference in attitude. Asking students to name THE subject and predicate of a sentence fails to recognize that the subject-predicate pattern is the *favorite form* in English, but by no means the only type, especially when spoken English is included. Witness:

> *Where are you going, Sally?*   *To the Library.*
> *Let's go together.*
> *O.K.*

These are all common English speech patterns. One has subject and predicate, one has predicate only, and two have neither subject nor predicate.

Furthermore, picking out subjects and predicates plus a host of subordinate constructions does not account for a very important fact about our language—that it is composed of a series of skeletal (kernel) sentences from which we form our utterances by means of suppletion, inversion, or expansion. Even this method of analysis has limitations in depth, as will be evident after a look at transformational grammar in the next chapter.

GRAMMAR AND SPEECH

It has already been pointed out that there is no sharp dividing line between traditional and linguistic grammars, that the terminology of the tradition spills over into linguistics, and that the linguist frequently uses familiar words by describing them carefully. The major change that has taken place is that the grammarian no longer considers himself the policeman of the language, the arbiter of what is right and wrong.

Once freed from this false and uncomfortable position, the teacher of language can investigate his material without having to make excuses for English that does not conform to the "standard." He recognizes that the student who says "I ain't got no pencil" is being every bit as communicative—and perhaps a bit more colorful besides—as the one who says it "correctly." The teacher knows exactly what the student is saying, the student knows the teacher knows exactly what he is saying, so why go into long explanations about two negatives making a positive? And if the student has read his literature assignment carefully he knows that Mark Antony managed to stir the hearts and minds of Rome to mutiny and rage despite his double superlative.

> *This was the most unkindest cut of all.*[17]

If the student happens to be a Mexican-American, Puerto Rican, or other Spanish speaker, he can demonstrate that the double negative: *Yo no tengo nada.* (literally, *I don't have nothing*) is considered grammatical or ungrammatical on the basis of custom, not logic or communicativeness.

Besides, to tell a student that his speech is incorrect is to imply that his family and his friends are inferior. The student will probably never have the nerve to say it to his teacher, but he may very well be thinking: "My father says 'I ain't got no . . .' and he's making good money driving a truck." Can we expect this young man to accept his teacher's judgment that he must somehow alter his way of speaking?

On the other hand, the student may be thinking: "My father says 'I ain't got no . . .' and he's been unemployed much of his life. I guess we're just ignorant." In this case the teacher has performed an even more serious disservice. He has struck a blow at the fundamental dignity and self-respect of that student and his culture. He has lowered the student's self-image at a time when it is vital that his self-image be boosted.

However, to leave it at that is not carrying out the teacher's responsibility to teach. As long as the student's speech is tied to certain usages, he may find himself trapped in a particular economic or social level. The teacher's job is to help the student to break the language barrier.

It should not be the purpose of education to make all students into college-educated professional people. Education should be a process of helping each individual to find his own identity—to develop his own talents, to make his own decisions, and to live comfortably and in harmony with himself, his fellow man, and his environment.

Because language is such a vital part of ourselves and our relationship with our surroundings, it would seem reasonable that these ends can be served by helping the student attain some understanding of language and some control over it. But telling him that the language he uses is incorrect, when in *his* environment and for *his* needs that language has served him well, will help him gain neither understanding nor control. We need a sounder, more convincing approach.

Language has long been used as a means of social separation. Speakers of a language

---

[17] William Shakespeare, *Julius Caesar*, Act III, scene ii.

often associate certain prestige factors with particular modes of speech, or dialects. It is not that any one dialect is superior to the others, but that the people who speak it are people of prestige. It is the prestige of the individuals that rubs off onto the language, not anything inherently better about the language that makes the individuals prestigious.

Once a society has established a prestige dialect, the people in power can use that dialect to maintain their power. This is particularly true of our present American society, where generations of living in a democratic framework with no formal class structure have produced a society in which many of our traditional status symbols have been erased. This situation has been abetted by our mass production system, which has produced such an abundance of inexpensive clothing, automobiles, and television sets that it is increasingly difficult to tell by looking at a person whether he is rich or poor.

If a citizen of the slum should come into prosperity, with an assist from the bank and the FHA, he may move his family to a more expensive neighborhood. He may purchase any number of luxuries that mark his transition into a higher economic level, but one thing he cannot readily change is his speech. Speech patterns are acquired at a very impressionable age and are practiced regularly for too many years for a person to invade the prestige dialect as easily as he moves his furniture into a newer and larger house. As Henry Higgins stated in the musical comedy *My Fair Lady*:

> It's _aw_ and _gone_ that keep her in her place,
> Not her wretched clothes and dirty face.[18]

Higgins' feat of passing off this former flower girl as a lady of quality is particularly astounding when one realizes the difficulty of changing a human being's speech habits.

If the children of a former slum dweller wish to enroll in the university, to be admitted to the country club, to be accepted in many social circles, and to be allowed to work in the more remunerative, steady, and prestigious jobs, they must learn to speak the prestige dialect. The job of the teacher is to help students operate in whatever type of society they choose, to free them from the shackles imposed by the "wrong" dialect. But this must be done without taking away from the student's self-respect or the respect he has for his family and the culture that nourished him. It must be done with sufficient honesty to admit that learning to speak prestige English is not a matter of improving communication, but just what the word implies—prestige.

Even traditional grammarians have been recognizing this recently. Most of the modern texts contain explanations about "formal" and "informal" usage, urging

---

[18] Alan Jay Lerner, "Why Can't the English." Reprinted by permission of Coward-McCann, Inc.

the student to retain his easy, relaxed speech for use at home, but to change his manner of speech to fit the occasion with the same facility one might change from a pair of old jeans to a business suit. But with speech patterns as deeply ingrained as they are, the change of clothing is a much simpler metamorphosis.

In such a setting the teacher is free to take his place as helpmate and guide, and the student is free to look at language and dialect, at himself and his place in society, with some measure of objectivity. Once he understands that *I brung it* is quite communicative but will keep him out of law school, or *He done real good* is a frequently used English pattern but will keep his sister out of a job in the better department stores or offices, he is in a position to make some realistic decisions concerning his life and what he wants to do with it.

Even at this point the teacher's job is far from finished. It is a common human tendency to seek the path of least resistance, even when it may not lead to the most desirable ends. As every teacher knows, this is a particular hazard for students. Thus the teacher can become a vital influence in the lives of young people. It is not to impose but to challenge, to stimulate, and to inspire that the teacher enters the scene. It is not to tell the student which path to take but to equip him to follow any path and to see that he is informed of what lies at the end of each and what will be needed for the journey. The old English teacher was a paper corrector, an assignment maker, and a disciplinarian; the New English Teacher is an opener of doors and a builder of new pathways.

7

playing with sentences
transformational grammar

Chapter 5 pointed out that the morpheme and not the word is the basic unit of meaning in language. In the previous chapter our review of structural analysis was conducted in terms of words. The use of the word as a unit of analysis is not without merit as long as the linguist is analyzing his own language, for a native speaker of a language knows approximately what constitutes a word in that language. But analysis based on words alone has the limitation of ignoring the importance of the morpheme as an analytical tool.

In 1957 Noam Chomsky's *Syntactic Structures* presented a method of linguistic analysis that not only breaks sentences down into constituent morphemes but also reveals more of the inner structure of the language than any other method available at the time.[1]

Some linguists have hailed the *transformational grammar* of Noam Chomsky as the most important and valuable grammatical system ever devised, whereas others have been more cautious. Robert Hall, characterizing the more cautious school, pointed out that transformational grammar can be useful in teaching a foreign language, in the elementary phases of language instruction, and with such mechanical devices as teaching machines and programmed instruction in language, or in devising

---

[1] Noam Chomsky, *Syntactic Structures* (The Hague: Mouton and Company, 1957).

systems of machine translation.[2] He concludes, however:

> At its best, a transformational grammar is a helpful—though, occasionally, somewhat artificial—guide for those unacquainted with the language through whose mazes it leads them. At its worst, it can degenerate into an arid, artificial game of inventing rules for constructing series of abstract formulae, pure "hocus-pocus" ... with little necessary relation to the facts of language as it is spoken and as a functioning aspect of the behavior of humans living and interacting in society.[3]

Despite the misgivings of such linguists as Hall and others, transformational grammar has gained popularity in the past decade, largely because it affords a precise and comprehensive approach to linguistic analysis.

But whether it ultimately receives widespread support or rejection from linguists should not be the only consideration in deciding its value as a school grammar. Linguists conduct their research for a wide variety of reasons. Knowledge about any subject so intrinsic to being human is in itself a worthwhile pursuit. But linguistics also has a range of practical applications, from anthropological research to translating the Bible into non-Indo-European languages. Linguists are not necessarily school teachers, and there is no more reason to feel compelled to bring their latest findings into the classroom than there is to incorporate all of the latest discoveries in medicine into a course in high school physiology.

The term *transformational grammar* might better be considered alongside another term: *generative grammar*. In a generative grammar each part of the utterance is assigned a symbol, and the symbols are arranged on a diagram, somewhat as a mathematical formula is used to show numerical relationships. A series of rules is devised to show how the constituents of a language are placed in proper relationship to *generate* new utterances.

The transformational phase of the operation involves certain word-order changes, or *transformations* necessary to produce variations of the simple kernel sentences of Chapter 6. Thus transformational and generative grammars are closely intertwined, and the terms are often confused. A *complete* generative grammar of a language contains all the grammatical structures that are possible in that language, plus all possible ways (rules) by which these structures can be combined into sentences. These generative rules, added to a *vocabulary* or *lexicon*, should be sufficient to form a complete description of that language.

It takes only a brief glance at the many complex forms a language can take to

---

[2] Some linguists are attempting to devise a system of feeding language into a computer that will automatically translate into another language. At this writing much research and development is still needed to make machine translation a reality.

[3] Robert A. Hall, Jr., *Introductory Linguistics* (Philadelphia: Chilton Company, 1964), p. 227.

realize what an undertaking a complete grammar would be. Fortunately, it is not necessary to name every star in the heavens to study astronomy, and a course in linguistics need not account for every possible English sentence. We can, however, examine some of the most common forms our language can take.

In a brief chapter such as this it is not possible to offer a comprehensive transformational grammar of English. Owen Thomas, in his *Transformational Grammar and the Teacher of English*, presents a fairly compact statement of his theory in 225 pages of text.[4] Paul Roberts devotes about two-thirds of his 577-page *Roberts English Series, Complete Course*, to a presentation of his grammatical theory.[5] This chapter explores the terminology and methods of transformational grammar, taking some basic formulas as models and looking in depth at certain areas that will serve as examples of how transformational grammar is developed.

BASIC REWRITE RULES

The first stage of transformational analysis generally consists of breaking each structure into its immediate constituents and expressing this relationship by means of *phrase structure rules*, or *rewrite rules*. The first rewrite rule consists of:

R. (Rewrite Rule) 1: S → NP + VP

S stands for *sentence*, *NP* and *VP*, respectively, for *noun phrase* and *verb phrase*. A phrase, as used by transformationalists, is a head word with all of its attributes, if any. It may consist of a single word or a long series of words. The symbol → means *is rewritten*. Rewrite Rule 1 thus means: *Sentence may be rewritten Noun Phrase plus Verb Phrase*. In other words, in any formula in which *S* is used to symbolize a sentence, the symbol *NP* + *VP* may be substituted. The sentence itself has not been changed— only the symbol. *NP* in this rule is similar to the subject of the sentence, and *VP* is equivalent to the predicate.

This rule does not mean that every sentence *contains* a noun phrase and a verb phrase, but that it is treated grammatically on the basis of these two parts. For example, the sentence *Let's have lunch* contains a null (ø) NP. The treatment of sentences on an *NP* + *VP* basis is satisfactory for grammatical analysis of English, particularly written English, for the *NP* + *VP* construction is the favorite form

---

[4] Owen Thomas, *Transformational Grammar and the Teacher of English* (New York: Holt, Rinehart and Winston, Inc., 1965).

[5] Paul Roberts, *The Roberts English Series, Complete Course* (New York: Harcourt, Brace and World, Inc., 1967).

(most common) sentence of the language, and in the cases in which a sentence lacks one of these parts, that part can be expressed as null (ø). *R1* (rewrite rule #1) can also be illustrated by means of a *branching tree diagram*:

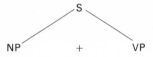

Rewrite rules are universal. If, in our system, *S* is to be rewritten *NP + VP*, then all sentences of this type can be so rewritten.

No grammar of English is complete that does not account for intonation patterns, because intonation plays a major part in determining the meaning of English sentences. Therefore, many grammarians begin transformational analysis with a pattern we shall call *Rewrite Rule A*:

R. A: S → Nuc + IP

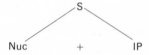

S stands for *sentence*.
Nuc stands for *Nucleus*—the words, or segmental portion of the sentence.
IP stands for *intonation pattern*, sometimes expressed phonologically:

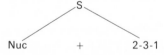

Successive rewrite rules call for a further breaking down of each constituent:

R. B: Nuc → NP + VP

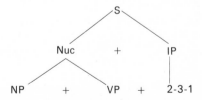

In this brief introduction to transformational grammar we shall use a system common to much linguistic analysis: IP is presumed to exist as a suprasegmental phase of language but brought into the analysis only when it plays a role in grammatical patterning. The symbol *S* for sentence will be broken into *NP + VP*, as in Rule 1, without entering *Nuc* for *nucleus* on the chart.

Note that this grammar does not attempt to define either a sentence or its parts, but simply to state that certain *relationships* exist within the sentence and that the parts are called what they are on the basis of standing in this relationship to other constituent parts.

Let us state *R1* again, this time expanding it to include more of the language:

R1:   S → {Interjection}
{Fragment}
{NP + VP}

The brackets indicate a *choice*. The item to the left of the arrow may be rewritten as any *one* of the items inside the brackets. This is not a random choice. There are three kinds of English sentences. *S* may symbolize any one of them.

An *interjection*, as traditionally defined, is an unstructured utterance of strong feeling: *Gee whiz. Golly. Wow! Yipee!* A number of considerably stronger expressions of feeling may be so classified. They are written with a capital at the beginning and a period or exclamation point at the end. A diagram for an interjection is usually quite simple:

S
|
Interjection
|
Wow

A *fragment* is an utterance that is not structured *NP + VP*. Fragments are frequently spoken in answer to questions:

Where are you going?   Upstairs.
Down the block.
Wherever necessary to do my job.

Fragment diagrams may be simple or complex:

S
|
Fragment
|
Upstairs

The more complex diagrams are illustrated throughout the chapter. Fragments and interjections give smoothness, pace, and color to the language but seldom furnish interesting material for grammatical analysis. Therefore, we shall limit the balance of this discussion to the third type of sentence, the *NP + VP* variety.

After *R1*, each constituent is subject to further analysis.

R2: NP → $\begin{Bmatrix} \text{Det} + \text{N} \\ \text{Proper N} \\ \text{Pers Pron} \\ \text{Indef Pron} \end{Bmatrix}$

Det (determiner) includes words that regularly precede nouns and mark them as nouns: *a, an, the, my, this, somebody's, Joe's,* and many others.

N (noun) refers to common nouns.

Proper N as traditionally defined includes names of specific people, places, things: *Jack, Phoenix, Mount Whitney, Ohio, Mississippi, Mr. Throckmorton, America, Plymouth,* and *Taming of the Shrew.*

Pers Pron (personal pronoun) includes *I, you, he, she, it, we, they,* and *who.* Objective forms (*my, your, his, her, its, our, their*) of the personal pronoun are determiners and pattern with nouns.

Indef Pron (indefinite pronoun) includes three forms that can be used alone or with one of three suffixes. The forms are *every, some,* and *no*; the suffixes are *—one, —body,* and *—thing,* making a total of ten indefinite pronouns—*everyone, nobody, something, nothing, some,* and so forth. (*No* and *every* cannot be used as indefinite pronouns without one of the suffixes.) A branching tree diagram for each type of NP is illustrated:

R2.1: *We gobbled up the remains of the cake.*

```
                    ─S───────
         NP          +        VP
          |          +         |
     Pers Pron       +    gobbled up the remains of the cake
          |          +         |
         We          +    gobbled up the remains of the cake
```

R2.2: *Somebody goofed.*

```
                    ─S───────
         NP          +        VP
          |          +         |
     Indef Pron      +       goofed
          |          +         |
       somebody      +       goofed
```

R2.3: *The chipmunks ran along the log.*

```
                      ─S──────
           NP          +        VP
        /     \        +         |
      Det  +   N       +   ran along the log
       |       |       +         |
      The  + chipmunks +   ran along the log
```

R2.4:   *Ichabod fled in terror.*

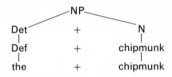

NP	+	VP
Proper N	+	fled in terror
Ichabod	+	fled in terror

R3:   Det → { Def / NonDef }

Def: definite
NonDef: nondefinite

Definite determiners are *the, this, that, these, those, my,* and so forth. *Nondefinite determiners* are *a, an, some, ø,* and so forth. We can now add one more step to our diagrams:

R3.1:   *the chipmunk*

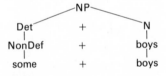

Det	+	N
Def	+	chipmunk
the	+	chipmunk

R3.2:   *some boys*

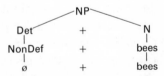

Det	+	N
NonDef	+	boys
some	+	boys

R3.3:   *bees*

Det	+	N
NonDef	+	bees
ø	+	bees

Note that the diagrams do not begin with *S*. A fragment of a sentence, as well as a complete sentence, can be diagrammed. Each time another *string* is added to the diagram, another layer of analysis—another bit of information—is added. In the third diagram, the NP is *bees,* with *ø* added to indicate the determiner is *null,* or there in theory but not expressed in words. Branching trees can be read from the top down to see how an utterance is divided and subdivided until a string of morphemes is derived, or they can be read from the bottom up to show the grammatical origin of each construction and its relationship to other elements in the expression

R4: N → $\begin{Bmatrix} \text{Count} \\ \text{NonCount} \end{Bmatrix}$

Count nouns can literally be counted. An English speaker can say *one book, three yo-yos, eighteen nations, twenty-two people.* Noncount nouns cannot be preceded by a number. One is not likely to hear **six wheats, *four flours, *eighty-one airs* (in reference to a gas), or **twelve bloods.* Differences between count and noncount nouns are arbitrary, not necessarily logical. Wheat is a grain, yet we say *four grains* but never **four wheats.* Grain can also be noncount: *Look at all the grain,* but *wheat* cannot be changed to count. Henry Gleason points out that *pebbles are* (count), while *gravel is* (noncount), only because of custom, not logic.[6]

Note that some nouns change meaning when they change from count to noncount. *Coffee* is noncount, but *one coffee* generally refers to one cup of coffee. *Iron* is a noncount word for a metal, but *an iron* is a tool for taking wrinkles out of clothing.

R5: Count N → $\begin{Bmatrix} \text{Count} \\ \text{Count} + \text{Pl} \end{Bmatrix}$

Singular nouns are sometimes written N_s or $N + Sing$, but usually a noun is *presumed* to be singular unless the plural morpheme is added. In diagramming, sometimes R4 and R5 are simplified by combining the rules and going directly from *N* to *Count + Pl,* resulting in the rule:

$$N \rightarrow \begin{Bmatrix} \text{NonCount} \\ \text{Count} \\ \text{Count} + \text{Pl} \end{Bmatrix}$$

Distribution of determiners is restricted by the noun. Singular count nouns can take *the, a, an, his, our,* and others, but cannot take ø or plural determiners such as *these* and *those.* Plural count nouns can take *more, some,* ø, *her, its,* and *the,* but cannot take *a* or *an.* Noncount nouns can take all determiners except *a, an, these, those, one, two, three,* and so forth, which indicate number. Noun types can be indicated as follows:

R5.1: *some boys*

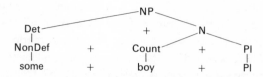

[6] Henry Allan Gleason, Jr., *Linguistics and English Grammar* (New York: Holt, Rinehart and Winston, Inc., 1965), p. 135.

R5.2: *The information*

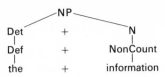

R5.3: *a house*

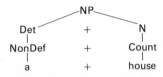

Notice that inflectional morphemes are indicated in the final string. We do not write *boys*, but *boy* + *Pl.* When all the rules of phrase structure have been worked out, a complete morphological analysis of the utterance can be seen.

In a grammar written for native speakers, it may be assumed that the reader knows the common words of the language. A grammar written for students of a foreign language should include a *lexicon,* or list of words that can be used as nouns, verbs, and determiners, as well as information concerning the proper inflectional forms. In a school grammar, information about how to form irregular verbs or any other constructions that may not be obvious to all students would also be helpful. This might include information about which constructions are the *favorite forms* of the language, including noun-verb agreement, determiner-noun correspondence (*this kind—those kinds*), or other areas of confusion.

R6: VP → Aux + Verbal

Aux (auxiliary) contains all of the *characteristics* of the verbal, including tense and certain words needed to develop the meaning. The verbal is the main verb plus its attributes. Auxiliary and verbal are indicated in the following diagram:

R6.1: *The trees grow tall.*

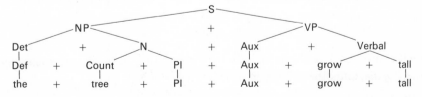

The phrase structure rules encountered thus far do not analyze the verbal beyond the level shown in diagrams R6.1 and R6.2. As more rules are brought in, however, increasingly detailed analysis can be made.

R6.2: *Some work is fun.*

```
                                    S
        NP                  +              VP
    Det      +      N       +      Aux   +      Verbal
     |               |              |
  NonDef   +   NonCount   +   Aux   +   is   +   fun
     |               |              |
   some    +      work     +   Aux   +   is   +   fun
```

R7: *Verbal* →
$$\begin{Bmatrix} V_i \\ V_t \ + \ NP \\ LV \ + \ \begin{Bmatrix} NP \\ Adj \\ Adv \end{Bmatrix} \end{Bmatrix} \quad (+Adv)$$

V_i: intransitive verb
V_t: transitive verb
LV: linking verb   as described in the previous chapter
Adv: adverb (Class IV word)
Adj: adjective (Class III word)

Note that a sentence may contain more than one *NP*, but only the *NP* directly under the *S* in the diagram is the subject of the sentence.

R7 states that there are three kinds of verbals. Intransitive verbs are not followed by *NP*:

Mary sleeps.
Joe tried.
The dog ran.

Transitive verbs are followed by NP, known as the *direct object*:

Mother carried the groceries.
Scott has eaten the hamburgers.
The dog frightened us.

Verbs are transitive or intransitive depending upon the construction of the sentence:

Harry ran away.   *Harry ran a race.*
Judy ate last night.   *Judy ate all the pizza.*

Linking verbs include *be* as well as such copulative verbs as *feel, seem, appear, become, remain,* and others. They may be followed by NP:

Condors are birds.

Or by an adjective:

Condors are rare.

Or by an adverb:

Condors are here.

(At this point it might be worthwhile to review Chapter 6, page 132, concerning the relationships of *be* and the other verbs.)

Any of the constructions in R7 *may* be followed by an adverb, or possibly even more than one adverb: The parenthesis around the adverb indicates it may or may not be present.

V_i + two adverbs: *Mark will work hard today.*
V_t + three adverbs: *He aimed his gun slowly, carefully, deliberately.*

Adjectives and adverbs are indicated in the diagrams:

R7.1: *The trees grow tall.*

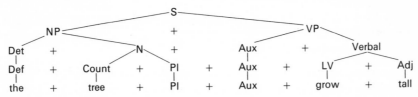

R7.2: *Tigers roar loudly.*

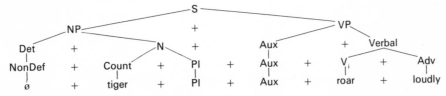

R7.3: *Mother baked the cake this morning.*

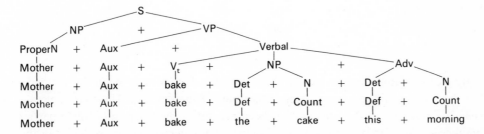

The transitive verb in the terminal string is *bake* rather than *baked* because the past tense ($\{D_1\}$) morpheme is part of the auxiliary (see Rewrite Rule 9). The adverb phrase *this morning* contains an internal structure *Det* + *N*.

The following sentence chart based on R7 illustrates the relationship between transformational and structural grammars. Each sentence type listed in R7 is one of the basic kernel sentences of the previous chapter.

Transformational		Structural
VP → Aux + V$_i$	*The puppies play.*	Det + N + V
Aux + V$_i$ + Adv	*The puppies play happily.*	Det + N + V + Adv
Aux + V$_t$ + NP	*The puppies play games.*	Det + N + V + N
Aux + V$_t$ + NP + Adv	*The puppies play games today.*	Det + N + V + N + Adv
Aux + LV + NP	*The puppies are rascals.*	Det + N + LV + N
Aux + LV + NP + Adv	*The puppies are rascals today.*	Det + N + LV + N + Adv
Aux + LV + Adj	*The puppies are cute.*	Det + N + LV + Adj
Aux + LV + Adj + Adv	*The puppies are cute now.*	Det + N + LV + Adj + Adv
Aux + LV + Adv	*The puppies are there.*	Det + N + LV + Adv
Aux + LV + Adv + Adv	*The puppies are there now.*	Det + N + LV + Adv + Adv

Transformational grammar is also deeply rooted in morphology, for one of the major purposes of the diagram is to show the morphological relationships of the sentence parts. Even derivational morphemes can be shown on the diagram:

R7.4:　*Nobody bought my automobile:*

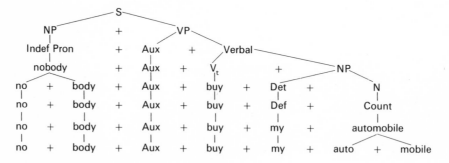

By means of this diagram we can show not only each morpheme in the sentence, but the relationship it bears to every other part of the sentence. However, unless a *complete* grammar of the language has been presented, the diagram is only a partial breakdown. We can only show those linguistic phenomena that are included in the rules studied to this point. For example, one of the major gaps in our present system is our inability to show *tense* and other verb characteristics. *Aux + buy* could stand for any one of a great number of verb forms:

buy	is buying	be buying
bought	were buying	could be buying
did buy	might have been buying	has bought
may buy	shall have bought	should have bought

might buy	could have been buying	can be buying
shall buy	had bought	must buy
would buy	have been buying	must have bought

A systematic method of analyzing the important verb forms is needed. R8 gives us the rule:

R8:   Aux → tense ($+$M) ($+$Have $+$ Part) ($+$be $+$ ing)

From Rule 8 it can be seen that all English verbs must have tense. The stem form (see Chapter 5, page 109) is known to transformationalists as the *present tense*, and the $\{D_1\}$ form is the *past tense*. In addition to tense, three other attributes *may* be present, as discussed in R9, R9.1, and R9.2. For tense we have a rule:

R9:   Tense → $\left\{ \begin{array}{c} \text{Pres} \\ \text{Past} \end{array} \right\}$

R9.1:   *The dog barked.*

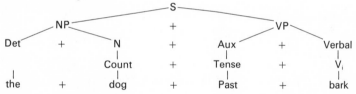

R9.2:   *Raisins are delicious.*

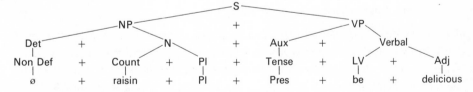

TRANSFORMATIONS

Branching tree diagrams begin with an *initial string* (usually *S*), proceed through a series of *intermediate strings* by rewrite rules to a *terminal string* (such as ø $+$ raisin $+$ Pl $+$ Pres $+$ be $+$ delicious). The terminal string represents the morphological and syntactic breakdown, carried as far as it can be carried with the rewrite rules available at that point in grammatical study.

Other operations, however, can be carried out *on the terminal string*. For example, the terminal string can be converted into everyday English speech or writing. To change the terminal string to writing, apply the *morphographemic rules*.

This is done by converting the symbols of the terminal string to conventional writing (graphemes):

ø = null
raisin + Pl = *raisins*
Pl + Pres + be = *are*
delicious = *delicious*
Add capital letter and end punctuation.
ø + raisin + Pl + Pres + be + delicious = *Raisins are delicious.*

The same sentence may be represented in spoken English by applying *morphophonemic rules*, which simply involves rewriting the terminal string in phonemic symbols:

ø + raisin + Pl + Pres + be + delicious = /rejzənzardəlíšəs/

But when we attempt to apply morphophonemic or morphographemic rules to the other sentence shown, we run into trouble with the verb:

morpheme	grapheme	phonemes
the	*the*	/ðə/
dog	*dog*	/dɔg/
past {D₁}	*ed*	/t/
bark	*bark*	/bark/

Putting this string of graphemes together in their usual left-to-right order, we come up with:

the + *dog* + *past* + *bark* = **The dog edbark.*

Obviously the form *edbark* will have to be reversed to *barked,* for tense morphemes are suffixed, not prefixed to the verb. This problem did not reveal itself in the string ø + *raisin* + *Pl* + *Pres* + *be* + *delicious* because the verb *be* is highly irregular and inflects by suppletion instead of suffixation: *be* → *is, are, was, were,* and so forth. Nevertheless, for uniformity of rule, we handle irregular verbs in the same manner as regular verbs. *Pres* + *be* is *transformed* into *be* + *Pres.* The rewrite rule states: *Aux* + *Verbal,* not *verbal* + *Aux.* Because of the rigid word order of English, all rules must be carried out in the left-to-right order stated.

But would it not be simpler to change the rule to *Verbal* + *Aux?* This cannot be done because *Aux* includes many words, as we shall presently see, such as *shall, must, would, have, had,* and many others that regularly precede the verb. Also, *verbal* includes adjectives, adverbs, and noun phrases, so if we try to put the *Aux* after the verb, we might come up with : *The dog bark loudlyed*. It is simpler to have *Aux* precede the verb, then by means of a *transformation* to put things back in proper order. A transformation is a change in word order or an insertion or deletion performed upon a terminal string for some grammatical purpose. Transformations can be performed to change a sentence from declarative to interrogative, to make a statement negative or passive, or to accomplish a wide variety of purposes. The first transformation we shall look at is a *mandatory transformation*, one that must be performed to make the terminal string grammatical. This is the affix reversal (Owen Thomas aptly called it a "flip-flop."),[7] needed to get the past tense morpheme (and other verb affixes) on the right side of the verb. The rule is:

T-Af :   Af + v $\Rightarrow$ V + Af

Transformation rules are assigned *names*, whereas rewrite rules are designated by number. Rewrite rules begin with *R*, transformation rules with *T*. In addition, transformation rules use the double ($\Rightarrow$) instead of the single arrow.

After all rewrite operations have been performed, T rules are applied to terminal strings, making a second step in analysis. Or in some cases T rules can be applied directly to the sentence as written in conventional spelling, using words instead of morphemes as the basic unit of meaning. Both methods are illustrated in the following pages.

One more process is necessary before the *T-terminal string* is derived. This is to place *double bar juncture* between words and before and after the sentence, separating complete words from morphemes. The following diagram shows all of the processes we have learned thus far:

Nina wanted some horses.

S							. . . Initial string
NP	+	VP					. . . Intermediate string
Proper N	+	Aux	+	Verbal			. . . Intermediate string
Nina	+	Tense	+	V$_t$	+	NP	. . . Intermediate string
Nina	+	Past	+	want	+	Det	+	N . . . Intermediate string
Nina	+	Past	+	want	+	NonDef	+	Count	+	Pl . . . Intermediate string
Nina	+	Past	+	want	+	some	+	horse	+	Pl . . . Terminal string
Nina	+	want	+	Past	+	some	+	horse	+	Pl . . . Terminal string with T-Af transformation
#Nina	#	want	+	Past	#	some	#	horse	+	Pl #. . . T-terminal string with double bar juncture between words

Nina wanted some horses . . . . Morphographemic presentation

/nîĵnəwâńtidsəmhȯ́rsiz/ . . . . Morphophonemic presentation

---

[7] Thomas, *Transformational Grammar and the Teacher of English*, p. 60.

MORE REWRITE RULES

The Auxiliary

Thus far we have examined only tense of rewrite rule 8:

R8:   Aux → Tense (+M) (+have + Part) (+be + ing)

Let us now examine the three optional parts. The first of these is *M*, which stands for *modal*. Modals are those auxiliaries that give additional information about the time and manner of the verb. English has five major modals, four of which are generally considered to have both past and present tense forms, making a total of nine:

present tense:	*shall*	*will*	*may*	*can*	*must*
past tense:	*should*	*would*	*might*	*could*	

Note that tense is not necessarily related to time, although *shall* and *will* are generally related to the future. The others can be used to form a sentence in any time:

I should go now.
I should have gone yesterday.
I should go tomorrow.

Modals have other characteristics. As shown in the rewrite rule, if used with other auxiliaries, the modal comes first:

I <u>might</u> be going.
I <u>shall</u> have gone.
I <u>should</u> have been there.

If modals are present, the $\{Z_3\}$ third person singular morpheme is not used, either in the modal or in the main verb:

John flies his kite.	but	*John can fly his kite.*
The horse runs fast.	but	*The horse will run fast.*
Someone is here.	but	*Someone must be here.*

Modals are diagrammed by dividing *Aux*:

R8.1:   *Students will enjoy English.*

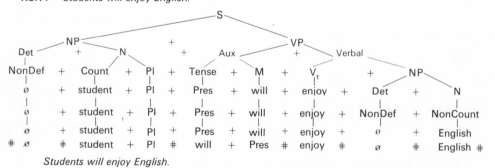

Students will enjoy English.

Note that the affix transformation and double bar juncture can be performed in a single step. When a modal is present, *tense* attaches to that modal, not to the verb.

Have + Part, like *M*, is optional. When it is included with the sentence, it must be in the proper order.

Have stands for any form of the auxiliary to have:

> Have + Past = *had*
> Have + Pres = *have*
> Have + Pres + $\{Z_3\}$ (third person singular) = *has*
> *Part* is the past participle ($\{D_2\}$) form added to the verb.

Have + Part is also a subdivision of Aux:

R8.2:   *The man has gone there before.*

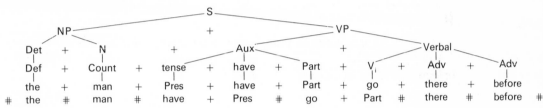

The man has gone there before.

Note that the verbal contains two consecutive adverbs. Notice also that the T-Af transformation is applied twice in the T-terminal string, once to *Pres + have*, again to *Part + go*. The T-Af transformation may be applied to any inflection that requires inversion.

If a sentence contains both *modal* and *have + Part*, the modal is always first:

R8.3:   *Martin may have found happiness.*

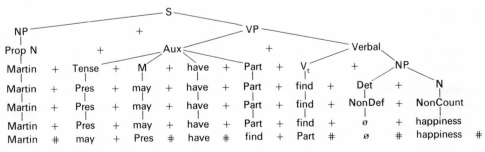

Martin may have found happiness.

The last optional part of *Aux* is *be + ing*, which forms what is often called the progressive:

R8.4: *Some spacemen were coming.*

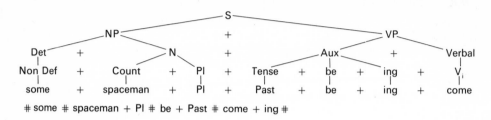

some # spaceman + Pl # be + Past # come + ing #

Some spacemen were coming.

Because the subject noun is plural, *be + Past = were*, not *was*. Note the T-Af applied to *ing + come*.

In summary, auxiliaries have eight possible constructions:

tense:	The trees <u>grow</u> tall. (Diagram R6.1)
tense + M:	Students <u>will</u> enjoy English. (R8.1)
tense + have + Part:	The man <u>has gone</u> there before. (R8.2)
tense + be + ing:	Some spacemen <u>were coming</u>. (R8.4)
tense + M + have + Part:	Martin <u>may have found</u> happiness. (R8.3)
tense + M + be + ing:	I <u>must be going</u> now.
tense + have + Part + be + ing:	I <u>have been going</u> there for many years.
tense + M + have + Part + be + ing:	(See Diagram 8.5)

R8.5: *Mary could have been helping us.*

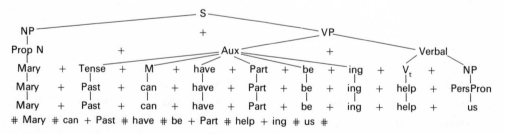

Mary # can + Past # have # be + Part # help + ing # us

Mary could have been helping us.

This sentence requires three applications of the affix transformation.

The Determiner

Proper nouns, personal pronouns, and indefinite pronouns do not take determiners, but common nouns do:

Romeo loves Juliet:	NP ⟶ proper noun
He loves Juliet:	NP ⟶ personal pronoun
Somebody loves Juliet:	NP ⟶ indefinite pronoun
The young man loves Juliet:	NP ⟶ determiner + adj + noun

All common nouns have one determiner, which may be a single word (the), a series of words (all three of the), or no words at all (ø).

A careful investigation of the determiner reveals a much more complex structure than the simple *definite-nondefinite* used so far:

R10:   Det → (PreDet +) (PreArt +) $\left\{\begin{array}{l} \text{Art} \\ \text{Demon} \\ \text{Gen} \end{array}\right\}$ (+ PostDet)

As with *Aux*, *Det* consists of one part that must be present (one of the items in brackets) plus three options. However, two characteristics can be seen from the R10 formula: The mandatory item is not first, but *third* in sentence order; and the mandatory item consists of *three possible constructions*, one of which must be present. Let us examine first that part of the determiner that is mandatory:

Art stands for *article*, a construction that can be subdivided in a manner similar to R3:

R3:   Det → $\left\{\begin{array}{l} \text{Def} \\ \text{NonDef} \end{array}\right\}$

R11:   Art → $\left\{\begin{array}{l} \text{Def} \\ \text{NonDef} \end{array}\right\}$

11.1:   *the flowers*

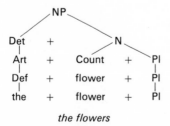

the flowers

11.2:   *weather*

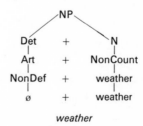

weather

Definite article is *the*; nondefinite articles include *a, an, each, every, ø,* and so on.

Demon stands for *demonstrative*. The demonstratives are *this*, *that*, *these*, and *those*.

10.1: *that storm*

that storm

10.2: *those horses*

those horses

Plural added to nouns changes the demonstratives *this* and *that* to *these* and *those*.

Gen stands for *genitive* and can be further subdivided:

R12: Gen → $\begin{cases} \text{PosPro} \\ \text{PropN + Pos} \\ \text{NP + Pos} \end{cases}$

PosPro stands for *possessive pronoun*. These include *my*, *your*, *his*, *her*, *its*, *our*, and *their*. *Pos* added to a noun or proper noun includes all allomorphs of $\{Z_2\}$, represented morphographemically by *'s* or *'*.

Examples are: *The man's, Harold's, Mr. Jones', the boys', for his conscience' sake.*

Demonstratives and genitives are generally considered *definite determiners*, but because they are all definite, there is no point is classifying them as such on a diagram. Only with the article do we need to distinguish between definite and nondefinite.

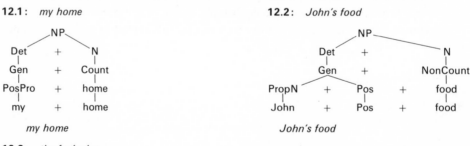

12.1: *my home*

my home

12.2: *John's food*

John's food

12.3: *the fox's den*

the fox's den

Note in 12.3 that the NP within the determiner can be subdivided. A genitive or demonstrative could also have been used with the smaller NP:

12.4: *my sister's friend*   **12.5:** *that man's family*

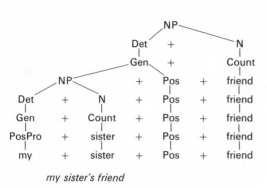

my sister's friend

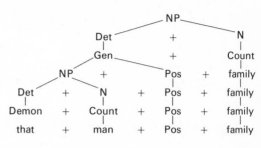

that man's family

The Prearticle

Immediately before the article, genitive, or demonstrative there may be a *prearticle*, consisting of a word such as *only, half, just, both,* or *all*:

10.3: *half the roads*   **10.4:** *all that money*

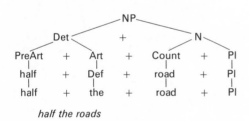

half the roads

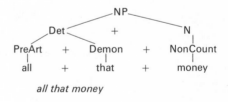

all that money

10.5: *only his coat*

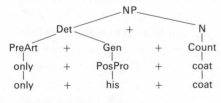

only his coat

The Post Determiner

After the article, genitive, or demonstrative there may be a *post determiner*. The rewrite rule for post determiners is:

R13:   PostDet → $\begin{Bmatrix} \text{Cardinal} \\ \text{Ordinal} \end{Bmatrix}$

The *cardinals* consist of the numbers *one, two, three, four*, and so forth. The *ordinals* are *first, second, third, fourth*, and so forth.

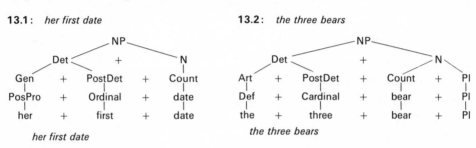

13.1: *her first date*   **13.2:** *the three bears*

13.3: *the ten million people*

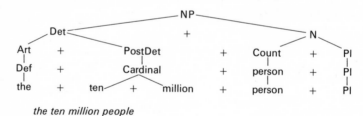

the ten million people

The Predeterminer

The optional construction that comes first in the determiner is the *predeterminer*. Predeterminers consist of a determiner plus the *predeterminer morpheme*, *of*. The lexicon of predeterminers consists of any word that can be used to make a prearticle, article, genitive, demonstrative, or post determiner, plus any *noun of quantity*, such as *slice, wedge, piece, box, can, jar, quart, mile,* or *barrel*. These constructions are made predeterminers by the predeterminer morpheme *of* immediately after: *some trees* is nondefinite article + noun + plural; *some of the trees* is predeterminer + definite article + noun + plural.

Predeterminers can be diagrammed:

10.6: *all of my children*

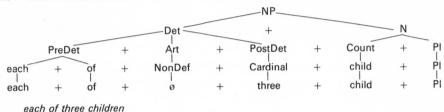

all of my children

10.7: *all my children*

all my children

10.8: *each of three children*

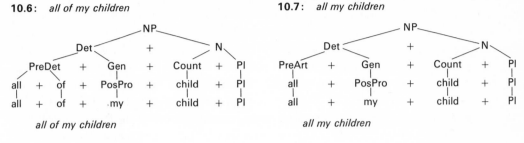

each of three children

Notice in 10.8 that the mandatory element (article, genitive, or demonstrative) is present but null. Construction is the same as if it had been *each of the three children*. Regardless of how many optional determiner constructions are present, word order is maintained according to the rewrite rule for determiners:

$$Det \rightarrow (PreDet +)\ (PreArt +) \begin{Bmatrix} Art \\ Demon \\ Gen \end{Bmatrix} (+ PostDet)$$

10.9: *most of all those sixteen children*

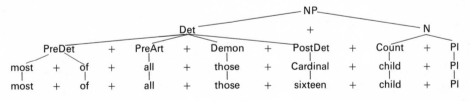

most of all those sixteen children

The more deeply one investigates the complexities of the English determiner, the more intricate the pattern becomes, and, also, the more difficult it becomes to draw a sharp, clear line between determiner and adjective. Owen Thomas, for example, includes in his postdeterminer category not only cardinals and ordinals but *comparatives* and *superlatives*. He would thus classify as postdeterminers *more* in *some more people* and *smallest* in *the smallest boy*.[8]

One difference between determiner and adjective is the flexibility of order. Adjectives may occur in more than one possible order; but the order of determiners is fixed. One can have a *refreshing, cool glass of lemonade* or a *cool, refreshing glass of lemonade*. One can have *some of this lemonade*, but never **this some of lemonade*. But even in some adjective groups, word order has become fixed. I have heard of the *little red schoolhouse*, but never of the **red little schoolhouse*. But determiner word order is not perfectly rigid either. One can speak of *the first three prizes* or *the three first prizes*.

Also, any number of adjectives that the writer feels are consistent with good writing style can be applied to any one noun: a *big, ugly, sprawling, dilapidated two-story building*, but never **a this the building*. This text has not included comparatives and superlatives as determiners partly because they fit previously established criteria for form class words (large lexicon, inflectional endings, lexical meaning), and also because John can be *shorter, fatter*, and *older* than Harry.

Some transformational systems include such forms as *next, last*, and *final* with the ordinals, and *many, few*, and *several* as cardinals. In this case one can take *a few final strokes* or *a final few strokes*. Obviously, postdeterminers are the least rigid of the determiners. It would take a grammar far more comprehensive than we can contemplate in this introductory work to account for all the subtleties of determiners.

ADVERBS

Adverbs (often called *adverbials*) were described in the previous chapter as one of the four form classes. They are attributive to verb phrases, and may consist of single words:

> *annually, now, forever, here, carefully, well, slowly,*
> *quite, never, upstairs*

They may also consist of groups of words:

> *in the drawer, when you are ready, every year, like a frightened gazelle*

The English language contains a number of different types of adverbs, each with a different function and different distribution:

1. Adverbs of time: *now, tomorrow, this morning, in a few days, some day*
2. Adverbs of place: *here, in the city, downtown, at home, under a tree*
3. Adverbs of manner: *well, slowly, beautifully, in great haste, with regret*
4. Adverbs of frequency: *regularly, every few days, annually, whenever it rains*

---

[8] Thomas, *Transformational Grammar and the Teacher of English*, p. 82.

There are other types of adverbs whose distribution is quite different from that of those listed. *Sentence adverbs* are attributive to the entire sentence rather than to the verb head word alone:

> *I would <u>definitely</u> like to go.*
> *This <u>certainly</u> is a beautiful day.*
> *<u>Surely</u> you don't mean it.*

Adverbs of degree are frequently classified as *intensifiers* (see Chapter 6, page 135). Examples are *very, quite, hardly, really, partially,* and *exceedingly.*

Preverbs usually follow the first word in the auxiliary:

> *That puppy is <u>never</u> quiet.*
> *I could <u>hardly</u> recognize him.*
> *The cook has <u>rarely</u> done so well.*
> *I could <u>almost</u> guess the answer.*

However, this is not a rigid rule, as adverbs have the most flexible sentence distribution of any word class in the language.

Distribution of Adverbs

In R7 we discussed five major sentence patterns of the English language. These are:

$$\text{Verbal} \rightarrow \left\{ \begin{array}{l} V_i \\ V_t + NP \\ LV + NP \\ LV + Adj \\ LV + Adv \end{array} \right\} \quad \begin{array}{l} \text{(intransitive verb)} \\ \text{(transitive verb + noun phrase)} \\ \text{(linking verb + noun phrase)} \quad (+ \text{adv}) \\ \text{(linking verb + adjective)} \\ \text{(linking verb + adverb)} \end{array}$$

The different types of adverbs have different distributions. After transitive or intransitive verbs one can use most of the adverb types:

$$\left\{ \begin{array}{l} \textit{Mary sings} \\ \textit{Joe hit the ball} \end{array} \right\} \quad \left\{ \begin{array}{l} \textit{today.} \\ \textit{in the park.} \\ \textit{beautifully.} \\ \textit{every day.} \end{array} \right\} \quad \begin{array}{l} \text{(time)} \\ \text{(place)} \\ \text{(manner)} \\ \text{(frequency)} \end{array}$$

After a linking verb only the adverb of place is common:

> *Mary is   here.*
> *upstairs.*
> *away.*
> *in New York.*
> *at bat.*
> *on vacation.*

But we are hardly likely to hear:

> *Mary is   today.
>   beautifully.
>   every day.

However, after we have added an adverb of place to the linking verb, the LV + AdvP pattern, like the other LV patterns, can take an adverb of time, place, or frequency:

> *Joe is here:*   now.   (time)
>   at school.   (place)
>   in good weather.   (frequency)

Adverbs of degree are in a class by themselves. They cannot be used in any of the constructions shown. One cannot say *Mary sings quite*, *Joe hit the ball rather*, or *My friend is very*.

Adverbs of degree are preposed with adverbs of manner:

> Mary sings <u>quite</u> well.
> Joe hit the ball <u>rather</u> skillfully.

Or sometimes with other types of adverbs:

> We have lamb chops for dinner <u>fairly</u> often.
> We arrived <u>very</u> late.

The entire distribution of adverbs can be expressed in an expansion of rewrite rule 7:

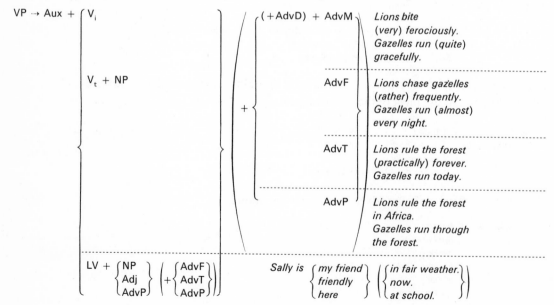

Adverbs can be placed on a branching tree diagram:

Sally plays her violin quite expertly.

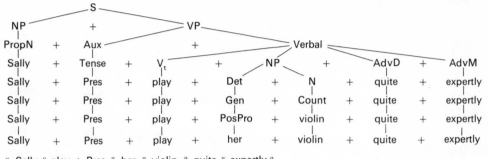

\# Sally \# play + Pres \# her \# violin \# quite \# expertly \#

Sally plays her violin quite expertly.

That man has been a teacher in this school.

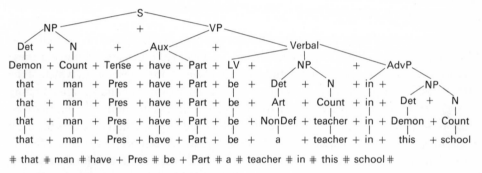

\# that \# man \# have + Pres \# be + Part \# a \# teacher \# in \# this \# school \#

That man has been a teacher in this school.

T-Adv

Adverbs, as we have already noted, are among the few English constructions that can easily be moved from one position in the sentence to another. This can be demonstrated in a transformation rule.[9]

$$\text{\textbf{T-Adv}:} \quad X + Y + Adv \Rightarrow \begin{Bmatrix} Adv + X + Y \\ X + Adv + Y \end{Bmatrix}$$

[9] The adverbial transformation, as well as many other transformations of English, involves not only a change in word order but an accompanying change in intonation. Space limitations do not permit discussion of intonation, but a complete grammar of the language would include detailed description of the intonation patterns of linguistic constructions before and after the transformation.

The use of X and Y here is similar to that of a mathematical formula; that is, they can stand for any construction. Beginning with the morphographemic string on page 175, we have:

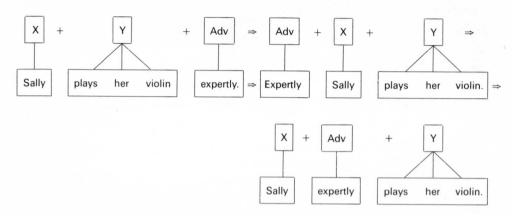

This does not imply that all transformations will produce smooth and effective English, only that the transformations are *grammatically* possible. Knowing these transformations should focus the student's attention on the question: In which of the three positions is the adverb most effectively placed for smooth and dynamic writing style? In composition the writer or speaker must select from numerous alternatives, just as the painter selects his most effective colors and a cabinetmaker selects the most beautiful or functional pattern and most desirable wood. But before the most effective selection can be made, the alternatives must be clear. A major rationale for the teaching of transformational grammar in the public schools is that it explores the many alternatives available to a writer, giving numerous examples of the various forms an utterance can take.

Thus the teaching of modern grammar can be *a search for alternative forms*, not a series of right-or-wrong exercises. By expanding the students' repertoire of synonyms, the teacher demonstrates that there is frequently more than one word to fit a given situation and that each word carries a different value. Likewise, there is a variety of sentence forms available to say any given thing, and the selection of the form to be used, as well as the selection of the appropriate synonym, will determine the student's *writing* style.

Closely tied to style is the development of the *sensitivity* of the writer. The New English Teacher is careful not to impose his own preferences and his own writing style on his students but rather to encourage each one to develop a personality and style of his own.

"Look at these synonyms," the teacher might urge. "Try the active and the passive forms; try a two-sentence construction, then transform into an adverb clause. Which form really says what you mean? Which one "grabs" the reader and makes him believe it? Which one sings the sweetest song?" The New English Teacher does not supply ready-made answers; he just asks the questions and focuses the students' attention on their work. How much more exciting is this approach to teaching than merely filling a page with red marks!

SINGLE BASE TRANSFORMATIONS

Thus far, most of our inquiry has involved *rewrite rules*, those rules that show how each linguistic form can be broken into its constituents and how the constituents fit together morphologically into kernel sentences or expanded kernel sentences. But these rules still do not account for a great number of English sentences. For example, they do not show how a statement can be transformed into a question, how an affirmative utterance can be made negative, or how an active sentence can become passive. These are done by means of transformations, or changes of word order, including additions, deletions, or reversals. We have already looked at two English transformations:

T Affix: Affix + Verb $\Rightarrow$ Verb + Affix

This is the mandatory transformation that puts the *tense*, *participle*, or *ing* affix after, rather than before, the verb. We also looked briefly at the adverb transformation:

T Adv: X + Y + Adv $\Rightarrow \begin{Bmatrix} \text{Adv} + \text{X} + \text{Y} \\ \text{X} + \text{Adv} + \text{Y} \end{Bmatrix}$

This is just one of a number of possible formulas showing the flexibility peculiar to English adverbs. The transformations discussed so far and those in this section are called *single base transformations* because they involve a single kernel sentence (base) and its variations. *Double base transformations* will be discussed later.

Interrogatives

Interrogative transformations change a statement into a question. English contains a number of different types of questions. Beginning with a statement:

Mary was sipping cider in the cellar.

we can form a number of questions:

Yes/no: *Was Mary sipping cider in the cellar?* (Can be answered yes or no.)
Tag: *Mary was sipping cider in the cellar, wasn't she?*
          Mary wasn't sipping cider in the cellar, was she?
Echo: *Mary was sipping cider in the cellar?* (No change except intonation.)
Wh: *Who was sipping cider in the cellar?*
          What was Mary sipping in the cellar?
          What was Mary doing in the cellar?
          Where was Mary sipping cider?   (Cannot be answered yes or no;
          How was Mary sipping cider in the cellar?   involve *how* or a word beginning
          When was Mary sipping cider in the cellar? with *wh.*)

Beginning with the *yes/no* question, we have the following transformation formula:

$$\text{T Yes/no:}\quad NP + Tense \left(+\left\{\begin{matrix}M\\ have\\ be\end{matrix}\right\}\right) + X \Rightarrow Tense \left(+\left\{\begin{matrix}M\\ have\\ be\end{matrix}\right\}\right) + NP + X$$

These transformations can be illustrated without drawing an entire branching tree diagram. We can start with the terminal string of a sentence and apply the transformation rule:

T Yes/no: 1

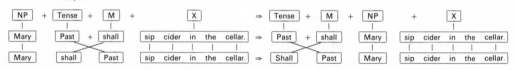

Mary should sip cider in the cellar   ⇒   *Should Mary sip cider in the cellar?*

T Yes/no: 2

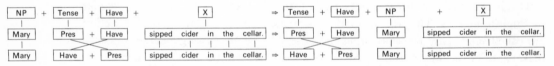

Mary has sipped cider in the cellar   ⇒   *Has Mary sipped cider in the cellar?*

T Yes/no: 3

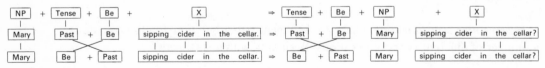

Mary was sipping cider in the cellar   ⇒   *Was Mary sipping cider in the cellar?*

In diagrams 2 and 3 it was convenient to treat X as a single, unified construction. For that reason we did not break *sipped* and *sipping* down into *sip + Part* and *sip + ing*.

T Yes/no: 4

The final *yes/no* transformation will require some special comments. When the optional *modal*, *have*, or *be* are not present, another step must be added:

When the transformation is applied to this sentence, the verb and the tense morpheme become separated. This is not possible in English. Tense is a completely bound morpheme. It cannot appear unless it is attached to a verb. There is no way to write *tense + Mary + sip*. Therefore, at this point in the formula, English speakers add *Do* to *Past* in order to be able to say the past tense morpheme. *Do* in this sentence has no lexical meaning. It is a function word, put in simply to enable the speaker to express tense morpheme:

#Mary # sip + past # cider # in # the # cellar ⇒ # Do + Past # Mary # sip # cider # in # the # cellar #

Mary sipped cider in the cellar. ⇒ *Did Mary sip cider in the cellar?*

The addition of *do* to the formula may be considered a separate transformation:

T Do: NP + Tense + X ⇒ Tense + Do + NP + X

Another example of a *Do* transformation would be:

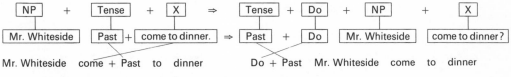

Mr. Whiteside came to dinner. ⇒ *Did Mr Whiteside come to dinner?*

Note in the examples that the tense morpheme transfers from the verb to Do (*sipped* ⇒ *did sip*; *came* ⇒ *did come*). If tense is *present*, *Do* takes the form *does* or *do*, depending on number:

Mr. Whiteside comes to dinner. ⇒ *Does Mr. Whiteside come to dinner?*
They come to dinner.   ⇒   *Do they come to dinner?*

It is interesting to note that when the verb is one of those used to form auxiliaries —*be* or *have*—the *Do* transformation is not *needed* even if there is no auxiliary verb present. In that case a simple yes/no transformation can be applied. This can be illustrated by applying the formula directly to the morphographemic string:

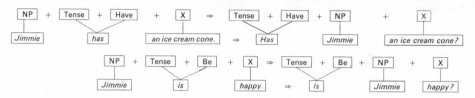

Students frequently have difficulty interpreting Shakespeare and other early writers because of changes in the language. The *Do* transformation is an example. Today we seldom see yes/no questions without *do*, except for sentences with *be* and *have*, as shown. Even with *be* and *have* the *Do* transformation may be applied: *Does Jimmie have an ice cream cone?* But in *Macbeth* we find:

Elizabethan English	Modern English
And wakes it now . . . ?	*And does it wake now?*
(Act I, scene vii)	
How came she by that light?	*How did she come by that light?*
(Act V, scene i)	
Know you not he has?	*Don't you know he has?*
(Act I, scene vii)	

This is also true in negative transformations, which we shall investigate presently.

Elizabethan English	Modern English
Hear it not, Duncan;	*Do not hear it, Duncan;*
(Act II, scene i)	

A teacher guiding his charges through such literature might do well to give some basic instruction in these language changes.

T Wh

Wh questions are those that cannot be answered by yes or no. They usually begin with *how* or a word that begins with *wh*. The first step in forming a *wh* question is to apply the yes/no transformation. For brevity we will work directly with the morphographemic string:

Then we take the yes/no question and apply to it the *T Wh* formula. This can be done a number of ways, depending on the type of sentence with which we are dealing. In this example we shall assume the presence of an adverb and proceed to "question" the adverb:

T Wh:

$$X \;+\; \begin{bmatrix} \text{AdvP} \\ \text{AdvT} \\ \text{AdvM} \\ \text{AdvF} \end{bmatrix} \;+\; Y \;\Rightarrow\; \begin{bmatrix} \text{Where} \\ \text{When} \\ \text{How} \\ \text{How often} \end{bmatrix} \;+\; X \;+\; Y$$

The square brackets signify that each item in one bracket matches the item on the same line in the other. If the adverb is of *place*, the *wh* word will be *where*; if a *time* adverb is used, *when* is the *wh* word. *Manner* and *frequency* adverbs take *how* and *how often*, respectively. Continuing the transformation we have:

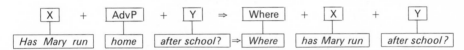

In these transformations X represents all words on one side of a particular construction; Y represents everything on the other. As we change from the *T yes/no* to the *T Wh* transformation, *X* and *Y* may change. Within the formula, however—on either side of the double bar arrow—*X* and *Y* remain identical except for the possible addition or deletion of a capital letter or end punctuation to account for movement to or from the beginning or end of a sentence. These changes in punctuation, of course, only occur in the morphographemic string.

To question the adverb of time in the sentence shown, begin by using the sentence derived from the *Yes/No* transformation:

X		AdvT	+	Y	⇒	When	+	X		Y
Has Mary run home	+	after school?		ø	⇒	When		has Mary run home?		ø

With the adverb of time coming at the end of the sentence, *Y* is null. The null portion of an utterance is generally shown on the branching tree diagram and the terminal strings, and is dropped in the morphographemic string. *Y* is illustrated in this example to show that it exists in the formula, although it is null.

Next let us look at an adverb of manner placed at the beginning of a sentence.

The adverb can be added to the sentence without altering the formula. First apply the yes/no transformation:

The product of the transformation produces a sentence that is grammatically correct but poor writing style. Applying the *Wh* transformation, we have:

(X+) AdvM   +   Y   ⇒   How (+X)   +   Y
Filled with joy,   is Mary running home?   ⇒   How   is Mary running home?

Note that X is null.

Our final example of the *Wh* transformation involves an adverb of frequency:

NP + Tense + M + X ⇒ Tense + M + NP + X
Mary   can   walk home from school every day   ⇒   Can   Mary   walk home from school every day?

X   AdvF   (+Y)   ⇒   How often   +   X   (+Y)
Can Mary walk home from school   every day?   ⇒   How often   can Mary walk home from school?

T-Neg

In addition to changing a kernel sentence from affirmative to interrogative, we can change it from positive to negative. The simplest transformation is that which inserts the word *not* into the formula. This transformation is similar to the question in that the formula is very simple when *modal*, *have*, or *be* is present, but requires the *Do* transformation without one of these optional elements.

T-Neg: NP + Tense + $\begin{Bmatrix} M \\ have \\ be \end{Bmatrix}$ + X ⇒ NP + Tense + $\begin{Bmatrix} M \\ have \\ be \end{Bmatrix}$ + not + X

Applying T-Neg to a morphographemic string we have:

NP + Tense + Have + X ⇒ NP + Tense + Have + Not + X
Somebody   has   eaten my porridge.   ⇒   Somebody   has   not   eaten my porridge.

But if the optional *have* is removed, we must first apply *T-Do*. We begin with the terminal string:

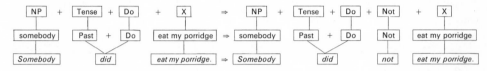

Somebody ate my porridge. ⇒ Somebody did eat my porridge.

Now apply *T-Neg*:

Have can be used as either a verb (to own, to possess) or as part of an auxiliary (have + Part). It can be made negative with or without the *Do* transformation. Compare these morphographemic strings:

Judy has a new bicycle. ⇒ Judy hasn't a new bicycle.

(*Has not* contracted to *hasn't*.) This sentence can also be made negative by applying the *Do* transformation first:

Judy has a new bicycle. ⇒ Judy does have a new bicycle. ⇒ Judy does not have a new bicycle.

But the same flexibility does not apply in the case of *be*, the other auxiliary:

Scott is here now. ⇒ Scott is not here now. But: *Scott does not be here now.

Nor does this flexibility apply to transitive and intransitive verbs. Longfellow wrote:

Tell me not in mournful numbers . . .

But such constructions would be unusual today. Modern English speakers are more likely to use the *Do* transformation unless *modal, have*, or *be* is present.

T-Passive

Another transformation that can be performed on a kernel sentence is the passive. This can be done to any sentence built on a transitive verb. The formula is:

T-Passive: $NP_1 + Aux + V_t + NP_2 \Rightarrow NP_2 + Aux + be + Part + V_t \ (+by + NP_1)$

The following example shows the formula applied to the morphographemic string of a kernel sentence:

In this example, Aux (tense) transfers from the verb *read* in the active sentence to *be* in the passive. In both sentences the base form of the verb *read* is the stem (/rijd/). In the active sentence the past tense is added; in the passive sentence the participle, making the final pronunciation in both sentences /red/. All three forms (stem, past, and participle) are spelled alike because *read* is an irregular verb. In grammatical analysis, however, these must be considered as three separate forms. Usually the tree diagram is performed on the kernel sentence, and then the transformation is applied to the terminal string. However, a diagram of a transformation is possible.

This diagram may require some form or forms that have not been included in the phrase structure rules listed thus far. An example is the passive transformation, in which *be*, *participle*, and *by* have been added by the passive formula. These forms can be added to the diagram:

That text was read by Mr. Walker's class.

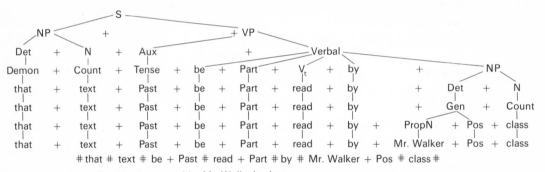

That text was read by Mr. Walker's class.

If the auxiliary contains optional forms, these are diagramed as usual:

That article should have been read weeks ago.

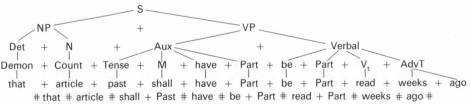

That article should have been read weeks ago.

DOUBLE BASE TRANSFORMATIONS

Among the most interesting aspects of transformational analysis are the *double base transformations*, which explain how two different thoughts are combined into a single sentence. If the speaker of English—or any other language—were unable to perform these transformations, his speech and writing would consist of childish snatches that lack the complexity and beauty, the drama and emotion that our language is capable of attaining.

To a native speaker these transformations are not a conscious process. They are performed intuitively, and the capacity to handle them develops as the individual matures in language competence. The linguist, on the other hand, attempts to analyze these intuitive moves and to express by means of a formula those processes that have taken place.

The double base transformation consists of three utterances: It begins with a *matrix*:

> *If man is to survive he must keep the air he breathes pure.*

to which an *insert* is added:

> *If man is to survive he must keep the water he drinks pure.*

producing an expanded utterance, or *result*:

> *If man is to survive he must keep the air he breathes and the water he drinks pure.*

This does not imply that either the matrix or the insert actually existed as separate linguistic utterances. The double base transformation is merely a symbolic way of showing that the *concepts* are combined into a single utterance.

T Compound

One of the simplest double base transformations is that which *compounds*, or combines, two parallel thoughts into a single utterance. In this transformation the matrix and the insert sentences are identical except for the compound construction. In other words, the speaker is saying the same thing about two different elements:

> **Matrix:** *Transformational grammar has interesting implications* ⎫
> **Insert:** *Structural grammar has interesting implications.* ⎬ ⇒
> **Result:** *Transformational and structural grammar have interesting implications.*

Note that the information about structural grammar is literally *inserted* into the matrix sentence. This is frequently referred to as *embedding*.

The transformational process can be illustrated by a flow chart:

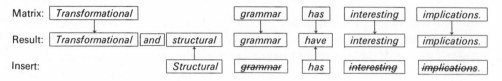

This can be expressed by a formula:

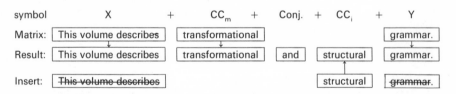

CC_m and CC_i, respectively, refer to the compound construction in the matrix and the insert. In making the transformation, X and Y of the insert are deleted. X and Y may be null if the compound construction is at the beginning or the end of the utterance. In this example, X is null. The *conjunction* does not come from either the matrix or the insert but must be added to complete the transformation. Other changes may also take place, such as a change of verb form for agreement.

In this example the *subject* was compounded, but any part of the utterance can be so treated, as shown by the following:

Matrix: *This volume describes transformational grammar.*
Insert: *This volume describes structural grammar.* $\Rightarrow$
Result: *This volume describes transformational and structural grammar.*

These transformations can also be indicated in the formula:

symbol	X	+	CC$_m$	+	Conj.	+	CC$_i$	+	Y
Matrix:	This volume describes		transformational						grammar.
Result:	This volume describes		transformational		and		structural		grammar.
Insert:	~~This volume describes~~						structural		~~grammar.~~

Compound prepositional phrase:

Matrix: *More information can be found in the bibliography.*
Insert: *More information can be found in the appendix.* $\Rightarrow$
Result: *More information can be found in the bibliography and (in the) appendix.*

(Y is null in this example.)

T Comparative I

In the comparative transformation both matrix and insert contain a *Noun + Verb + Adjective* pattern, the adjective of the two utterances being identical. The result sentence gives the additional information that the quality expressed by the adjective is present to a greater degree in the noun of the matrix:

Matrix: *The water is cold.*
Insert: *The wind is cold.* $\Rightarrow$
Result: *The water is colder* (*than the wind*) (*is*).

Parentheses around *than the wind* and *is* indicate that these constructions may be deleted if doing so improves the style. The verb may be deleted without taking out the construction in the first parenthesis, but if the *than* ... construction is deleted, the verb must also be deleted. These may be flow charted as follows:

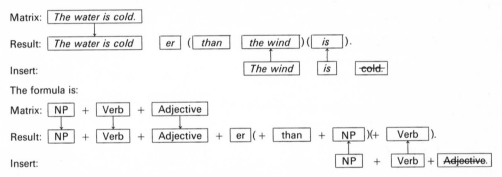

The formula is:

The *er* (comparative morpheme discussed in Chapter 5) and *than* are added by the transformation. They do not come from either insert or matrix. The adjective of the insert must be deleted.

This example used the linking verb *be* in the matrix and insert. If, however, the verb is transitive or intransitive, the verb *do* (or its proper inflected form) is substituted for the verb in the result sentence:

Matrix: *We try hard.*
Insert: *They try hard.* $\Rightarrow$
Result: *We try harder* (*than they*) (*do*).

The example shows that the comparative transformation can be applied to adverbs as well as adjectives. With irregular adjectives and adverbs, the irregularity is maintained in the transformation:

Matrix: *Margie plays the piano well.*
Insert: *Sally plays the piano well.* $\Rightarrow$
Result: *Margie plays the piano better* (*than Sally*) (*does*).

With transitive verbs, as illustrated in this sentence, an additional NP (object of verb) is introduced into the formula:

Matrix: $\boxed{\text{NP}_m}$ + $\boxed{\text{Verb}}$ + $\boxed{\text{NP}_2}$ + $\boxed{\text{Adverb}}$

Result: $\boxed{\text{NP}_m}$ + $\boxed{\text{Verb}}$ + $\boxed{\text{NP}_2}$ + $\boxed{\text{Adverb}}$ + $\boxed{\text{er}}$ (+ $\boxed{\text{than}}$ + $\boxed{\text{NP}_i}$) + ($\boxed{\text{Do}}$)

Insert: $\boxed{\text{NP}_i}$ + $\boxed{\text{Verb}}$ + $\boxed{\text{NP}_2}$ + $\boxed{\text{Adverb}}$

T Comparative II

As noted in Chapter 5 not all adjectives and adverbs inflect *er*. Some use the phrasal construction with *more*. This changes the formula:

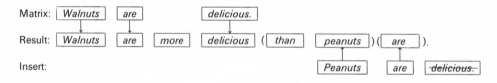

T Superlative I

The superlative transformation involves the same adjectives and adverbs and the same $Noun + Verb + \begin{Bmatrix} Adjective \\ Adverb \end{Bmatrix}$ sentences for the matrix and insert. The transformation is more complex, however, involving more optional deletions in both the matrix and the result. Note below that *the* and *est* are introduced into the result sentence. As with *er* and *than* in the comparative transformation, they do not come from either matrix or insert. This is the pattern:

Matrix: *Redwoods are old.* ⎫
Insert: *(All) (of) these trees are old.* ⎬ ⇒
Result: *Redwoods are the oldest (of) (all) (these) (trees).* ⎭

The insert sentence could read any of three ways:

> *These trees are old.*
> *All these trees are old.*
> *All of these trees are old.*

The result sentence contains a number of options:

> *Redwoods are the oldest.*
> *Redwoods are the oldest of all.*
> *Redwoods are the oldest of these.*
> *Redwoods are the oldest of these trees.*
> *Redwoods are the oldest of all these trees.*

The formula can be shown on a flow chart:

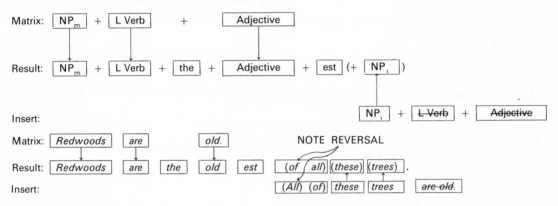

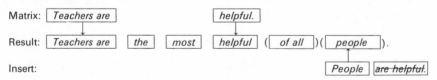

T Superlative II

Those adjectives and adverbs that take the *more* rather than the *er* transformation are also different in the superlative:

Matrix: | Teachers are | | | helpful. |
Result: | Teachers are | the | most | helpful (of all)(people).
Insert: | People | are helpful. |

The only real difference between superlative I and II is the free form *most* placed before the adjective or adverb instead of the bound morpheme *est* after it.

T Possessive I

In the previous chapter we looked at the genitive morpheme as part of the morphological system of the English language. It is also possible to regard the genitive as a transformation, the product of two thoughts that are combined into a result sentence. In a possessive transformation the insert sentence is built with a *Noun + Verb + Noun* pattern, and the verb is always some form of *have*. The pattern for the matrix sentence is NP$_1$ + X. The noun of the matrix is the same as the second noun of the insert (NP$_2$). To make the transformation, change the *have* of the insert to the genitive morpheme and add it to the first noun (NP$_1$). This construction replaces the determiner of the matrix. An example is:

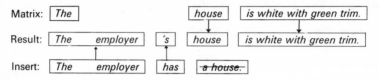

The formula is:

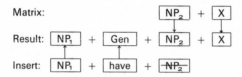

More commonly this is written:

Matrix: *The house is white with green trim.* ⎫
Insert: *The employer has a house.*   ⎬ ⇒
Result: *The employer's house is white with green trim.* ⎭

T Possessive II

When the transformed determiner is an attribute of a nonliving thing, an *of* preposition frequently replaces the genitive morpheme:

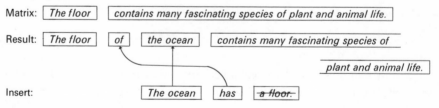

This can be shown in the formula:

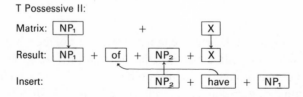

The usual method of expressing this is:

Matrix: *The floor contains many fascinating species of plant and animal life.*
Insert: *The ocean has a floor.* ⇒
Result: *The floor of the ocean contains many fascinating species of plant and animal life.*

T Adjective

The adjective transformation results from an insert sentence of the *Det + Noun + Be + Adjective* type, with a matrix containing the same NP plus *X*. The adjective of the insert is placed between the determiner and the noun of the matrix:

Matrix: | The | | children | | sang and danced. |

Result: | The | | happy | | children | | sang and danced. |

Insert: | ~~The children~~ | | ~~are~~ | | happy. |

The formula for the adjective transformation can be charted:

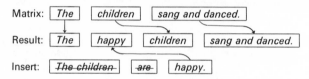

Matrix: | Det | + | Noun | + | X |

Result: | Det | + | Adjective | + | Noun | + | X |

Insert: | ~~Det + Noun~~ | + | be | + | Adjective |

Frequently these transformations are treated in terminal strings:

Matrix: Det + Noun + Pl + V$_i$ + Tense + and + V$_i$ + Tense
         The + child + Pl + sing + Past + and + dance + Past   ⇒

Insert: Det + Noun + Pl + be + Tense + Adjective
         The + child + Pl + be + Pres + happy

         Det + Adj + N + Pl + V$_i$ + Tense + and + V$_i$ + Tense
         The + happy + child + Pl + sing + Past + and + dance + Past

T Relative

Let us examine the processes that take place when two utterances are combined by means of a relative clause: Relative clauses begin with *who*, *which*, or *that* and are inserted into a matrix. Do not confuse relatives with interrogatives:

Relative	Interrogative
I saw the little man <u>who</u> wasn't there. *It was the report <u>which</u> pleased me.*	*<u>Who</u> wasn't there?* *<u>Which</u> report pleased me?*

The relative clause pattern is:

Matrix: *The little clown hit the big clown with a balloon.* ⎫
Insert: *The big clown started to cry.* ⎬ ⇒
Result: *The little clown hit the big clown, who started to cry, with a balloon.* ⎭

The same process can be put on a flow chart:

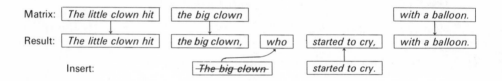

Note that the noun phrase *the big clown* is found in both matrix and insert. This is a necessary ingredient for a relative clause transformation. We label this common noun phrase *NP* (with the understanding that there may be other noun phrases involved, but only the common one will be labeled *NP* for this formula). Everything to the left of *NP* is *X* and everything to the right is *Y*. The following formula expresses the transformation:

T Relative

Matrix: X + NP + Y ⎫
Insert: X + NP + Y ⎬ ⇒
Result: X_m + NP + { who / which / that } + X_i + Y_i + Y_m

The subposed *m* and *i* $(_{m,i})$ stand for the *X* and *Y* of the matrix and insert respectively. *Who, which,* and *that* are relative pronouns introducing the relative clauses. *Who* and *that* can be used when the common *NP* is a person, *which* and *that* for a nonpersonal *NP*. Using symbols, we can show a formula that will fit all relative transformations:

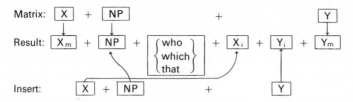

In many relative clause transformations, one or more of the *X* or *Y* constructions may be null:

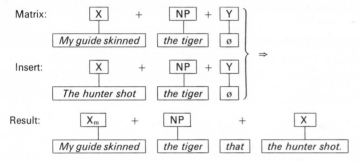

Sometimes the relative pronoun is omitted: (null relative pronoun)

My guide skinned the tiger the hunter shot.

Sometimes the order is reversed, particularly when one of the *X* or *Y* constructions is an adverb, which is highly movable:

Then, with a balloon, the little clown hit the big clown, who started to cry.

These reversals or deletions can be considered transformations that are applied to the original transformation. Their purpose is to improve the style.

RECURSIVENESS

Recursive transformations are those that can *recur*, or be repeated by adding new inserts to the result sentence. The compound transformation, for example, is recursive.

Matrix:	*Transformational and structural grammar have interesting implications.*
Insert:	*Traditional grammar has interesting implications.*
Result:	*Transformational, structural, and traditional grammar have interesting implications.*

There is one slight change in the formula after the first compound transformation. This is the use of a comma instead of a conjunction between all but the last two compounded constructions. The relative clause transformation is recursive:

Matrix: *The little clown hit the big clown, who then started to cry, with a balloon.* } ⇒
Insert: *The little clown had a deep voice.*
Result: *The little clown, who had a deep voice, hit the big clown, who then started to cry, with a balloon.*

One could go on indefinitely adding relative clauses. This does not mean that such practice would produce good, clear, readable sentences. It only means that it is *grammatically* possible. Correct grammar and desirable writing style are not the same thing, although this has long been a point of confusion within the teaching profession. The result sentence shown is already beginning to bog down with too many detours detracting from the main thought. To add more detail would make it very difficult to read, even though the known rules of grammar permit it.

The possessive and adjective transformations are also recursive:

Matrix: *The employer's house is white with green trim.* } ⇒
Insert: *Jerry has an employer.*
Result: *Jerry's employer's house is white with green trim.*

Matrix: *The happy children sang and danced.* } ⇒
Insert: *The happy children are young.*
Result: *The happy young children sang and danced.*

Comparative and superlative transformations are not recursive.

The water is colder than the wind.
Walnuts are more delicious than peanuts.
Redwoods are the oldest of all these trees.
Teachers are the most helpful of all people.

In English something cannot become "more" than "more," and if a thing is "most" that is obviously as far as the concept can be carried. Therefore you cannot add another comparative or superlative transformation to the result sentences shown. However, English provides a great variety of highly complex constructions. It is possible by combining a series of different processes, including expansion, deletion, and reversal, to produce an infinite variety of English sentences:

Although redwoods were once considered the oldest trees in the world, some bristlecone pine trees have been discovered that are older than the oldest known redwoods.

Although this sentence is not particularly complex for written English, it contains a superlative transformation, a comparative transformation, a relative clause transformation, and a number of other phenomena that can be analyzed in terms of transformations, rewrite rules, structural patterns, traditional grammar, morphology, or phonology. This brief section on descriptive grammar has provided only a glance at the processes of analysis.

TRANSFORMATIONS AND THE TEACHING OF LANGUAGE

Even in the short introduction presented in this chapter it should be evident that the branching tree diagram and other transformational devices permit a much closer scrutiny of the language than has any other system devised thus far. But transformational grammar is a growing, changing medium. The terminology and methods described in this volume are based mainly on the school textbooks with which many teachers will be working in the next few years. But already linguists on the forefront of knowledge are developing new systems and expanding present ones. What the future holds is anyone's guess, but it seems obvious that with language an ever-changing phenomenon, no system of grammar will ever become the final and ultimate one.

One of the major rationales for the adoption of transformational grammar in the public schools is that language, more than any other facet of human experience, has elevated man above the beasts, and simply understanding the nature of anything so intrinsic to man and so vital to his humanity is interesting and worthwhile in itself.

I find this view only partially acceptable. I can recommend it for myself, for observing the subtle differences in usage between the adverb of place and the adverb of manner, or the complexity of the common determiner satisfies an aspect of my intellectual curiosity. However, to impose this discipline on every schoolchild in a series of required English courses is akin to requiring a detailed study of the circulatory system because if our blood stops circulating we cannot survive.

But regardless of whether transformational grammar is offered as a school subject, the need remains for a language teacher to be familiar with the modern school of linguistics. This movement has had such a strong impact on the profession in general and on textbooks in particular that such knowledge has become inescapable if a teacher is to call himself professional. He needs this data, if for no other reason than to make an educated decision concerning what he is to teach. The alternative is to become a pawn in the hands of curriculum committees and textbook salesmen.

Even if the teacher rejects the idea of teaching transformational grammar—or any other phase of linguistics—to his students, he still needs to understand the intricacies of the language he professes to teach. A professional should be better informed than his clients. An automobile driver does not need to know the complexities of the internal combustion engine, but the mechanic does. The physician must be able to diagnose the patient's problem with far greater precision than the patient himself. Likewise, the teacher should be able to diagnose the student's language usage problems through a combination of a sensitivity to good language and a scientific understanding of the processes by which language operates.

Finally, the language teacher needs to keep in touch with the contributions of linguistics to teaching methodology in many related areas. Linguists will undoubtedly continue to give us valuable information concerning the teaching of reading, spelling, and composition and of foreign languages in addition to our own. And the schools may do well to offer transformational grammar or whatever linguistic systems become the method of the future. This may be done through an elective course in the English Department or by offering students who may develop a sincere interest in the subject an opportunity to explore transformational grammar in English classes.

But if we are to teach our students to communicate skillfully and intelligently we must make optimal use of every precious minute. And if it comes to a *choice* between exploring the relationships between *NP* and *VP* or the relationships between rich and poor, Whites and Blacks, or Americans and Asians, I think I would find understanding each other more pressing than understanding the subtle nuances of language.

On the other hand, is it possible that learning transformational theory will contribute to the student's ability to communicate with his fellow man? Does knowing about the relative clause transformation help the student use it?

Demonstrating that the two sentences *Jimmie plays the guitar* and *Jimmie's mother gave him a guitar* can be smoothed into *Jimmie plays the guitar that his mother gave him* by use of the relative transformation may help free the student from a stilted, childish style. But the question remains whether this can be done just as effectively simply by showing a student the different ways that words can be regrouped without teaching the theory. THUS FAR I HAVE SEEN NO CONVINCING EVIDENCE THAT KNOWLEDGE OF GRAMMAR RULES IS NECESSARY FOR GOOD USAGE. My gifted students have generally acquired writing style either intuitively or with a few suggestions from the teacher. The others, regardless of how skillful or unskillful they became in the use of language, did not learn the rules anyway.

William Shakespeare and Ernest Hemingway, John Keats and Eugene O'Neill did quite well without knowing transformational grammar, and the *Iliad* and the *Odyssey* managed to get themselves written in an age when, as far as we know, there was no grammatical theory of any kind. What this implies for your students and mine is not clear at the moment. What is clear is that the teaching of English is going through a major transition. The butterfly may still be in the cocoon.

The linguists have caused us to take a hard look at the teaching of grammar. While we are doing so it would seem natural to take an equally hard look at linguistics. Research is desperately needed. When the educational researchers use the knowledge gleaned from rat mazes and theory building to conduct extensive classroom experiments in various methods of teaching students to use language, we may begin to see some answers. At the moment, this possibility seems remote. More likely, the teachers will have to do it alone. In either case, finding a realistic solution to the whole question of the teaching of grammar is the great unfinished job before us. This is the challenge for the New English Teacher.

section three

---

alternatives

introduction to section three

One of the great problems in the teaching of English has been the extremely parochial view that language teachers have had regarding their function. A few prescriptions concerning *lie* and *lay*, a Canterbury Tale or two, and a schedule of book reports have too often characterized our anemic offerings. The difficulty with such an approach, in addition to the obvious fragmentation of instruction and lack of concern for anything resembling human values, is that language cannot logically be disassociated from our thinking processes and our emotions.

Traditional grammarians have acted as if everyone who speaks a common language speaks—or should speak—in the same patterns used by his neighbors. Even linguistic textbooks have not entirely avoided falling into this error. But the language of any individual is unique and highly personal. Although over-all patterns are established by imitation of the common mother tongue, these patterns are only generalities, the specifics of which are filled in by the individual.

Thus only in the broadest sense can it be said that you and I—and each of our neighbors—speak the same language. Part of our language heritage is shared in common with millions of other speakers of English, but this common heritage is modified by the sum of all the experiences to which our individual lives have subjected us. Thus our daily utterances reflect both the commonality of our culture and the individuality of ourselves. And in the total pattern of our language expression we reveal our personalities, prejudices, fears, inhibitions, and attitudes. Future events will continue to shape and alter our pronunciation and our style of putting words together. And how fortunate it is that it happens this way, for conversation and literature would be unbearably dull if everyone spoke and wrote in the same style.

201

The study of language, therefore, can proceed from two points of view : the common heritage of our English tongue, and the development of that which is unique to the individual. Unfortunately, the school tradition has concentrated on the former to the almost total exclusion of the latter, and there is little in the new linguistic curricula that changes this. This is true not only of the teaching of language. School programs generally have concerned themselves more with teaching a discipline than with the growth of the student. Yet ultimately the success of a school should be measured not in terms of how much history, mathematics, or grammar we have managed to cram into the heads of our charges but in terms of whether we have produced happy, healthy, functioning human beings.

Having completed our introduction to descriptive linguistics in Section Two, we now take the two-pronged attack on these language problems. First we shall examine language as a common human experience, noting the world's families of languages and their relationships, as well as the story of the development of our own native tongue. Then, through the insights of the general semanticists, we shall look at language as it concerns us individually. In the latter case we shall examine our emotions, our attitudes, and our thinking processes as they affect the way we use and react to words.

Some of the material in the following section is not commonly found even in many of the New English textbooks. At times we may not seem to be discussing language at all, but this is because of the impossibility of disassociating language from the sociological and psychological processes from which it develops. It is, in fact, this very tendency to study language out of its context of human activity that has produced the boring, useless, and irrelevant English curricula so well known to suffering school students and even many of their teachers.

8

the wonderful world of words
the story of language

IN THE BEGINNING

How did it all begin? When and where and by what means did the "miracle of language" take place? How did man start himself on the road to civilization by learning to modify the sounds in a small membrane of the throat? Wherever and however it happened is lost in antiquity, for man's use of language extends far beyond our most ancient records.

But if we do not know, we can speculate. A healthy curiosity and a lively imagination seem to be built into the nature of man. Psammetichus, an ancient king of Egypt, attempted to discover the "original" language of man by raising two children in a speechless environment to see what language they would "naturally" speak.[1] *Genesis* tells us that God created man, presumably with a gift for language, for He brought before Adam all the beasts of the field to be given names. Later He set man against man by giving him not one tongue, but many. So intrinsic to cooperative endeavor is the ability to communicate that when man lost the universal language, according to Genesis, he was unable to complete the Tower of Babel and perished in the flood. Such accounts of language being a Divine gift permeate religious thinking throughout the world. Even later, some interesting assumptions about language have been based

---

[1] Herodotus, Book II, ¶2.

on religious beliefs. It has frequently been assumed that Hebrew is the original language of man, spoken by Adam. Sir Thomas Browne, the seventeenth-century physician and author, believed that a child reared in solitude would speak Hebrew naturally.[2]

In addition to such imaginings, however, modern linguists have also been active. Hockett's "blending" theory—that language may have developed from the combining of two or more complex animal sounds—was discussed in Chapter 3. But other theories have also been advanced.

Human speech is by no means the only form of communication, and was probably not the first. Although such methods as American Indian smoke signals, African tom-toms, and the signal fires of classical mythology do not utilize words in the vocal-auditory sense, the significance of each of these signals was probably prearranged by means of spoken language. On the other hand, such nonspeech communication as the pictorial art found on the walls of the caves of Cro-Magnon man may have developed independently of speech or even preceded it.

Gestural language probably came before speech, and has never been completely replaced by it. The variety of messages that can be sent by means of hand and facial gesture rivals speech in complexity. This method of communicating, at some time in the dim past history of the species, may have been a rival of vocal language. But auditory speech was the victor, probably because it is quick and simple, leaves the hands free for other tasks, and can be used in the dark or even around corners. Today gestural language remains an important phase of communication. Hand gestures are built so inextricably into the speech of some people that there is a story about the two men who were forced to walk silently because it was too cold to take their hands out of their pockets.

In many professions standardized gestures are used as a form of communication. The director of a broadcasting studio cues his actors and technicians by a series of hand signals: index finger across throat meaning *cut* (stop), finger revolving in clock-wise circle for *faster*, palm up for *bring up volume*, and palm down for *bring down volume*. During athletic events umpires signal their decisions to the players and the crowd by hand signals, and in football a flag thrown into the air indicates a penalty. American Indians used pasimology (gesture language) to converse with members of neighboring tribes, for each Indian tribe had a language of its own. Boy scouts do the same, when conversing with scouts from other troops at inter-national jamborees.

---

[2] Helene Laird and Charlton Laird, *The Tree of Language* (Cleveland: World Publishing Company, 1957), p. 27.

Many gestures have taken on symbolic meaning in everyday human interactions. The handshake is a common greeting, as is the salute in military circles. Both of these gestures are reported to have grown out of chivalry, the former from the custom of extending the open hand to show no weapons, the latter from raising the visor so the other man could see whom he was facing. This may also explain why both of these gestures are associated more with men than with women.

Despite the importance of gesture, it is spoken language that dominates human communication, and modern linguists, as well as their predecessors, have speculated about its origin. Although we are not likely to discover how language, in some dim and distant era, developed out of animal cries and signals, we do have a number of theories, advanced by linguists, which have been given interesting, if somewhat playful names.

The "bow-wow" theory maintains that language originated from an attempt to imitate the sounds of nature. A man hears a sound and tries to reproduce it vocally. Such onomatopoetic words as *bang*, *screech*, and *bark* are evidence for this theory, but opposing it we find that the same sound is heard differently by speakers of different languages. Dogs, for example, make the same sound regardless of nationality, but an English speaker hears *bow-wow*, while a Frenchman hears *oua-oua*, and an Italian *bu-bu*. American cats *purr*, but French cats go *ron-ron*.

Mario Pei, in *The Story of Language*, explains a number of other theories:

The "ding-dong" theory sustains that there is a mystic correlation between sound and meaning. Like everything mystical, it is best discarded in a serious scientific discussion.

The "pooh-pooh" theory is to the effect that language at first consisted of ejaculations of surprise, fear, pleasure, pain, etc. It is often paired with the "yo-he-ho" theory to the effect that language arose from grunts of physical exertion, and even with the "sing-song" theory, that language arose from primitive inarticulate chants.

The "ta-ta" theory that language comes from imitation of bodily movements is further exemplified in the Darwinian belief described above.[3]

LINGUISTIC CHANGE

Whatever the origin of language—whether speech developed in one particular locality and spread throughout the world, or came into existence wherever *homo sapiens* roamed the earth—one fact seems to stand out: language, like the sand dunes of the desert, is a constantly changing phenomenon. There are many influences at

[3] Mario Pei, *The Story of Language* (Philadelphia: J. B. Lippincott Company, 1949), p. 19.

work to cause language change as well as a number of processes by which these changes take place. One of these processes is *accretion*, the addition of new forms to the language. Accretion may be the result of a number of influences.

Events of both great and small magnitude occur to require or inspire new words. During World War II, when Vidkun Quisling cooperated so willingly with the Nazi invaders who had taken over his native Norway, he became so despised for his actions that the name *Quisling* became synonymous with collaborator.

New morphological combinations are frequently made by compressing two words into one. *Motor hotel* has become *motel*, and a *hamburger* with *cheese* on it is a *cheeseburger*. Likewise, a *beefburger* or *steerburger* is a hamburger that costs more, while a burger named after the restaurant—Smithburger and Bob'sburger—has enough status to run from two to three times the price of a similar platter with the prosaic name of *hamburger*. Note that in the case of *motel* a single letter, *m*, took the place of the word *motor*, while in the latter words the full morphemes—cheese, beef, and steer—were retained. The former is an example of *blending* (see Chapter 3, page 58), while the latter are *compounds*.

Compounding can frequently lead to new words that have little relation to their original constituent parts. *Blackboard* is an interesting example. Originally just what the name implies, blackboards today are seldom black and never, in my observation, boards. The shift in color has bothered some people, for I have heard them referred to as *chalkboards*, but the fact that they are now made of pressed hardened wallboard painted with special green or tan or almost any color "slating" material does not keep most people from continuing to call them *blackboards*.

This example illustrates the tendency for the referent of a word to undergo a change, either gradually or suddenly, until we find ourselves using the same word for a different object. Many jokes have been made about what has happened to the modern *drug store*, which has changed so radically that we now have to use the phrase *prescription pharmacy*, to describe the thing a drug store used to be. A more dramatic example is the word *butter*, once used only for a dairy product made from milk fat. But despite the development of oleomargarine, my family (and I suspect most families) continues to say, "Please pass the butter." I don't think there is any snobbery involved, just force of habit, and although I have occasionally heard the term *margarine* used as a noun, I have never heard it used as a verb: **Please margarine my bread*, or as an adjective: **I'd like some margarined toast*.

We also create new words by adding distributional morphemes. I remember a school board meeting in which one board member criticized the assistant super-intendent for using the word "finalize" in a report. The board member showed his lack of familiarity with language patterns by claiming that such a word did not exist, and that the tendency on the part of "certain public officials" to use it was "debasing" the English language. Interestingly enough, the board member was instantly placated when it was pointed out that *finalize* is listed in Webster's *Dictionary*.

Borrowing from other languages is a major source of new words, particularly in English, for English is one of the most polyglot of languages, as we shall presently see. The Conlin, Herman, and Martin English series, *Our Language Today*, has an interesting sequence of lessons on the development of English.[4] The seventh grade volume of this series points out examples of words that have come into English from other languages: from the American Indians comes *moose* and *skunk*, as well as the inspiration for compounds such as *paleface* and *firewater*, and the idiom *bury the hatchet*. Every cluster of immigrants coming to this country brought a heritage of language. The Dutch left us *noodle* and *pretzel*, the French *levee* and *depot*, and the Mexicans a large group of words pertaining to ranching: *cinch, pinto, rodeo*, and even the word *ranch* (*rancho*). If the Mexican cowboys brought us words of the ranch and prairie, the Germans gave us foods and eating places, such as *frankfurter, delicatessen, rathskeller*, and the *hamburger*.

In lessons scattered throughout their grammar text are dozens of words that are derived from foreign languages. However, the authors also point out that words come into the language from occupations that need a terminology of their own—terminology that is frequently adopted by the public at large. Politicians, for example, either gave us or inspired *filibuster, lame duck*, and *caucus*; while the forty-niners of California's gold rush left us a legacy of *hoodlum, deadbeat*, and *pull up stakes*.

Slang, of course, is a rich source of new words. Charlton Laird discusses the injection of slang into language:

Human minds, at least human minds that are good for much, like to play. They like to play with all sorts of things, and since words are dear to minds, notably with words. The results of the play sometimes become standard speech, and even lose the color they had. Probably few speakers of English now think of the mouth of a river as spewing water into the sea. Other elaborations never gain currency. Once ranch hands had been called *cowboys*, somebody was likely to call them *cowpunchers*; once there were *cowpunchers* there were sure to be *cowpokes, cowprods*, cow-anything else that offered a likely synonym. Cowpunching became *cow-walloping*. Soon there were *Pennsylvania cowboys, drugstore cowboys*, the latter becoming *lounge lizards* in the evening. And so it goes. "Three cocktails and a chaw of terbacker" becomes a *Kentucky breakfast* and a dust storm becomes a *Mormon rain*. That is, leaps in semantics take place because people like to play with language, to make similes and concoct epithets, to have fun with the innocent game of juggling words.[5]

---

[4] Conlin, Herman, and Martin, *Our Language Today* (New York: American Book Co., 1966).
[5] Charlton Laird, *The Miracle of Language* (Cleveland: World Publishing Company, 1953), p. 68.

Much of our slang disappears as quickly as it arrives. Henry Gleason views slang as an attempt by some "in-group" to achieve a language of its own.[6] Teen-agers, professional groups, residents of a geographic area, hippies—many such cliques develop a jargon that distinguishes them from the rest of the world and keeps the "out" groups out. But the members eventually tire of any word or phrase that does not fill a semantic need—that merely duplicates existing forms. Thus most of these unusual expressions pass into oblivion.

But some slang is retained, mainly because it does fill a need. It says something that cannot be said as quickly, as precisely, or as colorfully any other way. Then the out-groups adopt it, and it begins its perilous journey into the formal language. *Fetch* and *ain't* are fighting their way into English despite tremendous opposition from purists, the former because *go get and bring back* requires too many words, the latter because we have no other contraction for *am not*. And once you can say *I ain't* (am not), it is natural to move on to *he ain't, she ain't* (is not), *we ain't, they ain't* (are not). Much of today's slang will be tomorrow's formal language, and there is little we teachers can do about it.

New social conditions, as well as new inventions, can bring in a rich new vocabulary. An interesting example of this is the concern of many of our contemporaries for the need of the individual to find happiness through some form of "self-fulfillment." As long as man had to spend practically all of his time and energy merely growing enough food to stay alive, there was little real opportunity to think about happiness. Happiness was a full belly and freedom from financial woes. But once the machine age freed man from the need to be continually grubbing in the soil, he was able to look for a more satisfying life. As a result, many new forms crept into the vocabulary, words and phrases describing emotional states, attitudes, and activities related to the pursuit of happiness.

Most of these forms are still in the realm of slang and are frequently viewed with the same contempt that characterized *ain't* and *fetch* a few years ago (and still does in some traditional circles). But I remember my first impression of the word *uptight*. No formal definition is needed to see what a beautiful description this is of the inflexibility, the formality, the prudery, and the tension that characterize much of our society! And expressions such as *turned on* and *turned off* describe with such eloquence two common states of the human psyche that I would need a paragraph to substitute for them. Whether such forms, along with *head trip, wiped out,* and *blow your mind,* will become part of the formal vocabulary is still uncertain, but the meaning of each is so well-adapted to a need, it is not surprising that their use is so widespread.

[6] Henry Allan Gleason, Jr., *Linguistics and English Grammar* (New York: Holt, Rinehart and Winston, Inc., 1965), p. 359.

In modern English, *echoism*, or *onomatopoeia*, and *reduplication*, discussed in Chapter 5, page 115, are comparatively minor influences, but may at one time have been more common. The former is the imitation of a sound by a word, accounting for the *rustling* of leaves, the *crinkling* of paper, and the *crack* of a splitting board. Reduplication gave us such words as *tut-tut* and *goody-goody*, with minor variations adding *razzle-dazzle* and *uh-huh*. Both onomatopoeia and reduplication can be seen in the word *tom-tom*.

Obsolescence can cause a language to lose as well as gain new words, as any school student struggling with Shakespeare can testify. Before *Macbeth* is over ten lines old the student has encountered *hurly-burly*, *Graymalkin*, *Paddock*, and *anon*. This is not unique, for the same amount of reading in *Romeo and Juliet* produces *carry coals*, *colliers*, *choler*, and *take the wall*. These forms have certainly not died out of the language completely but have become uncommon or archaic expressions. Only *collier* and *anon* are listed on the Thorndike-Lorge *Word List* as occurring once or more in a million words, whereas *hurly-burly* and *choler* are in the once in a million to once in four million group.[7] Today these words probably occur less frequently than even Thorndike and Lorge indicate, for their word lists were made from literature that goes back as far as the Bible, although the bulk of the material is modern. *Paddock* (with a capital letter) and *Graymalkin* are not on the list. English teachers, with their extensive reading experience, have become so accustomed to words and phrases such as these that they frequently fail to realize how much difficulty their students are having. There seems to be much less known, or at least much less written, about why some forms are dropped from the language than about how new words are brought in.

But a language does more than simply add or drop individual forms. Language undergoes many types of change, and these changes frequently occur with some degree of regularity. Careful study of linguistic change has led scholars to induce certain principles that occur with varying degrees of consistency.

Gleason distinguished between *phonetic change* and *analogic change*. The former is a regular change that takes place in a language, affecting a great number of words with similar patterns.[8] For example, when English dropped the pronunciation of the *ed* endings of the past and past participle as separate syllables, this change occurred in a great number of English verbs and adjectives. Shakespeare refers to "*their drenchéd natures*," giving two syllables to our one for *drenched*. This is a general

[7] Edward L. Thorndike and Irving Lorge, *The Teacher's Word Book of 30,000 Words* (New York: Bureau of Publications, Teachers College, Columbia University, 1944).

[8] Henry Allan Gleason, Jr., *An Introduction to Descriptive Linguistics*, Rev. Ed. (New York: Holt, Rinehart and Winston, Inc., 1961), p. 394.

phonetic change that has taken place in many English verbs. Analogic change, on the other hand, might occur in a single word without affecting any other word. It frequently tends to make the language more regular, if for example we were to change the plural of *ox* to **oxes*, but it can also produce irregularity, as would happen if for some unknown reason a trend should develop to change the plural of *box* to **boxen*. (*Es* and *s* are common, regular English plurals. *En* is an uncommon, irregular form.)

Generalization is a trend from the specific to the general whereas *specialization* is the tendency of words of general usage to be given specialized meaning. Laird gives the example of the word *tap*, which began as the peg pulled from a barrel to take a nip of liquor, and then developed into any kind of device used to draw something out. Instead of only pulling the *tap* out of a barrel, now we can draw water from the kitchen *tap*. Then the verb *tap* developed from the light blow that was generally struck the *tap* to loosen it or drive it in. Now *tap* means to draw out of, or drive into; hence *wiretap* came to mean getting information by means of an electronic listening device. When threads were substituted for the mallet in the modern faucet, the word *tap* had already become associated with the device, and because the inside of a faucet is threaded, a tool to make inside threads became a *tap*. Thus the etymology of *tap* illustrates how a specialized word can be generalized until it has a multitude of meanings, then specialized once more into something as particular as a tool for cutting threads inside a pipe.[9]

Deletion of a sound or morpheme is frequently responsible for changes. *Telephone*, for example, is becoming *phone*, *gasoline* is now *gas*, and *oleomargarine* is sometimes *oleo*, but more frequently *margarine* (unless it is *butter*).

Conditioning, the influence one sound has on adjacent sounds, was discussed in Chapter 4. Over a period of time certain sounds in the language will cause adjacent sounds to change. For example, a plosive voiced consonant followed by a voiced phoneme tends to become fricative, as the voicing is continued into the next phoneme. Thus the Anglo-Saxon /fǽdr/ became modern English /fáθr/ (*father*).

A change in stress, frequently the result of a change in the morphemic structure of the word, will usually result in a change in the phonemic structure as well. Thus *labor* /lejbər/ becomes *laborious* /ləbóʼwrijəs/ (ej → ə; bər → bówr). This principle is valid for historical as well as morphological changes. As words drop inflections and shift their accents accordingly, changes in pronunciation occur. Thus when the Middle English word for *April* dropped its third syllable and the stress fell on the first, that first syllable changed from /ə/ in /əprɪ́jlə/ to /ej/ in /éjprəl/ (April). A similar

---

[9] Charlton Laird, *The Miracle of Language* (Cleveland: World Publishing Company, 1953).

change, in reverse, took place in the second syllable when it changed from stressed to unstressed (/ɪ́j → ə/). Note that when English vowels lose their stress, they tend to go toward the center schwa, or /ə/ sound.

Sometimes languages undergo a major change in the entire phonemic structure for no reason that we have been able to discern. Thus it is with the "great vowel shift" that took place in the English language several centuries ago. This shift involved the forward and upward movement of the English vowel system, so that the word pronounced /šej/ is now /šij/ (*she*), and /rijd/ became /rajd/ (*ride*).[10] Why this shift occurred to the English language at that particular time is one of the great mysteries of historical linguistics.

Finally, as the languages that belong in the same group with English grow and change and evolve new languages over the centuries, there seems to be a general trend for agglutinative languages—those that put together long strings of morphemes into single words—to gradually organize these agglutinizations into a system of inflections, or word endings, and eventually to drop these inflections in favor of a more distributive language, one in which word order, not inflection, accounts for meaning. Old English, for instance, contained a complex inflectional system, but Modern English is a good example of a language that has evolved a more distributive grammar.

Does this general trend from these agglutinations to inflection to distribution indicate that there is such a thing as an "advanced" language, after all? Perhaps. But grammarians of the past took another view, maintaining that English was *inferior* to Latin because it lacked inflection. To argue whether this trend represents "advance" or "deterioration" is futile. As we have already noted, there is no evidence that any language is superior to any other in terms of filling the need of its constituents to communicate.

Taboo words are another interesting source of language change, enlarging our vocabulary through the invention of euphemisms to substitute for unacceptable forms. In traditional orthodox Judaism, the Hebrew word for *God* cannot be spoken or written by laymen, hence substitute words have been introduced, as well as abbreviations for writing. Religious taboo words and phrases are found throughout the world, this example having something in common with our own feelings against "taking the Lord's name in vain."

But restrictions against particular words come and go, as do other phenomena about language. Some English words that were once a bit shocking are now quite

---

[10] A number of linguistics texts contain a more detailed explanation of English sound changes. A very readable account can be found in Chapter 9 of Charlton Laird's *The Miracle of Language*, to which this section is indebted.

common. Nice Victorian ladies never used a word such as *leg*, or *breast*, even for chicken, but substituted *limb* for people, or *light meat* and *dark meat* at the table. *Jazz* used to be a vulgar word for *sexual intercourse*, but is now perfectly proper, having taken on a new meaning.

Frequently the nature of language restrictions tells something about the society. Probably no subjects have as many taboos in our culture as sex and bathrooms, with the result that we have an extensive vocabulary of synonyms for both, ranging from euphemistic attempts to be delicate to words of the "four letter" variety. In recent years, however, there seems to be a tendency toward *amelioration* of many words, that is a raising of their status from improper to acceptable. Although many people are still shocked by some of the language that is flowing from the mouths and pens of many of our "modern" philosophers, the use of words formerly taboo in polite society is spreading, and we may soon lose many of our restrictions. At present we are in that awkward "in-between" stage, in which nobody really knows what is acceptable in many situations and what is not.

A typical example of this confusion was reported to me by one of my student teachers. He was talking after class to two of his high school students—a boy and a girl—when the boy used a "four letter word" in the conversation. The student teacher, who considered himself one of the "turned-on generation," was not the least bit shocked, but he was sure the high school girl would be disturbed. As he was making a mental note to explain later to the boy about the use of indelicate language in front of girls, the girl said, "You shouldn't use words like that in front of a teacher."

VARIETIES OF LANGUAGE

Not only do languages evolve new forms and, over a period of time, new languages, but individual speakers of a language exhibit a great deal of variation in style. A number of factors determine how any individual will use his language at any given time. These factors are rooted in the individual himself, the person with whom he is communicating, and the situation.

The Speaker

Geography is one of the major influences on a person's speech. Groups of people living partially isolated from other speakers of the same language develop localisms that eventually become dialects. Social class, educational level, occupation, age, sex, and personality all come into play. Professional people have a dialect quite different from laborers. Some speech that is perfectly acceptable for men would be shocking if used by ladies or by men with ladies present. Although this language taboo has slowly been breaking down since the days of Victorian propriety, the women's dialect still cannot be used by men without serious repercussions. George S. Kauffman has built a hilariously funny one-act play, *If Men Played Cards As Women Do* on nothing more than the comic effect of men speaking the women's dialect.

The speech of a six-year-old would hardly resemble that of a teen-ager, while every older generation, hearing the current vogue in teen-age slang, wonders what has happened to "the King's English." But each generation of teen-agers matures into the solid citizens they are destined to become, and permanent changes in the language take place so slowly most people believe they do not happen at all. The way we use language can also reveal much about our prejudices, our attitudes, and our personality:

"Good morning," says Bill to the pretty receptionist as he arrives at work.

"Hiya, Sugar," blurts out Harry a minute later. Nothing has changed but the personality of the speaker.

The Audience

"Daddy be home later," said our office worker twenty minutes before greeting the receptionist. Then he kissed his wife and added, "Keep the home fires burning, Doll." Imagine reversing these remarks. Thus our speech is influenced by the person to whom we are speaking. Bill, stiff and formal with the pretty receptionist, greets his sixty-three year old private secretary with "Hiya, Sugar," while Harry, his mind still on the outer office, dismisses the whole thing with "Good morning."

Formal recognition of the rank of the person spoken to plays an important part in many languages. The Middle English second person forms *thou* and *ye* (nominative case) and *thee* and *you* (objective case) have all but disappeared, except for *you*. The others are used only in religious ceremony. We have thus developed a special second person for speaking to God, just as the Siamese have developed a special language for speaking to their king. Latin languages preserve more than one form of the second person (Spanish singular *tu* and *usted*, for example) for differentiating between people with whom one has a personal and a formal relationship.

Not only is the position of the hearer considered but, more important, the *relationship* that exists between the two. Sergeant Harris would not dare speak to a commissioned officer without adding "Sir," except with Captain Thompson, who was Harris's roommate in college.

The Situation

The third factor is the situation. Even with Thompson, Harris is as full of "Sirs" as he is with any other officer—in public. Only in the intimacy of a one-to-one relationship does their language change. Most of us automatically change our language as we move from intimate to formal situations. "Got a light?" in the inner office becomes "May I trouble you for a match?" once the board meeting begins. Gleason distinguishes five degrees of formality versus intimacy in human speech:[11]

At one end of the scale is *oratorical* speech, which is formal and elaborate, with carefully planned sentence structure and vocabulary. Attention is paid to old-fashioned prescriptions concerning "correct" grammar. It is generally used in formal oratorical situations—a clergyman addressing his congregation, a lawyer to a jury, or an orator to a large audience. To use this type of speech well requires considerable skill. Schools frequently concern themselves largely with oratorical speech to the neglect of other types, possibly on the theory that anyone who can handle this difficult medium can handle any speech situation. I am not convinced this is true, or even that a student is capable of such style until he has achieved considerable ease and fluency in the less formal aspects of speech. As a matter of fact, we may well be promoting stiffness and artificiality by stressing formal style too much and too soon.

Also in the formal key is *deliberative* speech, used with smaller but important and somewhat formal audiences. A teacher might use it with a class or a salesman with a prospect. Both situations, however, indicate that the relationship is not easy and casual. In the situations described, speech might begin on a deliberative level, then, as individuals begin to feel at ease with each other, move down the ladder to *consultative*.

Consultative speech is the most common. It is the usual medium for conversation and is generally spontaneous, with only slight attention paid to formal syntax. Speakers feel at ease with each other when using consultative speech.

An even more informal speech mode is the *casual*. This is reserved for speakers who have previously established a relationship of ease and trust. Casual speech is characterized by the use of slang and a sentence pattern that frequently includes fragments instead of the usual NP + VP construction. Function words are frequently omitted:

> *Got a match?*
> *Here. Had lots of fun yesterday.*
> *Where?*
> *Downtown.*

---

[11] Gleason, *Linguistics and English Grammar*, p. 358.

Gleason says little about *intimate* language other than that it "is a completely private language developed within families or between very close friends. Since it is not used in public, it is of little concern to the schools."

THE FAMILY OF HUMAN LANGUAGES

Because language changes, and because these changes frequently take place according to regular patterns over long periods of time, it is possible, by examining literature and other written documents of previous ages, to trace a language back and see how it was spoken centuries ago. If a language is traced back to a distant enough era, the changes observed are usually so profound that it is not the same language at all, but a "proto-language," or ancestor of the modern tongue.

By studying the proto-language closely, one may discover that at some time in history a group of people who spoke that language separated from the main body and settled in another area. The changes that took place in their speech were not the same as those of the parent group, and after sufficient centuries had passed, the two groups developed what would seem to the untrained observer to be two completely unrelated languages. These languages, in turn, branch off and are influenced by other languages, developing independently until an extended family of languages is formed, consisting of parents and siblings, plus a considerable number of grandparents and first, second, and third cousins.

The Indo-European

By tracing English back through its impressive bevy of sisters and cousins and aunts, linguists have concluded that our language, along with most of the major languages of Europe, northern India, the Americas, and a number of other areas throughout the world, are all related to a single, ancient proto-language about which we have no records. We feel confident, however, it was spoken by people of a prehistoric age who left us no artifacts as evidence of their presence. We call these people the Indo-Europeans, and believe our English tongue belongs to the Indo-European family of languages.

Who were these mysterious Indo-Europeans who vanished with almost no record of having been there except for a language inheritance that has spread to almost half the people of the world? We have no written accounts of their presence, not even of the language for which they are famous, but we are sure they were there, and we even think we know quite a bit about them. We believe they lived in central Europe.

How long they were there, whether they entered the area a few thousand years ago or tens of thousands of years ago, we are not sure. But we know they broke up as a unified culture before written records of the area were made—otherwise we would have more information about them. But how do we know they were there at all? Charlton Laird, in *The Tree of Language*, tells us:

The explanation which follows of how the scholars found out about the beginnings of English will be simpler than the process really was, but will give you some idea of it. The first thing the scholars did was to compare all the languages of Europe and Asia. Some of the Asiatic languages, like Chinese, were not at all like European languages. But some were—for instance, the modern languages of India which came from Sanskrit. Most of the languages of Europe seemed to be quite a bit alike, too. By comparing the same words in many different languages the scholars could be quite sure of this likeness. The words *mother* and *night*, for example, are similar in modern languages, as you see from this list.

ENGLISH	*night*	*mother*
GERMAN	*Nacht*	*Mutter*
SPANISH	*noche*	*madre*
PORTUGUESE	*noite*	*mae*
ITALIAN	*notte*	*madre*
FRENCH	*nuit*	*mère*
RUSSIAN	*nochy*	*maty*
SWEDISH	*natt*	*moder*
DANISH	*nat*	*moder*

But they are also similar in languages no longer spoken, the ancestors of modern languages.

MIDDLE ENGLISH	*nyht*	*moder*
OLD ENGLISH	*niht*	*modor*
OLD SAXON	*naht*	*modar*
OLD IRISH	*nocht*	*mathir*
LATIN	*nox*	*mater*
GREEK	*nyx*	*meter*
OLD SLAVIC	*noshti*	*mati*
SANSKRIT	*nakta*	*matar*

The dead languages in the list above were spoken in places as far apart as India and Ireland, but the words for *mother* and *night* are similar in all of them. As far back as the scholars could go, they found that these and many, many other words were similar. They finally worked back so far that there was no longer any writing in existence for the languages, back so far that no one knew anything about them. And then they started to deduce.[12]

---

[12] Laird, *The Tree of Language*, p. 28.

What these deductions were would seem fairly obvious. It must be more than coincidence that these and many other words bore such close resemblances. By comparing the word stock of modern with ancient languages, the evolution of many words could be traced. Eventually, as Laird tells us, linguists went so far back that there were no more written records and research could go no earlier. But having traced many languages back to the prehistoric, it seemed obvious that, considering the similarities, all of these languages must have come from a common ancestor. And because the children of that ancient tongue dominated the speech of Europe and northern India, linguists dubbed it *Indo-European.*

Of all the great families of languages, none has surpassed Indo-European in terms of the current number of speakers, the widespread distribution, or the power and influence in world affairs of its users. Who these Indo-Europeans were, when and where they lived, and what their culture was like can only be surmised from records of progeny languages. It was by examining their vocabularies that we came to believe they lived in a temperate climate, for they had words for *snow, winter, oak, pine, wolf,* and *bear*; but not for *camel, elephant, palm,* or *tiger.*[13] Their early culture was probably Stone Age, although they are believed to have been animal-raising nomads who moved about with their flocks, spreading their language.

The earliest surviving offshoot of the parent language was probably *Sanskrit,* which was brought to northern India by a group that broke away sometime about 2000 B.C. Other major offshoots were *Greek,* about 800 B.C. and *Italic,* about three centuries later. More Indo-European groups migrated to various parts of what is now European Russia, along the Danube River, south to the Mediterranean Sea, to the West Coast of Europe, including the islands of Great Britain.

Thus the Indo-European language family broke up into many branches and sub-branches. Today some of these comprise a comparatively small number of speakers, such as the *Baltic* branch, consisting mainly of *Lithuanian* and *Latvian*; *Albanian,* with no known closely related languages; and *Armenian,* also somewhat isolated in relationship. Although the ancient Greeks had a tremendous impact on Western culture, their spoken language remains today only in the form of *Modern Greek,* with a limited number of speakers.

But there are also a number of widespread and politically important branches of Indo-European. One of these, *Indic,* includes *Sanskrit,* no longer a spoken tongue but still used for literary and liturgical purposes. *Hindi* is the national language of India, as *Urdu* is of Pakistan. Hindi and Urdu are closely related and mutually understandable. Many other languages and dialects of this part of southern Asia belong to the Indic branch of Indo-European.

---

[13] Laird, *The Tree of Language,* p. 30.

The *Iranian* branch consists of *Kurdish*, spoken in eastern Turkey, Iraq, and part of Iran; *Persian*, spoken in Iran and as a second language in India and Pakistan; *Pashto and Afghan*, in Afghanistan and parts of Pakistan; and *Balochi* in Pakistan.

The *Slavic* branch contains *Russian*, whose use has become general throughout the Soviet Union, either as the only language or as a second language in those areas where other tongues are native. Also within the Baltic group are *Byelorussian* and *Ukrainian*, spoken largely within the Soviet Union; and *Czech*, *Slovak*, and *Polish*, frequently classified as dialects of a single language. *Serbo-Croatian*, with two written languages, is also among the major tongues of this group.

The *Romance* languages are the descendants of the Italic branch and include classical Latin of literary fame; Latin vulgate, or spoken Latin, which grew out of it, and the modern Romance languages. These are *Portuguese*, spoken in Portugal, Brazil, and areas formerly in the Portuguese Empire; *French*, spoken in parts of Canada, Switzerland, Belgium, and the Congo, as well as France; *Spanish*, with dialects spoken throughout Latin America (except Brazil) in addition to Spain; *Italian* and *Roumanian*, from their respective countries; and *Romansch*, one of the languages of Switzerland.

The *Celtic* languages consist of *Breton*, which is spoken in northwestern France but is disappearing in favor of French, and the three non-English languages of the British Isles: *Welsh*, *Irish*, and *Gaelic*, spoken in Wales, Ireland, and Scotland, respectively.

The *Germanic* languages are composed of *Icelandic*, *Swedish*, *Danish*, and two written systems of Norway, *Bokmal*, and *Nynorsk*. The Dutch-German branch contains *German*, *Dutch*, and *Flemish*. *Yiddish* is a language that the Jewish people developed in the course of their meanderings throughout Europe. It consists largely of German but is written in Hebrew letters. *Afrikaans* is spoken in Dutch-settled South Africa, and is a direct outgrowth of Dutch. The *English-Frisian* branch consists of *Frisian*, which is spoken by a small population around the North Sea, and *English*, spoken by more people throughout the Western world, and having more influence on the political and economic affairs of man than any other language.

Other Language Groups

Little by little, as linguists compared the word stocks of the world's many languages, classifying them into groups in much the same way that botanists and zoologists organize living things into classes and phyla, it seemed clear that the bulk of human speech could be traced back to five major proto-languages, including Indo-European. But the job of classification is by no means complete. There are still hundreds of languages throughout the world that have never been related to any major group. Perhaps they never will. Much research remains to be done before anything like a complete classification of the world's languages can be achieved.

It is difficult for us in America to visualize the complexity of human language distribution. In this country our population has exceeded two hundred million, with English as a national language. And that language is spoken by the bulk of the population of our nearest neighbor in the north, Canada, by our closest cultural ally, Great Britain, and by large segments of people as far away as Australia. And dialects are so slight, compared with those of many other languages, that although we may rib each other a bit about our speech, we can all sit down together and brag about our clever children or wonder if the threatened rain will spoil our picnic. Even in much of the non-English part of the world—at least in the more touristy spots—we can usually find someone who can direct us in English to a nearby restaurant.

But this situation is unusual. In Canada, French is more common than English in parts of Quebec. In the remote quarters of the British Isles one can still hear Welsh, Irish, and a remnant of Gaelic. Switzerland has four officially recognized national languages—German, French, Italian, and Romansch, with about 70 per cent of the people speaking German.

In India the national language is Hindi, but dozens of other tongues are also spoken, along with a host of minor languages and dialects. And even in the United States, millions of Americans speak German, Italian, Spanish, Yiddish, Polish and many other languages, with English being used either as a second language or not spoken at all.

On the North and South American continents over a thousand languages have been found among the Indians. Many of these have died or are dying as actively spoken tongues, as Indian culture becomes absorbed into the industrial twentieth century. In Africa, over five hundred languages are spoken by the native Black population. While the inhabitants of the northern part of the continent speak a descendant of one of the great proto-languages, the rest of Africa includes such diverse language groups as the *Sudanese*, the *West Atlantic*, the *Mande*, the *Kwa*, the *Gur*, and the many *Bantu* tongues, including *Swahili*, to name only a few.

The Pacific Islands comprise another area that contains many diverse languages that cannot be related to any of the major groups. In addition, there are many languages scattered throughout the world, spoken by a limited number of people in an area where the origin and relationship to neighboring tongues have not been established. An example is *Basque* of the French-Spanish border region. *Ainu*, spoken by a few thousand people of one of the Japanese islands, and *Etruscan*, of central Italy, are also in this group, along with the indigenous languages of Australia and New Guinea. Somewhat larger families include *Japanese*, *Korean*, the many languages of the Caucasus, and the *Dravidian* group of southern India.

Of the great language families of the world, we find five major groups, including Indo-European. The *Altaic* group contains three major branches: the *Turkic*, including Turkish; the *Mongol*, comprising several closely related Mongolian tongues; and the *Tungus-Manchu* group of east Asia.

The *Finno-Ugric* family contains such languages as *Finnish*, *Hungarian*, and *Estonian*, as well as *Lapp*, *Votyak*, *Cheremiss*, and *Mordvinian* of northern Europe, and the *Samoyed* languages of Asiatic Soviet Union. The Finno-Ugric and Altaic families have been found to be related, however, and are sometimes classified as a single major group, the *Ural-Altaic*.

The dominant family of oriental languages is the *Sino-Tibetan*, consisting of two main divisions. One branch is spoken in Tibet, Burma, and other parts of southern Asia. The other branch is *Chinese*. *Mandarin Chinese* is spoken in the northern half, and a number of other languages are spoken in the South, including *Cantonese*. All of these Chinese languages are related, but inhabitants of one area of China are unable to speak with many of those of another. *Mandarin*, however, is gaining popularity and is replacing some of the southern languages. The Sino-Tibetan group is second only to Indo-European in the number of speakers throughout the world.

Of tremendous influence in the history of Western civilization are the people who speak the *Semitic-Hamitic* tongues. The Hamitic group contains a number of distantly related languages, mainly in Africa, including the *Kushitic*, *Berber*, *Egyptian*, and *Chad* groups. The Semitic languages, however, are more famous, mainly because the *Arabic* group contains a great many speakers throughout northern Africa and the Middle East and because *Hebrew* is the main language of the *Old Testament*, although parts of it were written in *Aramaic*. The Arabic languages are frequently classified as dialects because of the cultural ties of the people, although they are as diverse as many separate languages. Hebrew was the language of the Biblical Jews, but was largely supplanted as a vernacular by Aramaic. It was preserved as a literary and liturgical language, however, as was Latin in Europe and Sanskrit in India, and has been revived in modern form as the spoken language of Israel. Semitic languages were also spoken by a number of important peoples during the early development of Western culture. *Phoenician* was an important language of commerce and the source of our modern English alphabet.

This has been a brief summary of the several thousand languages spoken by the human race. The great Indo-European family, consisting of the Indic, the Germanic, the Celtic, the Iranian, the Slavic, the Romance, and dozens of minor branches—minor only in terms of numbers of people speaking them—is the most widespread and influential of all the language groups. It includes English, Russian, Hindi, Spanish, and German, each of which has over a hundred million native speakers. The Semitic-Hamitic family is famous for its contribution to Western civilization, giving us ancient Egyptian, the Phoenician alphabet upon which our own is based, and Hebrew, the language of the Old Testament. The Sino-Tibetan group includes the languages (or dialects, depending upon how they are classified) of China, and dominates Oriental civilization almost as completely as Indo-European does our own. Mandarin Chinese, with over half a billion speakers, is by far the most popular of the world's languages. Finally, the Ural-Altaic completes the list of major language families, along with a host of others whose lineage and family ties are either lacking or are less thoroughly understood.

THE BIOGRAPHY OF ENGLISH

Now let us go back to the prehistoric time when our Indo-European ancestors wandered about central Europe, grazing their flocks and unwittingly spreading their language to the far corners of the earth. We shall confine our historical study to English partly because it is our native tongue and of greatest interest to us, and also because it is part of the Indo-European family that has been studied so extensively. From the early speculations of Sir William Jones on the similarities of Sanskrit and English, linguists have been tracing, analyzing, and studying the Indo-European heritage, and English has been given the greatest amount of attention. The result is that we have a surprisingly good account of what our language is and how it got that way, despite the fact that English is extremely mixed-up and complex in terms of established family ties.

The British Isles, where English developed, was the scene of much economic and military aggression, and the language word stock shows its indebtedness to almost every foreign people with whom the islanders came in contact. This may not have helped the spelling situation, but it has made English a language of tremendous color and versatility, not to mention its enormous vocabulary.

The earliest known Indo-European settlers on the British Isles were the Celts, who crossed over from the continent, bringing with them all their possessions, including their language. There were already settlers in the area, but we do not know what tongue they spoke. By the time the Celts reached Britain, they were in a somewhat advanced state of civilization, having developed the wheel and some metal tools. They probably had to fight and conquer the territory from the more primitive people who lived there.

But in 55 B.C., the Celts were in turn invaded. A still more advanced civilization crossed over from the continent and set about subjugating the residents. These newcomers did not come to colonize but to conquer and bring home booty. Under the generalship of Julius Caesar and his successors, the Celts and other British tribes were eventually subdued by the armies of Rome.

The Roman legionnaires also spoke an Indo-European language, Latin. The effects of the Roman occupation can still be seen on the British Isles in the form of great engineering projects. We can still see their roads, baths, and aqueducts—but the Latin conquerors from the mainland left almost no trace of their language.

Oddly enough, the same is true of the Celts, because once the Roman legions left Britain, other tribes came along. From the north came the Scots and Picts, and from the mainland came another wave of invaders in search of a place to live. These were the Angles, the Saxons, and the Jutes, all of whom spoke a different version of the Old German branch of Indo-European. The Celts were either driven from the choice farmland into the hills or made slaves. Those who escaped fled to the extremities of the island—to Scotland, Wales, or Ireland. The new invaders did not mix with the Celts but drove them out of the territory they conquered. They did not learn their language. The situation is similar to that in America, where the European settlers did not learn the language of the Indians, did not absorb much of their culture, and took only a handful of words from their language. For example, the Celtic *usquebaugh* (water of life) became *whiskey*, and some Celtic place names survive, just as the Indian idiom *fire water* became English slang, and Indian place names such as *Dakota* and *Minnesota* came into English. Thus, with few exceptions, Celtic disappeared from the mainstream of British life, but its descendants can still be heard in the Gaelic languages of Wales, Ireland, and Scotland.

Soon afterward, another invasion, this time the Vikings from Scandinavia, again challenged the people of Britain. The Vikings were a fierce and warlike people, and their destruction, robbery, and rape cast a pall of fear across much of Europe. But at last, after much bloodshed, the Vikings were stopped in Britain by an army led by King Alfred, and a treaty was made, giving the newcomers, called Danes, possession of the northeastern part of the Island, the southwest remaining Saxon. The Danes also spoke a Germanic language, and it was not difficult to blend their words with those of the other dialects to obtain something we call *Anglo-Saxon*, or *Old English*. But dialectal differences among the tribes were great, and when we speak of the Anglo-Saxon language we are really referring to a collection of dialects. In fact, the original boundary between the Danish and Saxon preserves, established by treaty around 886, is still a major dialect boundary in England.

The earliest Old English manuscript in existence is a poem called *Far Traveller*, which was copied, in all probability, by a monk around the year 1000 from a poem believed to have been written around 675. The famous epic poem *Beowulf* also comes from this early Anglo-Saxon period. Since that time the English language has changed so much that you and I cannot read these manuscripts without learning Old English as a foreign language. However, on a group of islands in the North Sea are people who speak a language called *Frisian*. Living in this remote, isolated area, these people have continued to speak the language of their ancestors, and today a modern Frisian could probably read *Beowulf*, although he could not read modern English without foreign language study.

If, at the end of the first millennium A.D., the people of the British Isles thought that the ownership and domination of their land was settled forever, they were about to be disappointed. In 1066 an army of invaders from northern France crossed the channel and at the famous battle of Hastings the residents were once again challenged in battle. These invaders were the Norman-French, descendants of other Vikings, who had settled in what is now Normandy, where they developed a civilization more sophisticated than that of their British neighbors. With their superior technology and military tactics, the Normans, led by William The Conquerer, defeated the Saxons and established a new set of masters on the island.

To this land the Normans brought French culture, including a French court, French literature, and their own special version of the French language. Latin became the language of the church and the school, and Norman-French became the language of the court, commerce and industry, literature and the arts, as well as the spoken language of society. Anglo-Saxon remained only as the spoken tongue of the common people, and because very few of them were educated, it virtually disappeared as a written language.

The British Isles developed into a three-language society, with Old English spoken by the peasants, Norman-French written and spoken for business and polite society, and Latin for religion and learning. Norman-French is based partly on the Scandinavian languages and partly on Latin. Because Latin has contributed so many words to the English language, it is frequently believed that it was during this period of Norman domination that much Latin crept into the language. I have taught high school English from textbooks that discussed the coming of Latin into English via Norman-French. Actually, the evidence does not support this. Because of Norman contempt for their lowly Saxon subjects, and because of Saxon pride and fierce determination to drive the invaders out some day, neither learned the language of the other, and neither language had a significant influence upon the other. Again the similarity between the European settlers and the American Indians is appropriate, except that in Britain there was considerable interaction between groups, the Saxon peasants tilling the fields of their Norman masters.

It is significant to note what happened to the three languages. To this day Latin remains the language of church and school, although to a lesser extent than formerly. Much of the Roman Catholic liturgy is spoken in Latin, and until recently knowledge of Latin was considered an indispensable part of the education of a gentleman. This is still true in many of the traditional private schools, but its use in public schools is declining rapidly. Nevertheless, Latin is still used for many scientific names, particularly in medicine, pharmacy, and biology.

Despite the complete domination of Norman-French as a written language and as a spoken language of polite society, when the Normans and Saxons eventually began to merge their cultures and mix socially, that language disappeared almost completely from the scene. Anglo-Saxon, the spoken language of the people, emerged instead as the national language of the British Isles. This story of the disappearance of French tells us again that the real language of a people is that which is spoken, not written; that of the masses, not the classes.

By this time the Anglo-Saxon dialects—the Old English of *Far Traveller* and *Beowulf*—had changed very radically. By the middle of the eleventh century a new language had emerged resembling the dialect we speak today. The years from the eleventh to the fourteenth century are generally known as the *Middle English* period. This is the language a modern speaker of English can read—but with considerable difficulty. It found its greatest fruition in the fourteenth century in the works of Geoffrey Chaucer. There were, of course, no sharp transitions from Old to Middle to Modern English, just a gradual evolution. But the 1066 battle of Hastings, more because of its historical significance than its immediate effect on the language, is frequently taken as the cut-off point between old and middle dialects, just as the publication of Shakespeare's work and the King James Bible usher in the era of Modern English.

It is interesting to note that during the Middle English period, the city of London emerged as the center of British commerce and industry. Thus the dialect popular in that area became the prestige language that ambitious English speakers everywhere sought to emulate. To this day the English of the south of London is frequently taken as "standard" English, and dialects derived from it are taught in the public schools as far away as America. And the only discernible reason seems to be that it is the dialect of prestigious people in the British capital.

But the Norman invasion did, in the long run, have a profound effect on the English language. Through the cultural advance of Norman life, England began to build economic and political ties to the mainland of Europe. Trade was established, and with it came European science, art, literature, and other influences. It was largely in the thirteenth and fourteenth centuries that English began to borrow heavily from the French, and once it started to borrow, like many a poor neighbor, it did not stop.

Borrowing language, however, unlike borrowing a cup of sugar or a lawn mower, enriches the borrower without taking anything from the lender, and rather than straining neighborly relations, may even improve them. Thus it has been with English. The early periods of the language were periods of great change. From *Beowulf* to

Canterbury Tales to *Taming of the Shrew*, English changed so radically it is difficult to consider Shakespeare, Chaucer, and whoever the mysterious author of Beowulf may have been as writers of the same language. But from the early fifteenth century to the present time, English has changed little. Instead, it grew. From all over the world, influences poured into the language. French dominates cooking, from *rotisserie* to *fondu* (with competition from the German *delicatessen*), and fashion from *lingerie* to *chemise*. Latin dominates not only the sciences mentioned earlier but also law. This is why we secure a writ of *habeas corpus* instead of a *have your own body* and why the school acts in *loco parentis* instead of as *parents on the spot*. It also explains why scholars cherish their *ibid*. (*ibidem*), *op. cit*. (*opus citatum*) and *loc. cit.* (*loco citato*) as so much more scholarly than the English *in the same place*, *in the work previously mentioned*, and *in the place previously mentioned*. As Latin dominates law and the biological sciences, Greek dominates chemistry, physics, and astronomy. And so goes the list. No other language on earth has been built up from so many languages, because when it comes to borrowing, English speakers have never been shy.

But if we have borrowed freely, we have also been generous. Terminology from such popular American pastimes as baseball and popular music have been taken over wherever these institutions have spread, from Mexico to Japan. And the Yankee tourist dollar has caused many a hotel and restaurant to look to its English.

An interesting example of English (or should I say *American*) influence on a foreign language was brought home to me during a recent trip to Mexico. Each time I thought I was beginning to understand Spanish, we went to another city, where I found that some of the words were different. For example, to get a piece of pie in Guadalajara, we asked for *pastel*. But in Mexico City *pastel* was cake. I did find among the *postres* (desserts) on the menu, however, an item called *pie*. *Pie* in Spanish (pronounced /pijéj/) means *foot*, which didn't appeal to me for dessert, but I was curious. I asked the waiter what that item was, and he looked at me with astonishment: "You, a Yankee, don't know what *pie* is (pronouncing it as we Americans do)!" Obviously, in a city so devoted to tourism, the restaurants were taking no chances of losing American business. I only hope the word never becomes standard Spanish, because this language, now so beautifully phonetic, would be mutilated by a glaring irregularity. I can hear the schoolchildren muttering as they bend over their spellers.

But if the word *pie* should spread from the tourist-type restaurants of Mexico City to general use in the Spanish language, a number of things could happen. The word could become Latinized. In this case, the pronunciation might remain the same, but the spelling could change to conform with Spanish phoneme-grapheme relationship, possibly to **pai*. More likely, the spelling will remain and the pronunciation change, probably to /pijéj/, making it a homonym of *pie* (*foot*). Or the word may not be

Latinized at all, keeping both its English spelling and English pronunciation. In this case, it would become one of the comparatively few Spanish irregular pronunciations.

There is a general tendency for languages to adapt a newly borrowed word to fit the phonemic structure of the receiving language. In English, however, this has been less the case than with most languages. English tends to retain the spelling of the parent language. This is why we have, for instance, not one but a number of plural morphemes. In addition to our favorite forms /—s ~ –z ~ –iz/, we retain the Greek /ə/ (data) the Hebrew /m/ (cherubim), and the Latin /aj/ (cacti), along with a host of others, including irregularities such as the Old English *oxen* and the replacives *mice* and *women*. This tendency also at least partially explains the utterly sadistic nature of English spelling. How do you build a regular spelling system for a language that includes the French *derrière*, Hebrew *eunuch*, German *zwieback*, Greek *cryptic*, Indian *moccasin*, Japanese *judo*, Chinese *chow*, Dutch *pretzel*, Italian *pizza*, Spanish *chile*, Swedish *smorgasbord*, and teen-age *tuff*? (The latter, as a slang word of enthusiastic approval, is generally spelled just as pronounced.)

OUR LANGUAGE TODAY

Today English is one of the most far-flung and widely spoken languages in the world, having over 300,000,000 native speakers. In total number of users, however, it does not compare with Chinese, which has over 700,000,000 speakers, if all dialects are considered. English is the native language of the United States and most of Canada, the British Isles, Australia, and New Zealand, and it is a major tongue among the White population in areas that once were part of the British Empire, such as The Union of South Africa and other colonies in Africa and Asia.

Its vocabulary has been estimated at well over half-a-million words, although obsolete words, recent foreign adoptions, and technical and slang vocabulary, all of which are used by limited communities of English speakers, would swell this figure considerably. The editors of *Webster's Third New International Dictionary of the English Language*, claim over 450,000 entries. Furthermore, they state, "It would have been easy to make the vocabulary larger..." except for space limitations.[14] This tremendous vocabulary is one of its strongest points: if we don't care to *leave*, we can *abandon*, *desert*, *evacuate*, *quit*, *vacate*, *withdraw*, *retire*, *retreat*, *resign*, *secede*, *abdicate*, or *tergiversate*. Each of these synonyms has a different connotation, and the writer or speaker of English can express many subtle shades of meaning.

[14] *Webster's New International Dictionary of the English Language*, Third Ed. (Springfield: C. and C. Merriam Company, 1960), p. 7a.

In spite of its Anglo-Saxon origin, over half the words of the language come either from Latin or from Latin (Romance) languages. Only about a third of the total vocabulary is derived from the parent Anglo-Saxon. The remaining sixth comes from hundreds of languages throughout the globe, including a liberal sprinkling of Greek.

But closer examination will reveal that our Anglo-Saxon heritage plays a greater part in the vocabulary than the figures would indicate. For example, let us look at the etymology of each word in the previous sentence:

```
AS  L       L      AS  L  AS AS  L     L       L      AS AS  AS  AS + L AS
But closer examination will reveal that our Anglo-Saxon heritage plays  a  greater  part    in
AS  L    AS AS  L    AS    L
the vocabulary than the figures would indicate.
```

This sentence has nine Latin words to twelve Anglo-Saxon, with one word, *part*, probably having roots in both. But compare the Anglo-Saxon words: *but, will, that, our, plays, a, greater, in, the, than, would*—with the Latin: *closer, examination, reveal, Anglo, Saxon, heritage, vocabulary, figures, indicate*. The common, everyday words— those we use over and over again—are largely Anglo-Saxon, while the longer, more technical, more specific, more literary words usually come from Latin. If we made a word count of a longer English work, counting each word only once, regardless of how many times it is used, the Latin words would outnumber the Anglo-Saxon words. But if each word were counted every time it is used, the result would be reversed. A general statement might be that most form class words come from Latin and most function words come from Anglo-Saxon, although this generalization has many exceptions.

English is essentially a *distributive* language, one that achieves its grammar through word-order rather than inflection or agglutination, although it does have a pattern of prefixes, suffixes, and roots, including a small inflectional system. Its history, grammar, phonetic structure, and vocabulary would classify it as a Teutonic language, inasmuch as it can be traced back through Middle English to Old English, which was really a collection of dialects that sprang from the West Germanic branch of Indo-European. Its closest relatives are Frisian, Dutch (Flemish), and a number of dialects of northern Germany collectively known as Low German.

TOWARDS A UNIVERSAL LANGUAGE

Every edition of the daily newspapers contains considerable evidence that humanity is engaged in a giant race between understanding and annihilation. It has frequently been suggested that as long as we live in a morass of several thousand languages, hope for understanding between nations is unrealistic. Many suggestions have been made concerning how to break down language barriers, including an increased program of teaching foreign language in the public schools. Undoubtedly this would be a help, particularly in the United States, where too many of us have lived in smug insulation from the rest of the world, unable to speak to our foreign neighbors, read their newspapers, or understand their values.

But learning foreign languages has its limitations. The question arises: learn *which* foreign languages? There are six languages in the world in addition to English that have over a hundred million speakers. Mandarin Chinese has over half a billion, whereas Russian has close to two hundred million. If the Latin American nations emerge from their economic deprivation, Spanish could become one of the world's great languages. But this still leaves Hindi, German, and Japanese in the hundred million plus class, with Arabic, Bengali, and Portuguese approaching the six-figure group. Some long-range predictions have been made that the emerging nations of Africa, with their enormous undeveloped wealth, may some day be the center of civilization and economic prosperity. But, as I have already pointed out, there are enough languages and dialects in Africa to keep a team of linguists busy for a lifetime. The enormity of the task of teaching American school students to speak the major languages of the world can be seen in proportion when we realize that of the world's nine leading languages other than English, only two—Spanish and German—are taught with any regularity in American public schools. (In terms of number of speakers, French is not in this group.)

Some local attempts have been made to break down language barriers without actually learning a foreign language. We discussed the American Indian's use of sign language as approaching a universal method of communicating, at least with tribes in his own language group. *Pidgin* languages come into being when one group, attempting to make themselves understood, speaks to people of another language, using what they consider a "simplified" vocabulary and grammar. If the motivation for understanding is mutual, the other people learn to imitate this distorted language, and what amounts to almost a new language is created. Such was the case with Chinese Pidgin English, with Yankee merchants desperately trying to open up trade with China. Other forms of Pidgin English developed in other parts of the world, each variety exhibiting some influence from the other language and the idiosyncracies of the individuals.

Closely resembling pidgin languages are *creole* languages. These are formed in a community in which a pidgin language has become a common form of communication, so common that children are brought up speaking it as their native language. A pidgin, in other words, is spoken as a *second* language, but if children are raised with it, it becomes a creole. Once a language is creolized, of course, it must be enlarged by its speakers to satisfy their needs. A child must be spanked, played with, taught to say his prayers, and later educated in the language. This requires many more words than are needed to determine the price of silk or a string of beads.

But creoles and pidgins also have their limitations. In the first place, they are really varieties of a language, not new languages. Pidgin English is a variety of English, just as Haitian Creole is a variety of French. You and I would encounter far fewer problems learning Chinese Pidgin English than would a Chinese, because the vocabulary is basically English. A second limitation is that pidgins and creoles have only local use, and seldom go beyond that. They are devised solely for reasons of expediency, and if they become a language at all (become creolized) they simply become one more local dialect, usually adding to, rather than alleviating, the problem of universal communication.

Another artificial attempt to break down the barriers of communication is *union-ization*. A union language is an artificially devised writing system that serves a number of languages. It may have a dual purpose to begin with, because a society with no written language cannot take its place among the family of industrial civilizations. But if only a handful speak a language, the difficulty of establishing a publishing industry and a literature becomes insurmountable. Only by combining like tongues into a single written language can a large enough base be established. In addition, a union language creates a cultural bond that can be a primary step in unifying a people.

These artificial languages must be carefully put together by skilled linguists, who are familiar with all the languages or dialects the union is intended to serve, and they cannot be devised at all unless the constituent languages are in close enough relationship to share reasonably common phonemic, morphemic, and grammatical structures.

An outstanding example of a successful union language is *Union Shona*, devised by linguistic missionaries for the production of a Bible to serve the needs of five of the six Shona dialects of Rhodesia and its neighboring territory. In all, about a million people are served, and a small publishing industry has arisen. *Union Ibu*, on the other hand, has been less successful in serving the needs of southern Nigeria. The failure may have been the result of methods of investigation and selection of features. It is both interesting and depressing to note that during the writing of much of this text a bloody war was raging in Nigeria, resulting in large-scale starvation. Whether a single language for all Nigerians could have had any influence on this tragedy, however, is doubtful.

Another alternative is the adoption of a single universal language to be learned, at least by the educated, as a second language that can be used for international trade, tourism, or developing a body of literature that can be read and discussed throughout the world without the need for translation. During the Middle Ages Latin served this purpose, at least in Europe. Learning Latin was the first requirement for an education, as it was used for all phases of religious, literary, and intellectual activity, and formed a common ground upon which educated people throughout the Western world could communicate, although at the time it was the native language of no one. Today, for all practical purposes, Latin is almost a dead language, kept alive only by the inertia of tradition. In America, the number of Latin classes in the public schools is decreasing rapidly.

After the decline of Latin, French assumed a similar position, as France became one of the leading commercial powers in Europe. French was in some ways even more "universal" than Latin. Although it was used less as a religious and scholarly medium, it was spoken as a native tongue by millions of people and it is still one of the major spoken languages of the world. But as French power declined and British and American power rose, English became much more popular throughout the world. Today English comes closer to being a universal language than French or Latin, whose use was limited largely to Europe, had even been.

In *The Miracle of Language*, Charlton Laird lists those qualities that he believes are necessary for a world language, and points out that English has all of them:[15]

Number of Speakers of the Language. Only Mandarin Chinese surpasses English in total number of speakers.

Distribution of Speakers. No language is spread throughout the world as widely as English. Chinese, Hindi, and Russian, the other three "big four," are more confined to single countries. French is widespread, but has far fewer speakers and is not growing in number. Spanish and German combine large numbers of speakers with widespread usage, but run far behind English on both counts.

Population Potential of the Areas in Which the Language Is Spoken. Three of the four major languages qualify here. Russia and China have great undeveloped resources. Spanish is also rapidly growing, but the nations in which it is spoken are not yet stable politically. Also, Spanish seems to be breaking up into many dialects and eventually may become many languages.

Adequacy of the Language Linguistically. English has the double advantage of a huge vocabulary and simple grammar. It has borrowed extensively from other languages, making the learning of English a little simpler for at least the majority of Europeans.

The major drawback lies in the inconsistent spelling, which makes English a difficult language to learn to read and write. Even many mature writers frequently

---

[15] Charlton Laird, *The Miracle of Language* (Cleveland: World Publishing Company, 1953), chap. 16. Topic headings are quoted from Laird. Comments are my own.

have to check their spelling. We have noted that our language is filled with foreign words and phrases, adopted into the language but not adapted for English spelling patterns. We have also noted some of the changes that have taken place in English pronunciation that were not accompanied by changes in spelling. Between these factors and the habit of printers of an earlier era of lengthening or shortening their lines by ingenious new spellings, we have a language with such confusing sound-letter relationships that we can make a game out of inventing new ways to write common words. For example, we present *phthaph* as our candidate to settle the dispute between the traditional (tough) and slang (tuff) spellings. All you have to do is take the *phth* from *phthisic*, *a* from *awake*, and *ph* from *photo*. Or take the *ti* from *attention*, the *o* from *women*, and the *pn* from *pneumonia* and you have *tiopn*, a delightful new spelling for *shin*.

A number of students of language have suggested spelling reform, including the late George Bernard Shaw. A few simplifications have been made, particularly in the United States, where *color* is more popular than *colour* and *catalog* and *theater* can be used for *catalogue* and *theatre*. But these are insignificant compared with the total pattern of language inconsistency. Changes such as *nite* for *night* and *thru* for *through* aim more directly at the problem, but are not accepted as standard English by the bulk of writers, copyeditors and teachers. As a matter of fact, what little spelling reform has been accomplished may have only complicated the language by introducing alternate spellings for the same word, a situation the language has only recently overcome.

Availability of the Language as a World Medium. English has already established a great publishing industry, making the written word available quickly and cheaply. Translators are readily available. It is fairly uniformly spoken all over the world; there is no need to translate Australian English into New Jersey English, or Texas English into London English.

Adequacy of the Language as a Medium of World Heritage. There is little in the human heritage—our philosophy, history, art, and literature—that is not available in publications in English. There is little of significance in any other language that has not been translated. Our system of libraries and reference tools, including dictionaries, ranks among the finest and most extensive in the world.

If man is to adopt anything like a universal language, English already has a head start, and would seem to be as good a candidate as any. But one can never tell. A sudden shift in world power can influence world language. The political and military situation being what it is today, we may well see two universal tongues emerge, English for Western civilization, Mandarin Chinese for the Orient. Or, if the Latin-American nations can achieve political as well as linguistic stability and economic growth, Spanish may prove to be a strong competitor, as could Russian, just as

Hindi or Japanese, each in its own section of the world, could challenge Chinese in the Orient.

Still another approach to an international language is the creation of a completely synthetic system, one that would be simple for the greatest number of people to learn because of a simplified grammar, lack of irregular forms, and limited vocabulary taken directly from other languages. A number of these artificial languages have been devised, but by far the most popular has been *Esperanto.*

Esperanto is essentially a Latin-based language, supplemented with Greek, Germanic, and other vocabularies. The hope that Esperanto would spread and become an international language is far from realized, although it has enjoyed some popularity, with Esperanto clubs scattered throughout the world. I have had the pleasure of attending meetings and study sessions of a local Esperanto club, and have found among its members an intense dedication to the "cause." Similar Esperanto societies in many parts of the world should make it possible for an individual to travel about the globe and be able to communicate with at least a small minority of people. But as a popular spoken language, as a language of commerce, scholarship, and universal appeal, Esperanto has not begun to take the place of any of the more popular modern languages.

Even if Esperanto—or any other language—should become internationally popular, the chances of its remaining universal are remote. Phonemic patterns of modern languages being as diverse as they are, dialectal differences are sure to appear in the French, English, and Russian varieties of any "universal" language, not to mention the Chinese and Swahili. And if the language becomes popular as a spoken tongue, the chances are that these dialects would become increasingly more pronounced until eventually they would be separate languages. Some control over this tendency could be exercised through the establishment of international standards of spelling and pronunciation, and by careful teaching in the schools throughout the world, including use of officially designated recordings of the language. Such measures would probably be effective as long as the language was used strictly for the purpose intended—a second language for interlingual communication. But once children began fighting in it, women gossiping in it, and men arguing politics in it, international control would be about as effective as our own feeble efforts to establish usage rules for *shall* and *will.*

The advantages of an international language for commerce, tourism, spread of learning, and translation of literature would be enormous. But the assumption that such a language would usher in a new era of Peace on Earth is, at best, risky. Within our own country, Whites and Blacks speak more or less the same language, as do rich and poor. But in a larger sense they do not speak the same language at all. I am not referring only to dialectal differences. Communication through language, in its broadest implications, involves more than whether we are going to call a book *libro* or *livre*. Communication about books—or about anything—depends upon recognizing the attitudes, the prejudices, and the point of view from which the subject is viewed. And keeping the peace is mainly a matter of *wanting* to keep the peace. An ounce of sincerity is worth a pound of translation.

The implications for educators in this last paragraph are perhaps the most significant in this volume. Having examined our language descriptively, historically, and comparatively, we have not done the real job at all, we have only prepared for it. The real action lies in using the language as a medium of communication, of learning to function as senders and receivers of oral and written messages. And this involves going beyond structure to meaning. It involves breaking through the mythology that surrounds language—the myth that some linguistic forms are superior to others merely because tradition holds them so; the myth that some languages are more advanced or more beautiful or more expressive; and finally another myth, one that will consume the bulk of our discussion in the closing pages of this volume—*the myth that meaning of a word is contained in the word itself, rather than in the mind of the speaker.*

It is to the quest for meaning that we direct the following chapter of this volume, for ultimately it is to the quest for meaning that the New English Teacher must direct his students. Anything else falls short of the goal, for language without meaning is not language at all.

9

---

myth and meaning

semantics

WORDS—WORDS—WORDS

It is a common fallacy to believe that all one has to do to find the meaning of a word is consult a dictionary. There seems to be a popular twentieth-century belief that writers of dictionaries, in some mysterious way, establish the "correct" definition of a word. Even English teachers, who ought to know better, too frequently admonish their charges to "look it up in the dictionary."

But all a lexicographer does is observe how a word is used in a great variety of situations and make an educated guess concerning the meaning, or meanings, intended. Then he has the problem of trying to find words to convey that meaning to the reader. Finally, the reader must decide what the lexicographer intended. Considering the difficulties, it is a monument to the skill of dictionary builders that things work out as well as they do.

But no matter how skilled and knowledgeable the lexicographer, he is working at one great disadvantage. He must base each definition on general usage of the word, arriving at a composite picture of the many shades of meaning given it by a host of writers. The reader, on the other hand, is interested in what a particular writer meant in a particular passage. When he reads that the United Nations is imposing economic "sanctions" against some nation, he wants to know just what the United Nations is doing. A dictionary can tell him that *sanction* can be either a term of approval or a type of punishment, but cannot tell him which is intended in this case. The reader must find out from the context of the passage. The key word here, of course, is *against*, for we hardly show *approval against* anything or anyone. In this problem the dictionary is valuable as a first step in deciphering the meaning of the word, but ultimately the reader must depend upon his own skill in interpreting, based on the entire passage.

The student who makes a habit of consulting the dictionary only when context does not provide sufficient information should eventually realize that different people often use the same word to mean slightly—sometimes even radically— different things. Whereas dictionaries list multiple meanings for most words, they cannot possibly include all the shades and nuances intended in each case.

Ultimately, students can develop considerable skill in making educated guesses about the meaning of new words without consulting the dictionary at all. In the example concerning sanctions, the entire article, perhaps giving excerpts of speeches condemning the country in question for its aggression, sets the stage for the reader to "guess" that the word *sanction* infers action against. The concept may be a bit hazy in the reader's mind, but this is preferable to a definition copied glibly from the pages of a dictionary. And because the reader has made the inference for himself, he is more likely to remember it. Each time he sees the word again, his understanding will be broadened and reinforced, along with his general perception of the multifaceted nature of the meanings of words.

How can you possibly arrive at THE definition of words that symbolize some of the complex, abstract, and controversial phenomena of the human mind? Take, for example, *patriotism*. Most of us consider ourselves to be patriotic, but we quarrel incessantly over politics and economics. We simply do not recognize the same courses of action as being patriotic. Both Republicans and Democrats disagree as to what these titles mean, and Catholics, Protestants, and Jews differ among themselves concerning the meaning of their own religions. Yet we glibly use words such as *love, freedom, sin,* and *honor* as if we all agreed what we are talking about. We discuss *molecular action, poverty,* and *a million light years* as if these concepts were within our understanding, and for *introversion* and *neurosis* we send students to the dictionary.

An interesting case was recently reported by United Press.[1] A man in Ann Arbor, Michigan, returned the food and department store advertising he had been mailed to the post office. Declaring the material *obscene*, he demanded that no more of this "junk mail" be sent to him. At first his local postmaster sent the mail back to him, maintaining that such material cannot possibly be considered offensive. When the case reached the legal counsel of the Post Office Department in Washington, a ruling was handed down that according to the law, the recipient is the sole judge of the

---

[1] From *The Sacramento Bee*, September 11, 1969.

obscenity of an advertisement. ". . . they (the recipients) can declare that an ad for a sack of potatoes looks sexy to them," ruled the counsel for the Post Office Department. Such a ruling is probably not as ridiculous as it may seem. As a matter of fact, it might be the only sensible approach to obscenity. After the comic opera proportions reached by some of our debates concerning just what constitutes obscenity, we may do well to recognize that nothing is—or is not—obscene. As is so frequently the case, the definition of the word lies not in the word itself, but in the mind of the speaker.

The dictionary, then, can only make *generalizations* about words. It can never tell us what Joe Smith means (or if he means anything at all) when he says "What this country needs is more *patriotism*," what Sadie McGrady has in mind when she asks her husband if he *loves* her, or what it feels like to be *poverty-stricken*. The generalizations contained in a dictionary make it a useful tool—one of the most useful tools of language study—but its overuse is like swatting flies with a sledge hammer. The semanticist is concerned with going beyond the generalities to communicate directly with Joe and Sadie.

THE POWER BEHIND THE WORD

Not only do words mean many things to many people; they are also frequently charged with emotional connotations that sometimes say more than their lexical denotations. Skilled propagandists can play on the hopes, the dreams, the fears, and the frustrations of people by careful manipulation of such emotionally charged words.

Clyde Miller calls the use of connotative values of words the *name calling* and *rosy glow* devices.[2] He reminds us how easy it was at one time to condemn Copernicus and Galileo simply by calling them *heretics*. Today we consider these people great men of science, but we can still draw violent reactions by calling a person a *communist*, a *reactionary*, a *nigger-lover*, or a *racist*. Notice that who we are and where and when an event takes place can determine which words carry which connotations.

Rosy glow words are designed to create an aura of warmth and approval. By referring to *price fixing* as *fair trade regulations*, everything is made right, and if a cause or product can somehow be associated with freedom, justice, purity, or anything else that sounds rosy, the struggle for acceptance is almost won. S. I. Hayakawa uses the terms *snarl words* and *purr words*, and points out that use of emotionally charged

[2] Clyde R. Miller, *Propaganda—How and Why It Works* (New York: Commission for Propaganda Analysis, Methodist Federation for Social Action, 1949), pp. 11–13.

words and phrases often reveals more about the speaker and his attitude toward the object he is discussing than it tells about the object itself.[3]

A politician might call himself a *liberal* and his opponent a *reactionary*, but the other man calls himself a *conservative* and his opponent a *radical*. And nobody is wrong. It's all a matter of semantics.

Cutting through ambiguity, emotionalism, and meaninglessness is a complicated and tortuous process. Often lexical meaning and emotional connotation are so intertwined that they cannot be separated. A good example of this is the recent confusion that has arisen concerning the proper word for Americans of the Negroid race. For years *Colored* was a standard term used in the South. In their current drive to find identity, however, many Black people have rejected this term, long a symbol of inferiority and condescension. At this time, *Negro* is still fairly common, although *Black* is preferred, particularly among the more militant groups, despite the fact that it is a misnomer. "Black" people are really a deep rich brown, and intermating has resulted in people of every possible shading of tan. Yet differences of opinion concerning a name exist even within the Black community. *Afro-American* seems to many to carry satisfactory identity implications. I still hear *Negro* used by some and denounced by others, and at this writing, the National Association for the Advancement of Colored People has yet to change its name. Similar confusion exists within the Mexican—Mexican-American—Chicano—Spanish Surname—community. The question of the proper name to apply to any racial, religious, or other ethnic group can

[3] S. I. Hayakawa, *Language in Thought and Action* (New York: Harcourt, Brace and Company, 1964), p. 44.

be a highly emotional one, despite the fact that all possible names have the same lexical meaning.

Our use of words, as well as our reaction to them, is a reflection of the totality of ourselves and our culture. Therefore, we cannot confine our study of semantics to words alone, but must turn our attention to the entire philosophical-logical system that has become part of the culture of Western civilization.

TWO POINTS OF VIEW

Throughout the centuries, much of Western man's thinking has stemmed from that eminent and venerable Greek philosopher, Aristotle, whose contributions to grammatical thinking have been noted in Chapter 1. But his influence on philosophy was even more profound. So deeply did Aristotle influence the way Western man thinks that our common system of reasoning is often referred to as *Aristotelian logic.*

Aristotelian logic is based on three premises, which are so interdependent that they could be considered three forms of the same principle. These premises are.

1. THE LAW OF IDENTITY: A thing is what it is. *X is X.* A tree is a tree. A house is a house. A man is a man.
2. THE LAW OF EXCLUDED MIDDLE: A thing is either a particular object or it is not that object. *It is either X or Non-X.* Either it is a tree or it is not a tree, a house or not a house, a man or not a man.
3. THE LAW OF NON-CONTRADICTION: *A thing cannot be both X and Non-X.* It cannot be a tree and also a house, a house and also a man, a man and also a tree.

These premises, at first glance, would seem so obvious, so fundamental, we may wonder why it took a genius like Aristotle to formulate them. If Aristotle did not actually originate this method of thinking, at least he observed that this is how most people think, and formulated a logic that has been a guide ever since. And today, although a relatively small number of people have studied Aristotelian logic— or even know that there is such a thing—most of us think and act on the assumption that these principles are valid, even though we are not conscious of the specific "laws." When we look at a tree we assume that a tree is a tree, either it is a tree or it is not a tree, and that it cannot be both a tree and not a tree. It all seems so obvious, so hard to refute, so safe.

But an interesting contrast with Aristotelian logic can be found by going back a couple of centuries earlier to the work of another philosopher, also Greek, whose writings can be a bit disturbing to anyone comfortably curled up in Aristotelian thinking. His name was Heraclitus, and his one known work exists only in fragments. Let us examine "Fragment 21:"

> You cannot step twice into the same river.

What could he possibly mean by such a statement? You step into a river, then step out. Can you possibly step into the same river again? Let Heraclitus explain: "Everything flows and nothing abides; everything gives way and nothing stays fixed."[4] The waters that once cooled your toes are in that brief instant gone forever, hurled down the inevitable course of time. Other waters may take their place, but these are never the same. But, you may argue, what difference does that make? Water is water, so why not say with Aristotle, "A river is a river?" But it is not the *same* river. Not only are the waters different—cooler or warmer, clearer or muddier, but the shape and size of the river has altered—imperceptibly perhaps—but undeniably altered. Bit by bit, grain by grain, our river is constantly changing. You don't believe it? Come back in a million years. You won't recognize the place. What new Grand Canyons or Yosemite Valleys will be carved out for your vacationing pleasure! Yet some people think they can actually step into the same river twice.

Not only has the river changed—you have changed. Also imperceptibly but inevitably, you grow, you develop, you age. Glandular-chemical reactions take place. New tissue replaces the worn-out cells that die and are eliminated. Just as inevitably, you develop new attitudes and a new relationship with the environment.

Returning to the river, we find it a very deceptive phenomenon. It changes form so slowly (with a few exceptional cases, such as sudden floods or droughts, or certain rivers whose beds are so unstable they have been known to change course frequently) that we are lulled into thinking it does not change at all. At the other end of the *stability-change scale* we might place a volcano, whose eruptions can bring on a sudden dramatic change from green fields to cinder-scarred wasteland. Volcanoes, with their sudden rush of hot lava, are a great physical danger to anyone in the area, but rivers, with their subtle, imperceptible maneuvers, are a danger to our thinking. They trick us into believing that R is R.

Between the extremes of river and volcano are most of the ever-changing phenomena in the affairs of man and nature. The concept of the universe as a complex, dynamic, moving, changing entity is extremely important, for the weakness of traditional Aristotelian thinking is its failure to account for change and differences of individuality.

---

[4] Heraclitus, Fragment 20.

It must be kept in mind that Aristotle epitomized the most careful and logical thinking of his time. For centuries Aristotelian logic has been the centerpost of organized thinking, the best and most comprehensive system available. But the march of civilization, like Heraclitus' river, is relentless in its progress, and we have come to the point, here in the twentieth century, at which Aristotelian logic is simply no longer adequate. If Aristotle were alive today, and had the benefit of centuries of scientific thinking, he would probably be the world's leading Non-Aristotelian.

Now let us compare the dynamic world of Heraclitus to the static world of Aristotle. Figure 9-1 represents a river flowing into a lake. Notice how gradually the water widens, how slowly the current ebbs. Little by little the terrain becomes less "riverish" and more "lakeish." But is *Point A* part of the river or the lake? *Point B*? *Point C*? At what point does *R* become *L*?

Definitions become blurred not only in space but also in time. Imagine Figure 9-1 as having been drawn in early June, when rain and melting snow swell our river and lake to capacity. But as the season wears on and the hot dry summer takes its toll, there is less and less water. At what point does our river become a stream? Is it a river in the spring and a stream in the fall? Or a river that goes almost dry about half the year? Or a stream that floods about half the year? Again definitions blur.

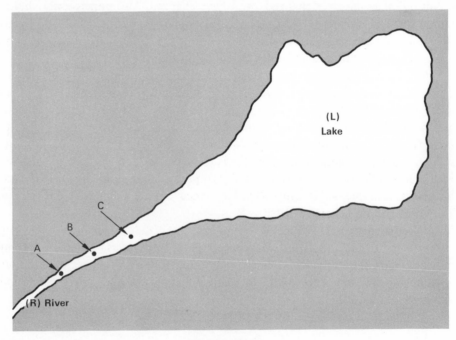

Figure 9-1.

Thus far our discussion has been on a rather theoretical level. After all, how important is it to discover when a river becomes a lake or a stream or whether you are re-entering the same or a different river? It really isn't important, unless you are working in some technical area that requires precise definitions. What is important, however, is the METHOD OF THINKING.

Many teachers who believe they are teaching their students to think, or who wish to teach schoolchildren to use language effectively might consider a semantic approach to education, calling for flexible thinking and a healthy respect for change. From a study of the opposing points of view of Aristotle and Heraclitus, a skillful teacher should be able to help his students transfer his learning to other areas in which we have been bound by a tradition that is static, unproductive, and incapable of solving twentieth century problems.

Nowhere is the need for flexibility more obvious than in the teaching of grammar. Traditional grammar is distinguished by its Aristotelian rigidity: A noun is a noun. Either it is a noun or it is not a noun. A word cannot be both noun and non-noun. Yet nouns, according to structural grammarians, are words that are frequently preceded by determiners. (See Chapter 6, page 129). But try:

> *The older* you get, my dear, *the prettier* you look.

Or try the rule (Chapter 5, pages 108–109) about adjectives having a three-part paradigm on *little*. Neither *littler* nor *more little* would be considered grammatical in any society of English speakers over the age of six. Yet *little* can be used in any construction that takes the uninflected form of *small*, and *small* meets every criterion in the chapter for an adjective. The most we can say about a word, then, is that under different conditions it can be a different part of speech, that it has *certain characteristics* of an adjective (but not others), that it seems to be at approximately some point along a continuum from "perfect example of adjective" (if there is such a thing) to "in no way related to adjective."

Finally, we recognize that a word is or is not some particular part of speech simply because we say so, because we establish or accept some particular criteria. Change the criteria and the word may change its part of speech. Use slot-and-filler methods, and *school* in *the school building* is an adjective (*the red building, large building, old building,* and so on). But by inflectional standards, school is a noun (*school, schools, school's, schools',* not *schooler, schoolest*). But even by slot-and-filler standards one cannot say a building is *very school,* even though it can be *very red.*

Nor are verbs immune. Verbs are definitely form class words with strong lexical meanings. But compare:

> *Did you take a book? Why, is one missing?*
> *Did you take a bath? Why, is one missing?*

The reply that makes a perfectly natural reaction to one question is only a rather stale joke in relation to the other. Despite the identical structure of these two sentences, *take* in the second sentence has very little lexical meaning but has certain characteristics of a function word in the form *take a bath*. It is similar to *have* in *let's have lunch*.

Or consider our sacred rules for punctuation: "Put a question mark after a sentence that asks a question."

> Tell me whether you love me.

It may seem unimportant whether X is X or the verb *take* is a form or function word, as long as we are speaking in the abstract, but when we discuss more vital matters our thinking needs clarification.

Take people, for example, and the way we classify them. We say, quite glibly, that Smithers is a *conservative* or a *reactionary* or a *hippie* or a *bookworm* or a *communist* without realizing that we have only the vaguest sort of idea what these terms mean. If the word *river* can include everything from the mighty Amazon to our favorite fishing stream, surely any term applied to people can include just as wide a variety of individuals. If a river is a constantly changing process, surely even poor old Smithers, for all his conservatism, is capable of being a different person today from the one he was yesterday. All we can say about an individual, if we know him well and understand his mental processes, is that on any given issue he will *probably* have predictable attitudes, that he has *certain characteristics* (but not others) of particular factions, that he falls somewhere along a continuum. Finally, we recognize that he is only conservative or liberal, peacenik or war monger, ignorant or knowledgeable because we say so, because we establish or accept certain criteria for defining these categories.

THE MAP AND THE TERRITORY

In 1933 Alfred Korzybski published *Science and Sanity; an introduction to Non-Aristotelian Systems and General Semantics*, the fountainhead of the general semantics movement. In this lengthy and somewhat technical volume, Korzybski laid the foundation for what he called a non-Aristotelian system. Although he was not the first to develop the basic concepts, his thorough investigations into the area have earned a special place for him in the early development of semantic thinking.

A number of other writers have amplified and explained some of the same principles found in *Science and Sanity*. In 1923 Ogden and Richards used the term *referent* to signify an object as it exists, as opposed to the object as it is viewed.[5]

---

[5] C. K. Ogden and I. A. Richards, *The Meaning of Meaning* (New York: Harcourt, Brace and Company, 1923), p. 11.

Figure 9-2 portrays what happens when Mr. X tells Mr. Y about an object he has seen:

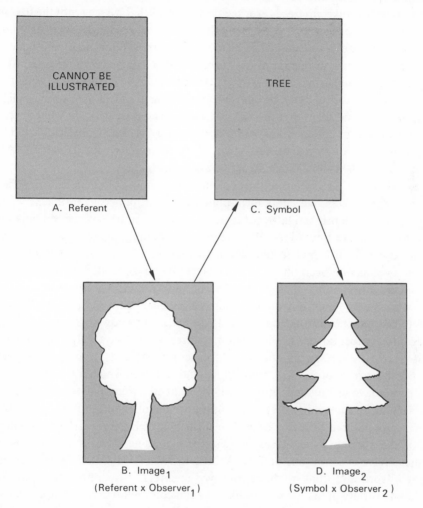

Figure 9-2.

At the left (A) you see the object itself, say a tree. This is the *referent* of Ogden and Richards, the object as it really is. From this referent comes Image₁ (B). Image₁ is a cross between the referent and the observer. That is, it is the referent as the observer sees it. The human organism is incapable of visualizing a tree as it really exists, for the real tree is not a thing at all, but a *process*. Like Heraclitus' river, it is a constantly changing affair, growing in places, dying in other places, shuttling moisture, food, and energy up and down and back and forth in a never-ending symphony of movement. No two trees are alike, no tree is ever the same twice. What we see is not the tree, in all its changing complexity, but *our image* of the tree, the tree as it appears to us. And not everybody sees the same thing when he looks at the tree. Your image and mine have some characteristics in common, but there are also significant differences. At best we get a general impression of a greenish thing held up by a trunk. The details blur.

Our image is also colored by who we are. The artist's trained eye may pick up details of color and form that the rest of us miss. The poet may see values even the artist misses, although perhaps without observing as much physical detail. The lumberman is sure the tree should be cut down immediately for its valuable board footage, but to the camper such an act would be sacrilege.

Not only is our perception of *things* clouded by a host of human factors, so is our grasp of many *issues*. We glibly form opinions about numerous problems we have never studied in depth and have either never experienced or experienced only under the grossest human limitations. We scream at the umpire for what we saw with an untrained eye from a seat in the bleachers, and we talk about people on welfare without ever having been on welfare ourselves. We know what is best for nations a hemisphere away, although we know nothing about their history, their culture, or their value system; and from our armchairs we can deal with every problem from high taxes to rebellious youth. Yet on each of these issues our knowledge may be as superficial and as parochial as our observation of a tree. Just as we see that part of the tree that is above the surface but not the root structure that feeds it, so do we frequently see only the surface of an issue, missing the vital causes in which it is rooted.

After we have formulated an image, if we want to communicate it to others it is necessary to find a symbol that will conjure up a similar image in the mind of the other person. So we turn to words. The third box of Figure 9-2 (C) represents the *symbol*, the word or words we use to describe the image in our mind. Here we find another source of confusion, for THE WORD IS NOT THE OBJECT. How often do we say a word and think we have conveyed meaning! How often are we aware of the infinite variety of images a word like *tree* can conjure up in someone else's mind? And no matter how many adjectives we add, or how poetic, or how literary, or how scientifically accurate our description, we can never describe the image in our mind so perfectly that the image in the mind of the listener matches ours *exactly*. As we acquire skill with words we can learn to bring Images$_1$ and $_2$ closer together, but communication is like the mathematical problem of dividing a quantity in two, then dividing the remainder in two *ad infinitum*. We can continue the process infinitely, but can never arrive at absolute zero. We can only make the difference so small it becomes imperceptible and unimportant.

The fourth square of Figure 9-2 represents the image as it could be communicated to another person. It is three steps removed from reality; three major alterations have been made in the referent before it is formulated in the mind of the second person. It is a mixture of the symbol and two observers. It is like the party game in which one person begins by whispering something into the ear of his neighbor, who tells the next person what he thinks he heard, and so on. Remember some of the crazy results?

The difficulty is that when the party is over we leave and continue to play the game, but this time in deadly earnest. We formulate opinions about people, nations, races, religions, and political movements on the basis of images many times removed from reality. And we vote, spend our money, and fight wars on the basis of these images.

THE MYSTERIOUS MARY MALONE

Take the case of Mary Malone. "You must meet Mary Malone," you are told, so you set out to discover what sort of person she is. Your first clue comes from the little girl next door, age four. She assures you that Mary Malone is an "old lady." Mary's mother, on the other hand, tells you that Mary is "just a baby." The boys at the office call her a "beautiful blonde," but one of the other secretaries confides that she is "rather plain, really—just uses too much make-up." Her boyfriend says she is a "bundle of energy," but the boss considers her "somewhat lazy." To an ardent communist, because she works in an office, she is a "dupe of the capitalist bosses," while another gentleman of equally extreme political viewpoint wonders if she shouldn't be investigated as a "dangerous radical."

Will the real Mary Malone please stand up. Impossible. You cannot talk about the real Mary. You can only find your image of her. The real Mary, like our tree, isn't a thing at all, but a happening, an event. Like Heraclitus' river, she is a constantly changing process—a process of growth and decay; of food ingestion and digestion; of blood rushing through veins and arteries; of millions of cells being created, reproducing, and dying; of an aging, growing, expanding, contracting. You can never find THE real Mary Malone. You can only hunt for symbols that come reasonably close, and hope for the best.

Thus far we have assumed a sincere interest by everyone concerned in trying to communicate as accurately as possible. But suppose, as frequently happens, an individual has a vested interest in *deliberately distorting* Image$_2$. He may be a politician attempting to sway his constituents, a businessman advertising a product, or a newspaperman sensationalizing a humdrum event to sell more papers. By the skillful use of snarl words and purr words or by the careful arrangement of elements (symbols), all of which may be true in themselves but create in the aggregate a totally false, sensationalized, or exaggerated impression, it is quite possible to create an $Image_2$ that has almost no relation to the referent.

This can be seen in many areas of communication, particularly in the mass media. Politicians are concentrating increasingly on their "image," and less and less on issues and realities (referents). *Image*, in this case, means $Image_2$, the impression you and I receive from a press agent's description of $Image_1$. $Image_1$ is the picture the politician and his agents have in their own minds. Advertisers, in selling the products of industry, are more concerned with producing an image of that product than with the actual qualities of the product itself.[6]

Daniel Boorstin uses the term *pseudo-event* to describe a news item that is created either by contriving the whole thing from the beginning (a "grand opening," a "testimonial dinner," or any event concocted to call attention to itself) or by sensationalizing or otherwise distorting the $Image_2$ of an existing event.[7] He gives numerous examples of how words and pictures are used by the mass media to create whatever $Image_2$'s will serve a particular purpose. One of these is an account of the televising of Chicago's 1951 parade in honor of General Douglas MacArthur on his "triumphal" journey across the nation after he had been relieved of his command of the American forces in Korea:

> For the television watcher, the General was the continuous center of attraction from his appearance during the parade at 2:21 P.M. until the sudden blackout at 3:00 P.M. Announcers continually reiterated (the scripts showed over fifteen explicit references) the unprecedented drama of the event, or that this was "the greatest ovation this city has ever turned out." On the television screen one received the impression of wildly cheering and enthusiastic crowds before, during, and after the parade. Of course the cameras were specially selecting "action" shots, which showed a noisy, waving audience; yet in many cases the cheering, waving, and shouting were really a response not so much to the General as to the aiming of the camera. Actual spectators, with sore feet, suffered long periods of boredom. Many groups were apathetic. The video viewer, his eyes fixed alternately on the General and on an enthusiastic crowd, his ears filled with a breathless narrative emphasizing the interplay of crowd and celebrity, could not fail to receive an impression of continuous dramatic pageantry.[8]

Another account of how $Image_2$ can be deliberately manipulated without saying a word that is not scrupulously accurate—this time through skillful manipulation of numbers—is Darrell Huff's *How To Lie With Statistics*. In his volume Huff describes a number of devices, including a careful selection of the information to be broadcast and to be withheld, by which the most impeccable figures can give a lopsided impression.

---

[6] A popular exposé of the methods of image builders is found in Vance Packard's *The Hidden Persuaders*.

[7] Daniel J. Boorstin, *The Image, or What Happened to the American Dream*. (New York: Atheneum Publishers, 1962), Chap. I.

[8] Boorstin, *The Image*, p. 27.

Some semanticists speak of the referent, the real thing as it exists in the extensional world, as the *territory*, and one's concept or image of the territory as the *map*. *Do you have an accurate map of the territory* is a reminder that the image and the referent, the map and the territory are no more the same thing than a geographic map is the same as the territory it represents. This difficulty, however, should not preclude our efforts to make our maps as accurate as possible, to bring together image and referent, and to strive to see the world as free as possible from prejudices, preconceptions, and the cultural blinders that limit our vision.

ABSTRACT AND CONCRETE

S. I. Hayakawa used a device he called the *abstraction ladder* to illustrate a similar principle.[9] Beginning with the simple, everyday word *cow*, he pointed out that *cow* is simply an abstraction, a word we use to stand for a host of complex creatures, which might be as different from each other as New York City is from Davis, California. But because New York and Davis have *certain* characteristics in common—they are both places where people live—we identify both by such common terms as city or town. We use the word *cow* in much the same way to identify a host of dissimilar creatures that have one or more characteristics in common.

Cow is a higher level abstraction than the word *Bessie*, which stands for only one of those creatures (See Figure 9-3). When we move our conversation from *cow* to talk about *Bessie*, we move *down the abstraction ladder*. But even *Bessie* is an abstraction. As illustrated in Figure 9-3, the word *Bessie* is only the symbolic representation of that which we perceive. The perception (Image$_1$), the picture in mind when you look at Bessie or remember Bessie, is a lower level abstraction still. But as already pointed out, it cannot be communicated directly. We can only use abstract symbols (words or pictures) to express our images. So we say, "I have a cow named Bessie," and allow our companion to form his own image (Image$_2$).

We do not reach the bottom of the abstraction ladder until we realize that our image of Bessie is only that which we are able to perceive with our limited human sensory system. Our understanding of Bessie depends upon whether we are a dairyman or beef rancher, school teacher or veterinarian. We also see Bessie in the light of such factors as our age, sex, previous experiences, and attitudes. The real Bessie, "The

[9] Hayakawa, *Language in Thought and Action.*

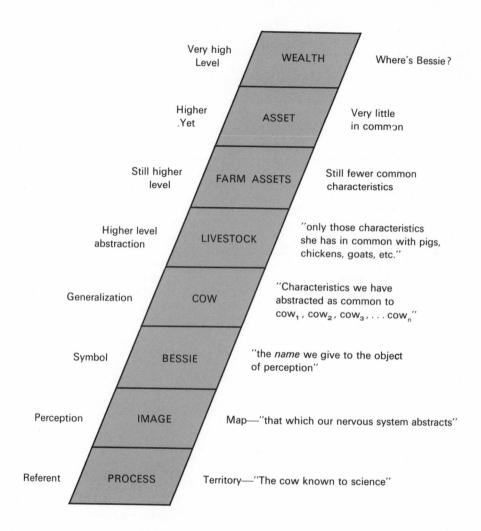

Figure 9-3. THE ABSTRACTION LADDER*

* Adapted from S. I. Hayakawa, *Language in Thought and Action*, p. 179. Courtesy Harcourt, Brace and World, Inc., and S. I. Hayakawa.

cow known to science ultimately consists of atoms, electrons, etc., according to present-day scientific inferences . . . . This is the *process level*."[10]

Figure 9-3 also shows that from *cow* one can go to ever-higher levels of abstraction, but at each jump the dissimilarities become more pronounced and the similarities fewer. When we talk about *livestock* we now include characteristics of chickens, pigs, sheep, and other animals. *Farm assets* includes still more territory, *assets* more yet, and by the time we get to the word *wealth*, we are on such a high level of abstraction there are comparatively few statements we can make that would still apply to Bessie.

What is the significance of all this discussion about levels of abstraction? If we would help our students use language effectively and think clearly, we must teach them that certain statements can be made at each abstraction level, but that most of us are confused about which statements are valid at which levels.

Frequently we think and speak at a higher level abstraction than our experience justifies. We discuss cows after knowing only Bessie. We know that football players never study, having had one in class, or that Orientals are shrewd business people, having read an article somewhere. So our perceptions of teen-agers, hippies, Black people, Jews, and Irishmen are formed on the basis of experiences with too small a number to represent the group. Like the blind men of Hindustan, we generalize about elephants without having seen one. And this condition is aggravated by the problem discussed earlier. Many of our limited impressions are not even formed by our own experience but by interpreting someone else's words (Image$_1$ → symbol → Image$_2$). It is hardly surprising that we develop inaccurate maps of our territories.

I recently observed a twelfth-grade class discussing the problem of alcoholism. The following statement was made and accepted by the group without challenge from either the teacher or the students:

Germans are big beer drinkers.

Let us subject that statement to semantic analysis. To begin with, how do you define the word *Germans*? Some possible definitions are:

All human beings who live in Germany. (East Germany? West Germany? Both?)
All human beings over the age of twenty-one (or nineteen? or whatever you consider the beer-drinking age?) who live in Germany.
Males over the age of   ?   who live in Germany.
Any of those listed, but including Americans of German ancestry (or Americans born in Germany? or second-generation German-Americans? or third generation? or ?).
Any of those listed, including people of German ancestry anywhere in the world.

---

[10] Hayakawa, *Language in Thought and Action*, p. 179.

Obviously, the number of possible definitions is as endless as the variety of rivers or cities or trees. In this sentence *Germans* is meaningless.

Let us arbitrarily define *Germans* as anyone living in the United States, either born in Germany or who has one or both parents born in Germany. This is less ambiguous than *Germans*. Other questions arise: "Am I *competent* to make a statement about *all* German-Americans? Have I observed them all? Have I even observed a representative sample? Have I observed Germans in St. Louis, Germans in Arizona, Germans in Connecticut, and Germans in Olympia, Washington? Have I observed Germans of many ages, both sexes, and a good sampling of socioeconomic levels?"

"Well," I might reply, "There are two Germans living across the street from me, and they sit on their front porches all evening and drink beer!" Now we're beginning to get somewhere. We have not only clarified the vague term *Germans*, we have gone *down the abstraction ladder* to make a statement that might begin to have some validity. I can make many statements about $Hans_1$ and $Fritz_1$ that I cannot make about the higher level abstraction. $Hans_1$ and $Fritz_1$ I have personally observed, but *all Germans*—even all German-Americans—represents too high a level of abstraction for me to make a valid statement. I need to come down the abstraction ladder to a subject I am qualified to discuss.

Now let us take a look at the complement of the sentence. How does one define "big beer drinkers?" How much beer must one drink to qualify? One can of beer every day? Does it require two cans? Three? Six? What about the person who doesn't touch beer all week and then drinks himself silly (or asleep) on Saturday night? Or the one who has such a low alcohol tolerance he becomes drunk on two cans of beer? Obviously, *big beer drinkers* is as meaningless as *Germans*.

But we left Hans and Fritz sitting on the porch. Suppose careful observation reveals that these two men like to sit outside after dinner, chatting with each other, with their neighbors and friends, their wives and children, until bedtime. And most of the time they have a can of beer in their hands. But how much beer do they actually *consume* in an average evening? Do they guzzle a six-pack apiece, or have they each learned to nurse a single can through a three-hour sitting? Suppose we observe that they put away an average of two cans each evening they sit out, which averages five evenings per week. We still don't know if this is being a "big" drinker. A beer salesman or a confirmed drunk might consider this not really drinking at all. Fritz's mother or wife, or a member of the WCTU might think it disgraceful. Like the many facets of Mary Malone, it's all in one's point of view.

Words such as *big* and *little*, *good* and *bad*, *near* and *far* are often meaningless, and lead to many questions that are unanswerable. A child might ask, "Is it far to Grandma's house?" but an adult should know that Grandma's house may be three miles, six miles, or a thousand miles from our house, or it may be farther than Aunt

Emma's. But how far is far? The public school system has been seriously negligent about teaching these vital thinking skills.

We might, therefore, conclude that Hans drinks more beer than my Uncle Joe and less than my Uncle Will, or that he drinks an average of ten cans of beer per week. Once we realize that statements such as *Germans are big beer drinkers* really mean *Hans₁ and Fritz₁ average ten cans of beer per week*, we are beginning to understand some of humanity's (including our own) deep-seated sources of misunderstanding and prejudice.

I selected the statement about Germans drinking beer as an example because I had heard it on three different occasions in the past year. This would seem to indicate that at least part of our population associates beer drinking with Germans. Whether there is any truth to the belief is a question I am not qualified to answer. I can only say that on three occasions I have observed the association.

But wouldn't the fact that this statement was heard three times made by different people indicate that there must be some truth to it? Possibly, but not necessarily. Every age has its mythology. The Greeks thought Zeus hurled thunderbolts at the earth, the Aztecs sacrificed human beings to their gods, the Puritans burned witches at the stake, and the Nazis blamed the Jews for most of their troubles. The student of semantics attempts to filter as much mythology as possible from his thinking to update his maps of the territories.

This is not to imply that the only way to obtain information is through personal observation. The observations of others can also be worthwhile, but they must be evaluated. A statement made by a friend may reveal more about the friend than about his subject. When Bill says he married the most wonderful woman in the world, we know far more about Bill and his domestic relations than we know about his wife. Harry's statement that foreigners are not to be trusted is a statement about Harry and his personal prejudices, not about foreigners. Bill and Harry, however, may not know this. The report of a research scientist concerning his recent experiments is in a different class but is still subject to verification. What you know about the individual—his possible prejudices and his competence to say what he does—must be considered along with the nature of the report itself.

Teen-agers are careless drivers is a high-level abstraction, difficult to prove, and suspicious because of its careless generalizing. *Insurance companies charge a higher rate for drivers under twenty-five because statistics indicate a higher accident rate* is a more carefully thought-out statement. It is still an abstraction, but subject to *verification.*

This does not imply, therefore, that high-level abstractions cannot be used. Quite the contrary, abstractions are vital in human affairs. Without the power to abstract and to express abstract ideas in language, civilization as we know it would not be possible.

Statistical information on a great variety of topics—including the per-capita consumption of beer by Germans and the insurance rates for drivers under twenty-five—can be of utmost importance in a great variety of decision-making situations. But it is because such information is so important that it must be examined. Before accepting or rejecting the sentence about insurance company rates, the reader would do well to check with enough companies to feel confident he has a representative sampling. Do *all* insurance companies charge a higher rate for young drivers? Do they *all* use age twenty-five as the cut-off point? Considerable research is needed to accept or reject the statement, but at least the question can be researched.

The higher the level of abstraction, the more need there is for interpretation. A generalization may be accurate on the basis of all known evidence, or it may mean any of the following:

> *I have seen two such cases, so I am guessing that it is always true.*
> *This is what I would like you to think.*
> *I want this to be true, so I subconsciously map the territory this way and ignore all evidence to the contrary.*
> *I've been brought up to believe this, and have never questioned it.*

Stuart Chase uses an interesting device in semantic analysis. He looks for words or phrases in a statement which, like our *Germans* or *big beer drinkers*, are so undefined they are meaningless. For them he substitutes the word "blab." Below he analyzes a typical speech of a typical demagogue:

> The Aryan Fatherland, which has nursed the souls of heroes, calls upon you for the supreme sacrifice which you, in whom flows heroic blood, will not fail, and which will echo forever down the corridors of history.

This would be translated:

> The blab blab, which has nursed the blabs of blabs, calls upon you for the blab blab which you, in whom flows blab blood, will not fail, and which will echo blab down the blabs of blab.

The "blab" is not an attempt to be funny; it is a semantic blank. Nothing comes through. ... If, however, a political leader says:

> Every adult in the geographical area called Germany will receive not more than two loaves of bread per week for the next six months,

there is little possibility of communication failure. There is not a blab in a carload of such talk. If popular action is taken, it will be on the facts.[11]

According to Mr. Chase's formula, our statement about Germans would be written:

> Blabs are blab beer drinkers.

[11] Stuart Chase, *The Tyranny of Words* (New York: Harcourt, Brace and World, Inc., 1938), p. 21.

Try the technique with your classes some time. After a bit of semantic training, bring in some magazines or newspaper articles and let the students hunt for blabs. Start them looking for examples of semantic nonsense, or have them write speeches or editorials illustrating how meaningless words are used to influence people.

A word of caution is needed, even though training in this type of thinking is desperately lacking in our school curricula. Despite our need for greater understanding not only of words but of the extensional world with which our words deal, it is possible to become so tied up with complexity and innuendo that we are plunged into a state of inactivity. Clarity of thinking is important, but meanwhile, back in the world of reality, there is work to be done. Frequently we are forced to make decisions on the basis of incomplete and poorly understood data. In these cases, we make the best decisions we can, based on whatever we do know.

Very few of us, for example, are properly familiar with the mechanical merits of one brand of automobile, washing machine, or typewriter in comparison with those of another. Seldom do we really understand the capabilities and limitations, the prejudices and prior commitments, the innermost convictions of the many political candidates we entrust with the highest decision-making powers in the nation. Yet we must decide what to buy and how to vote. We must make a host of decisions every day with little real depth of understanding. We decide to adopt a new textbook for the English program, to marry Susan, to vacation at the Grand Canyon, and to trade in the old sedan for a new station wagon—all on partial evidence and an emotional bias. It is necessary that we do so, for if we demand complete understanding of every issue before taking action we will paralyze ourselves into a stupor.

Electrical engineers are still trying to find out exactly what electricity is and why it works as it does. They have learned much, but the essential nature of their medium remains partly cloaked in mystery. But this has not prevented us from building a civilization based largely on the marvels of electricity. All anyone can do is recognize the incompleteness of his data, continue to search for reality, and *change his thinking or his behavior when new data indicate the wisdom of such a course.*

FLEXIBILITY AND MENTAL HEALTH

Wendell Johnson offers some interesting sidelights on the relationship of semantics to personality adjustment. In *People in Quandaries* he claims that inability to operate in a flexible, changing world can result in many personality disorders.[12] It has been his observation that the majority of people who develop mental illness and come for therapy tend to have certain characteristics in common. One major pattern is a tendency toward extremely high ideals. Their self-expectations are often beyond their capacities, even though these capacities may be considerable. The *I'm no good* complex can result from too high an expectation of oneself. The woman, for example, who will settle for nothing less than being the efficient secretary, meticulous house-keeper, loving mother, understanding wife, and glamour girl after eight may work herself into a state of neurosis over her failure to live up to her impossible objective. The same may be true of a highly successful vice-president of a major corporation who has set his goal on the presidency. The ideals of such individuals are not only high, they are unrealistic. In addition, the attainment of these goals assumes an out-of-proportion importance.

Much of the trouble, Johnson claims, results from too strong an Aristotelian "either-or" orientation. In the world of many neurotics and near-neurotics there exist only two possibilities for everything (Aristotle's law of excluded middle).

Either I am a success or I am a failure.
If Jones gets the promotion I want, obviously he is the success and I am the failure.

Either you love me or you don't.
If you do not demonstrate your love as I feel you should, obviously you do not love me.

These unfortunates cannot visualize that success and love come in an infinite variety of forms and degrees.

A number of influences in our society promote the maladjustment of the individual. To begin with, there is the emphasis on competition. In school the competition for grades, for a place on the team, for acceptance into college, for the first-chair violin in the school orchestra all tell the student at a very tender age what school is about. The business world, with its emphasis on increasing sales and expanding profits, sets the pattern for much of our thinking. The job market, the marriage market, the house-in-an-exclusive-neighborhood market—all the trappings and status symbols of a status-conscious society encourage the individual to plunge headlong into the quest for bubbles as if it were a struggle for survival.

---

[12] Wendell Johnson, *People in Quandaries* (New York: Harper and Brothers, 1946), p. 10.

We are also constantly being shown, by our television sets, motion picture theaters, and other mass media, what life in a fairy-tale world can be like. The expensive settings and clothing being passed off as part of the "typical American family" are enough to make any middle-income social climber feel himself a failure. The glamorous adventures, the acts of courage, the amorous conquests, and the witty dialogue can make many of us feel discontent with a subdivision home, humdrum life, middle-aged spouse, normal but noisy children, and, most of all, ourselves.

The siren song of advertising screams a never-ending symphony of discontent: just drink our beverage, the advertisers promise, and you too will be transported to a never-never land of beautiful women and strong handsome men, where everyone is young and carefree, and on a constant round of fun and picnics. Just buy our automobile and you'll zoom up the steepest hills accompanied by a beautiful wife and a troop of handsome, laughing children. But when the money is spent and things don't really seem to change very much, the disappointed individual may well ask, "What went wrong? What's wrong with me?"

Johnson points out that the concept of failure is peculiar to man. In nature there is no such thing as failure. Things change; living organisms are born, develop and die, but where in nature can one see evidence of failure? Only man believes that such a thing is possible. Failure is not an absolute; it is simply the difference between expectation and result.

This *two-valued* orientation—success or failure, right or wrong—can affect one's expectation not only of himself but also of others. No thinking individual would expect to find a free society in which everyone agreed on such things as religion and politics. Differences in point of view are as natural as differences between trees or rivers. The well-adjusted individual knows and accepts and often relishes these differences. But the maladjusted person is more likely to have an Aristotelian two-valued system: Either you believe as I do, or you are wrong; either you belong to my political party or you are subversive, to my church or you will be denied the Kingdom of Heaven.

There are many individuals whose intolerance of other people stems from a simple failure to realize that many of our "facts" are merely points of view. They confuse the image with the referent, their own map with the actual territory.

One of the major tasks of the New English Teacher is to develop a generation that can live with change, with ambiguity, with differing points of view. The schools are finally beginning to emphasize the "scientific method" of investigation in such areas as chemistry, biology, and physics. But in the social sciences—the studies concerned with *people*—we have yet to deal with the problem. The result is that we are turning out an "educated" citizenry that is pitifully unable to cope with its most basic problems.

The difference between our way of looking at the natural sciences and our way of looking at the social sciences is illustrated by Stuart Chase. He contends that our thinking about government, economics, law, and politics is based upon "principles" (high level abstractions), whereas science is based on experimentation and observation. He notes, for example, that "The principles of Washington's Farewell Address are still considered sources of social wisdom; the methods of Washington's physician, however, are no longer studied. The social 'sciences' look to the past, the physical sciences to the present."[13] The river flows, and conditions change. History is an unreliable teacher, but if we examine many of our attitudes toward social phenomena, we find them to be composed of mythology that may or may not have had some modicum of truth a century or two ago. Too many of us are trying to step back into an ideological river that has long gone out to sea.

If we are to help our students survive in this competitive, commercialized world, if society itself is to survive its own onslaughts, the task for education is a considerable one. And the teacher of language holds the key, because language is the medium in which we think and by which we communicate. We must teach our charges to map the territory by observation instead of mythology, to realize the ever-changing nature of the universe, so maps can be redrawn as new evidence and new conditions require.

It is largely this capacity to change one's convictions, loyalties, and emotional biases that concerns the semanticist. No matter how carefully and rationally we map our territories, we can only map our images, not the realities. The living, growing, human being is constantly revising his maps; he who cannot alter his view of reality to meet new discoveries and changing conditions has already begun the torturous process of dying.

---

[13] Chase, *The Tyranny of Words*, p. 113.

SUMMARY OF SEMANTIC PRINCIPLES DISCUSSED IN THIS CHAPTER

1. *No man can step twice into the same river.* Everything is changing. That which seems truth today may be disproved tomorrow. Emerson said: "A foolish consistency is the hobgoblin of little minds.... Speak what you think now in hard words, and tomorrow speak what tomorrow thinks in hard words again, though it contradict everything you said today."[14] It was once well known that the earth was flat, and it seemed obvious that if one sailed too far he would fall off the edge. Many of our laws of economics, sociology, and physical science that were adequate yesterday are inadequate today. How many of today's facts will still be facts tomorrow?

2. *The map is not the territory.* One cannot see a thing as it actually is, but only as one perceives it. Our image is blurred by the limitations of human perceptions, by our age, sex, nationality, religion, political background, education, family life, social position, and a host of other factors.

3. *The word is not the thing.* It is not even the image of the thing. It is an abstract symbol, and it conveys only a rough picture. Someone else hearing the word may visualize something quite different from what was in the mind of the speaker.

4. *The meaning of the word is not in the word.* It is in the mind of the speaker. Words have many meanings, implications, and emotional connotations that vary as greatly as do the people who use them. Even the dictionary, while it is a useful tool, can only give a high level generalization.

5. *Human communication is difficult, subtle, and loaded with traps.* At best, we come close; at worst, we go to war over our misunderstandings. The student of semantics is constantly striving, as a speaker, listener, reader, and writer, to arrive at a meeting of minds with his fellow man.

[14] Ralph Waldo Emerson, *Self Reliance.*

10

where do we go from here?

The supposedly revolutionary structural textbooks of the fifties . . . have turned out to be wrong. In the Chomskyan sixties, textbooks are much more numerous, and somewhat better, but their standards remain too low and their claims too high. Meanwhile our educational Establishment has grown like Jack's beanstalk, though with no giant at the top. A good many of the establishmentarians have joined the campaign for schoolroom linguistics, providing us with some good teaching materials from Curriculum Centers and with some opportunities for in-service training in summer institutes; but a great deal of energy and money has been wasted in exhortation, the initial preparation of teachers has not been made adequate, and rash experiments have been inaugurated with imperfect textbooks and with staffs unready and sometimes unwilling. The millennium is not yet.[1]

The speaker is James Sledd; the occasion is the ninth annual conference of California Association of Teachers of English. It is the winter of 1967, eight years after the author brought out his textbook for classroom linguistics (See Chapter 2, page 39). Speaking before a representation of the state's language teachers, Sledd made it clear that all was not apple pie in Linguisticsland. He expressed his disillusionment with the failure of the linguistics movement—and particularly the failure of the pioneering school textbooks—to live up to their earlier expectations. And as the author of one of these early linguistically oriented college English textbooks, Sledd is in a unique position to look critically at this movement.

---

[1] James Sledd, "Schoolroom Linguistics: The Hazardous Transformation," *California English Journal* 1, No. 14 (Spring 1967), p. 9.

This early statement is not a lone ripple on a sea of tranquility. In 1968 Neil Postman, another pioneer in school textbook writing, delivered a scathing denunciation to the National Council of Teachers of English:

Why, of all the relevant and perceptive inquiries into human problems that linguistics allows, have English teachers fixed on the abstractions of grammatical systems? In answering, one must try hard not to be libelous. But we must admit there are those in the teaching of English who are, quite simply, fearful of life. The stuffy and precious ones. The lovers of symmetry and categories and proper labels. For them, the language of real human activity is too sloppy, too emotional and uncertain, and altogether too dangerous to study in the classroom.

Grammarians offer such teachers a respectable out. They give them a game to play, with rules and charts, with boxes and arrows to draw, and most of all, with right answers. Great big white Right Answers. What's more, it's scientific. You can attend meetings about it, even argue, a little and genteelly, about new theories. A grammarian recently told an audience of English teachers: "You can have a word-based grammar or a sentence-based grammar." And I do believe there was from the audience a more than slight trembling of delight at the prospect of its having such heavenly options.

Then, too, we have among us those who are fearful not so much of life as of children. These are the controllers and the syllabus-makers, who are afraid to go where the feelings, perceptions, and questions of children would take them. These are the sequence-lovers who can take you from form classes to terminal strings in just the right amount of time because they consult the structure of their grammar books and not the structure of their students. If only we could find for these teachers a sequential or spiral student, their sequential or spiral curriculums would really work.[2]

Enter the New English Teacher. The controllers and the syllabus-makers are being driven from the temple. The linguists have rocked a boat that was long due for rocking. No longer can English instruction traffic in platitudes about *who* and *whom*. No longer can a teacher be considered knowledgeable if he still believes in *the* grammar of the English language; it is too obvious that there are *many* grammars—traditional, structural, and transformational—and that each of these comes in a tempting variety of shapes and flavors. And it seems a reasonable assumption that more will follow. We have finally realized that language is a highly complex phenomenon, filled with inconsistencies that defy classification into neat little sets of rules.

Thus far the New English has taught us more about what English teaching should *not* be than what it should. And if teachers are still discontent with the confusion, frustration, and boredom that has plagued the teaching of English in our time, it is because we expect too much. Linguistics can no more save public school language education than Einstein's theory of relativity can save high school physics. Einstein did not generate his theory for the purpose of filling high school textbooks, but to advance our

---

[2] Neil Postman, "Linguistics and the Pursuit of Relevance," *The English Journal* 56, No. 2 (November 1967), p. 1,160.

understanding of the physical universe. And confirmation of the theory was not viewed as a mandate to revise the entire science education program from kindergarten through university. Instead, as the result of careful study by scholars and teachers, our science education programs have not only been updated but have become more interesting and relevant to the needs of the student.

In the field of language instruction, less emphasis on the prescriptive in favor of the descriptive, new emphasis on speech instead of on written language only, and a dynamic rather than a static theory of language represent a first—and very positive—attempt to achieve a similar metamorphosis.

The problem is not just James Sledd's observation that the textbooks in linguistics are inferior. Rather, it is that the profession as a whole has yet to come to grips with the fundamental question: What is *really* valuable, relevant, and interesting for young people? Perhaps it was the recognition—conscious or otherwise—that SOMETHING needs to be changed that caused educators to embrace linguistics as the savior of the language program. Perhaps to an English teacher there is an irresistible appeal in this new science, which is continually broadening our understanding of the nature of language.

Many of us are English teachers because we love language and derive satisfaction from the study of its literature and its structure. But we tend to forget that this is something of a specialized interest, like bird watching or chess, and is hardly shared by the bulk of young hopefuls who face us across their desks five times a week.

Although we have yet to prove that understanding the form of a language will produce competence in its use, we might still ask what could be more interesting, more fundamental to the understanding of man than a study of that which distinguishes man from beasts? On the other hand, if we wish to include in our school curricula those studies that most directly concern man and his culture, we have a wide field from which to choose. What could be more fundamental, more necessary to an understanding of man and his struggle for realization than the study of anthropology —the story of the many forms man has assumed in developing a culture? And for a real understanding of the mind of homo sapiens, why not include a good course in psychology, a study of the many directions the mind can take in its meanderings through a complex and confusing world? Or an equally good case can be made for the study of philosophy, the expression of man's most profound thoughts about the nature of the universe. Or, if one doesn't care to consider man the center of all things, why not learn more about the universe itself—geology, meteorology, or astronomy?

If we look deeply enough at our school curricula, however, we eventually come to the realization that they are deeply rooted—despite all the "new" programs in science, mathematics, foreign language, social studies, and now English—in the tradition of the Middle Ages. This was the tradition that firmly believed that all knowledge was known, that all one had to do to be educated was to master certain standard subjects, consisting of grammar, rhetoric, logic, mathematics, astronomy, theology, and music.

Since those dreary days we have seen many innovations in education. But they have been innovations, for the most part, within the framework laid down by a naive and simplistic society. This framework has confined the pursuit of knowledge in the schools to certain traditional areas of learning, with innovation limited to changes of emphasis from one area to another, or a change in instructional methods or materials.

Today every field of learning has expanded beyond the wildest imaginings of previous generations. But the expansion of knowledge has ushered into our lives a new complexity, a new affluence, and a new set of problems. We can no longer depend upon the old patterns, the old knowledge. The time has come for the school to involve itself in training people to meet the new requirement of the new society—the society of today and tomorrow. The old problems of how to produce enough goods to keep everyone fed, clothed, and housed disappeared with the horse and buggy. But the old educational system is still pretty much in harness.

We are still plagued by the bugaboos of tradition. Chief among these is the myth that knowledge is its own reward—that we read a short story to appreciate the short story form, that when we have learned the three ways to develop a "well-written paragraph," we have done our job. This is pure pedantry. We read a short story to communicate with an author who is trying to make an emotional or intellectual impact, or both. Readers should be encouraged to feel and to think; but to list the six major characteristics of the short story is at best a means to unlock the author's intent, and at worst pure academic busy work. We write paragraphs—or sentences, or notes, or letters, or reports, or books—so that others may communicate similarly with us, not to show our virtuosity at using chronological sequence to develop a paragraph. And we study structure in language, if at all, in the hope that structure will unlock the key to meaning.

If the study of language is to play a significant part in the life of the student, it must break the traditional mold and strike out for more productive territory. The first step is to change the English teacher's self-concept from that of policeman to explorer. This in itself will not be easy. But even more difficult will be the creation of an atmosphere of acceptance for such a program in the mind of the public. There seems to be a general belief that teaching grammar in the school can, in some way, uphold the "standards" of the language. Just what these standards are, who decides what is correct or incorrect, and why it is necessary to have any sort of standard are questions that have never been clarified, if they have been considered at all. Yet the abandonment of prescriptive grammar is viewed in some quarters as part of an undesirable general trend toward permissiveness, allowing the language to degenerate. What a familiar story in the history of language instruction!

A vigorous public relations campaign is needed with administrators, curriculum committees, school boards, and the public in general to present language as an ever-changing rather than static phenomenon. Many individuals, products of traditional grammar instruction, have long ago forgotten the rules for using commas, but will insist that when they write they get the commas in the correct place. Yet they fail to reason their way into the next step—to understand that we do not learn language by memorizing rules but by imitating what we read and hear.

The closest thing to a logical reason for teaching prescriptive grammar is to keep everyone speaking the same language. If education acts as a sort of common denominator, teaching the same tongue to the butcher and the banker, and to children in Norwich, Connecticut, and Portland, Oregon, there will be less tendency for English to break up into dialects that eventually would become so diverse that English speakers would not be able to converse or do business across great distances.

This would be a powerful argument, if we had substantial evidence that it were true. But thus far the evidence is against the argument. Spanish, for example, is breaking up into numerous Latin-American dialects despite the efforts of officially established language Academies charged with the responsibility of preserving the mother tongue. These Academies have great prestige among academic circles, but the men in the fields, the women in the kitchens, and the children at play continue to create the language that endures. All that the Academies can do is give official recognition to new words and new constructions after they have become well established in the language. The Academies are thus many years behind the times. If any major influence is being exerted to keep English stable today, it is more likely the mass media. More extensive use of international radio and television, especially if coupled with mass travel, might do more to impede splinter dialects than all the grammar books in the schools.

But in the teaching of language, syntax is not really the problem. Granted, enough uniformity of usage to insure mutual understanding is necessary, but whether we use *rise* or *raise*, or *shall* or *will*, or even have the commas in the right place will seldom affect the understandability of our utterance. The major problems of communication are semantic, not syntactic.

And our whole preoccupation with uniformity points up one of the major defects of our language program. For educators who give as much lip service as we do to providing for *individual differences*, we have certainly built a system dedicated to wiping them out. One of the major beauties of the New English Teacher is his deep appreciation for the individuality of the student, and for the development, among other things, of each student's writing and speaking style. Of course, that style must remain within the framework of commonly recognized English usage, but within that framework are vast opportunities for the student to develop his sense of humor, his use of imagery, and his gift for drama.

The old English teacher told his students to "use at least three metaphors in your next composition," but it was useless. By emphasizing *correctness*, by *judging* everything the student did, he had already doused the flame of creation. The New English Teacher, by being appreciative and nonjudgmental; by allowing his students the freedom to create, to experiment, to decide for themselves; nourishes and develops each little spark of greatness. He knows that a good writer uses language as a musician uses sound, as an artist uses pigment; a poor writer trudges off to look it up in the rule book.

Throughout this volume questions have been raised concerning relevance. But relevance must not be measured against yesterday's institutions. Today the pressing needs of society are for more effective methods of living with ourselves and with each other. New horizons in living must be matched by new horizons in education. The need exists for different approaches to everything from family relationships to racial relationships, from the problems of poverty to the problems of affluence, from urban renewal to pure air and water renewal. The action is no longer with declensions and conjugations, or even with new methods of diagramming. If these things justify themselves, it must be on the basis of the larger picture—of the contribution they make to the individual's capacity to live. And to live is to think, to feel, to understand, and to find joy and satisfaction in one's role as citizen, family member, worker, and self-fulfilled individual.

The New English Teacher is a leader. He can excite and inspire. He will build a new generation—aware of its opportunities, mindful of its responsibilities, and eager to meet its destiny.

afterword

A few years ago I planted a little redwood tree. But instead of growing tall and straight, it began to grow crooked. "Redwood trees should be erect and majestic," I said. So I drove a stake in the ground and tied the trunk of the tree to the stake.

Thereupon, the trunk grew straight, but the branches twisted into strange shapes. So I took a pruner and trimmed the tree as I wanted it. Thereupon, the tree became sickly and pale.

Finally, I gave up and let the tree grow as it would. All I did was provide plenty of water and plenty of food. I let the sunshine and the rain and the good valley soil do the rest.

My little tree is bigger now, with branches growing in the most interesting directions. I have seen many unique and beautiful trees, but I am sure that in all the world there is no other redwood just like this one.

list of references

Albright, Robert W. *The International Phonetic Alphabet: Its Backgrounds and Development.* Indiana University Research Center in Anthropology, Folklore, and Linguistics, Publication 7, January 1958. Also Part III of the *International Journal of American Linguistics*, Vol. 24, No. 1 (1958). Bloomington: Director of Publications of the Research Center, Indiana University.

Bloomfield, Leonard. *Language.* New York: Henry Holt and Company, 1933.

Bloomfield, Leonard, and Clarence L. Barnhart. *Let's Read: A Linguistic Approach.* Detroit: Wayne State University Press, 1961.

Boorstin, Daniel J. *The Image,* or *What Happened to the American Dream.* New York: Atheneum Publishers, 1962.

Bruner, Jerome S. *The Process of Education.* Cambridge: Harvard University Press, 1960.

Chase, Stuart, *The Tyranny of Words.* New York: Harcourt, Brace and Company, 1938.

Chomsky, Noam. *Syntactic Structures.* The Hague: Mouton and Company, 1957.

Francis, W. Nelson. "Revolution in Grammar." *Quarterly Journal of Speech,* 40 (October 1954), 299–312. Also in: Allen, Harold: *Readings in Applied English Linguistics.* New York: Appleton-Century-Crofts, 1958.

Francis, W. Nelson. *The Structure of American English.* New York: The Ronald Press Company, 1958.

Fries, Charles Carpenter. *American English Grammar.* New York: D. Appleton-Century Company, 1940.

Fries, Charles Carpenter. *The Structure of English.* New York: Harcourt, Brace and World, Inc., 1952.

Gleason, Henry Allan, Jr. *An Introduction to Descriptive Linguistics,* Rev. Ed. New York: Holt, Rinehart and Winston, 1961.

Gleason, Henry Allan, Jr. *Linguistics and English Grammar.* New York: Holt, Rinehart and Winston, 1965.

Gleason, Henry Allan, Jr. *Workbook in Descriptive Linguistics.* New York: Holt, Rinehart and Winston, 1966.

Hall, Robert A., Jr. *Introductory Linguistics.* Philadelphia: Chilton Company, 1964.

Hanna, Paul R., Jean S. Hanna, Richard E. Hodges, and Edwin H. Rudorf, Jr., *Phoneme-Grapheme Correspondences as Clues to Spelling Improvement.* Washington: U.S. Department of Health, Education, and Welfare; Office of Education, 1966.

Hayakawa, S. I. *Language In Thought and Action.* New York: Harcourt, Brace and Company, 1964.

Hockett, Charles F. *A Course in Modern Linguistics.* New York: The Macmillan Company, 1958.

Hockett, Charles F. "The Origin of Speech." *Scientific American* 203:1 (September 1960), 89–96.

Huff, Darrell. *How to Lie with Statistics.* New York: W. W. Norton Company, Inc., 1954.

267

Jespersen, Otto. *Essentials of English Grammar*. London: G. Allen and Unwin, Ltd., 1933.

Jespersen, Otto. *Language*. London: G. Allen and Unwin, Ltd., 1922.

Johnson, Wendell. *People in Quandaries*. New York: Harper and Brothers, 1946.

Korzybski, Alfred. *Science and Sanity: An Introduction to Non-Aristotelian Systems and General Semantics*. Lakeville, Connecticut: The International Non-Aristotelian Library Publishing Company, 1933.

Laird, Charlton. *The Miracle of Language*. Cleveland: World Publishing Company, 1953.

Laird, Helene and Charlton. *The Tree of Language*. Cleveland: World Publishing Company, 1957.

Lees, Robert B. *The Grammar of English Nominalizations*. Bloomington: Indiana University Research Center in Anthropology, Folklore, and Linguistics. Publication 12, 1960.

Lloyd, Donald J. and Harry R. Warfel. *American English in Its Cultural Setting*. New York: Alfred Knopf, 1956.

Loban, Walter. *The Language of Elementary School Children*. Champaign, Illinois: National Council of Teachers of English, Research Report No. 1, 1963.

Lockwood, Sara E. *An English Grammar*. Adapted from *Essentials of English Grammar*, by William Dwight Whitney. Boston: Ginn and Company, 1892.

Lowth, Robert. *A Short Introduction to English Grammar*. London: Printed by J. Hughs for A. Miller and R. and J. Dodsley, 1962. Reprinted by The Scolar Press Limited, Menston, England, 1967.

The Macmillan English Series:
Pollock, Thomas Clark, *et al.* (elementary), Third Rev. Ed., 1967.
Pollock, Thomas Clark, *et al.* (secondary), Second Rev. Ed., 1961, 1964.
New York: The Macmillan Company.

Miller, Clyde R. *Propaganda—How and Why It Works*. New York: Commission For Propaganda Analysis, Methodist Federation for Social Action, 1949.

Murray, Gilbert. *Greek Studies*. Oxford: Clarendon Press, 1946.

Ogden, C. K., and I. A. Richards. *The Meaning of Meaning*. New York: Harcourt, Brace and Company, 1923.

Our Language Today Series
Vols. III–VI: Conlin, David A.; H. T. Fillmer; Ann Lefcourt; and Nell C. Thompson, 1967.
Vols. VII, VIII: Conlin, David A.; George R. Herman; and Jerome Martin, 1966.
New York: American Book Company.

Packard, Vance. *The Hidden Persuaders*. New York: David McKay Company, Inc., 1957.

Peck, Harry Thurston. *A History of Classical Philology*. New York: The Macmillan Company, 1911.

Pei, Mario. *The Story of Language*. Philadelphia: J. B. Lippincott Company, 1949.

Plato. *The Dialogues of* ———. B. Jowett (trans.). Vol. III, Fourth Ed. Oxford: At The Clarendon Press, 1953.

Postman English Series:
Vol. VII: *Discovering Your Language*. Postman, Neil; Harold Morine; and Greta Morine, 1963.
Vol. VIII: *The Uses of Language*. Postman, Neil, and Howard C. Damon, 1967.
Vol. IX: *Exploring Your Language*. Postman, Neil, 1966.
Vol. X: *The Languages of Discovery*. Postman, Neil and Howard C. Damon, 1965.
Vol. XI: *Language and Systems*. Postman, Neil and Howard C. Damon, 1965.
Vol. XII: *Language and Reality*. Postman, Neil, 1966.
New York: Holt, Rinehart and Winston, Inc.

Postman, Neil. "Linguistics and the Pursuit of Relevance." *The English Journal* 56:2 (November, 1967).

Priestley, Joseph. *The Rudiments of English Grammar*. London: J. Johnson and F. and C. Rivington; G. G. and J. Robinson; J. Nichols; and W. Lowndes, 1798.

Roberts, Paul. *English Sentences*. New York: Harcourt, Brace and World, Inc., 1962.

Roberts, Paul. *English Syntax*. New York: Harcourt, Brace and World, Inc., 1964.

Roberts, Paul. *Patterns of English*. New York: Harcourt, Brace and World, Inc., 1956.

Roberts, Paul. *The Roberts English Series*, Vols. III–VIII, and *Complete Course*. New York: Harcourt, Brace and World, Inc., 1966, 1967.

Robins, Robert Henry. *Ancient and Mediaeval Grammatical Theory in Europe.* London: G. Bell and Sons, Ltd., 1951.

Rosten, Leo. *The Joys of Yiddish.* New York: McGraw Hill Book Company, 1968. Also in *Harper's Magazine*, 237 (October 1968), 83–87.

Sandys, Sir John Edwin. *A History of Classical Scholarship.* Three Vols. New York: Hafner Publishing Company, 1958.

Sapir, Edward. *Language.* London: Oxford University Press, 1921.

Sledd, James. *A Short Introduction To English Grammar.* Chicago: Scott, Foresman and Company, 1959.

Sledd, James. "Schoolroom Linguistics: The Hazardous Transformation." *California English Journal* 3:2 (Spring 1967).

Sweet, Henry. *A New English Grammar.* Oxford: At The Clarendon Press, 1892. Part II—Syntax, 1898.

Thomas, Owen. *Transformational Grammar and the Teacher of English.* New York: Holt, Rinehart and Winston, Inc., 1965.

Thorndike, Edward L. and Clarence L. Barnhart. *Thorndike-Barnhart High School Dictionary.* Chicago: Scott, Foresman and Company, 1957.

Thorndike, Edward L. and Irving Lorge. *The Teacher's Word Book of 30,000 Words.* New York: Bureau of Publications, Teachers College, Columbia University, 1944.

Trager, George and Henry Smith. *An Outline of English Structure.* Studies in Linguistics: Occasional Papers, 3. Norman, Oklahoma: Battenburg Press, 1951.

Webster's Third New International Dictionary of the English Language. Springfield: G. and C. Merriam Company, 1964.

White, Leslie A. *The Science of Culture.* New York: Farrar, Straus and Company, 1949.

Whitehall, Harold. *Structural Essentials of English.* Harcourt, Brace and World, Inc., 1956.

Whitney, William Dwight. *Language and Its Study.* London: Trubner and Company, 1876.

selected bibliography

Linguistic Reference Works

Pei, Mario. *Glossary of Linguistic Terminology* (Anchor Books, 1966). Presents, in dictionary form, a concise definition of most of the terminology currently in vogue in linguistic literature.

Allen, Harold. *Linguistics and English Linguistics* (Appleton-Century-Crofts, 1966). General bibliography on linguistics and the English language.

Introductory Textbooks in Linguistics

For a more detailed study of linguistic science, with emphasis on descriptive linguistics, a number of volumes are available, including Henry Gleason, Jr.'s, *An Introduction to Descriptive Linguistics* (Holt, Rinehart and Winston, Inc., 1961); Robert Hall's *Introductory Linguistics* (Chilton, 1964); and Charles Hockett's *A Course in Modern Linguistics* (The Macmillan Company, 1958). These textbooks are concerned with linguistics per se, and not with the place of linguistics in the public schools. Hockett seems a little more readable than the others, and a bit more inclined to philosophize about such things as the nature of the language experience and its relationship to culture. Gleason covers some areas more comprehensively, with excellent chapters on morphology and language geography. He also includes an annotated bibliography. *Language*, by Leonard Bloomfield (Henry Holt, 1933), is a linguistic milestone. Much of the information is still valid, although some has been updated in recent years.

Structural Linguistics

The Structure of English, by Charles Fries (Harcourt, Brace and World, Inc., 1952), is one of the first and still a classic statement of the structural position. In this volume Fries attacks classroom grammar, outlines the theory of Form Classes and Structure Groups and of slot-and-filler grammar, on which much of our current classroom linguistics is based. Two early works by Paul Roberts, *Patterns of English* and *English Sentences* (Harcourt, Brace and World, Inc., 1956 and 1962), expand and adapt the work of Fries and others for public school use.

Transformational Linguistics

Noam Chomsky's *Syntactic Structures* (Mouton and Co., 1957) laid the foundation for transformational grammar. This work, however, is esoteric and not recommended until other works, such as *Transformational*

Grammar and the Teacher of English, by Owen Thomas (Holt, Rinehart and Winston, Inc., 1965) have been mastered. *English Transformational Grammar*, by Roderick A. Jacobs and Peter S. Rosenbaum (Blaisdell Publishing Company, 1968), presents a new, streamlined approach to transformational grammar, more interesting and more understandable for the beginner than previous systems. For an example of their work see the review of *Grammar I* and *Grammar II*, p. 276. Thomas addresses himself to the teacher of English; Jacobs and Rosenbaum to the student. Also, the "Complete Course" volume of the *Roberts English Series* (Harcourt, Brace and World, Inc., 1967) treats the transformational system quite comprehensively.

Grammar and the Classroom

Linguistics and English Grammar, by Henry Gleason, Jr. (Holt, Rinehart and Winston, Inc., 1965), is one of the most comprehensive statements available on the subject of grammar in the classroom. Gleason treats descriptive linguistics, but also covers the history of linguistic thinking, grammar and its relationship to public school curricula, some comparative linguistics, and in the final chapters a discussion of problems related to the teaching of grammar. Neil Postman and Charles Weingartner's *Linguistics—A Revolution in Teaching* (Dell Publishing Co., 1967) is a hastily put together, repetitious statement of a philosophy of grammatical teaching. Yet, in the course of the volume, the authors make some extremely important statements. See particularly Part One, plus the chapters on semantics and lexicography. *Linguistics in Proper Perspective*, by Pose Lamb (Charles E. Merrill Publishing Company, 1967), discusses contributions of the linguistics movement to the teaching of language. He is concerned with the values of linguistic data for the teaching of reading and spelling as well as with syntax. Charles Fries' *American English Grammar* (Appleton-Century-Crofts, Inc., 1940) is worth at least a quick reading for the interesting discoveries he made—in 1940—about the language of the American people as it is actually written.

There are also a number of very fine articles dealing with English and the teaching of English. Two excellent collections of these articles are: *Readings in Applied English Linguistics* (Appleton-Century-Crofts, 1964), compiled by Harold B. Allen; and *Aspects of American English* (Harcourt, Brace and World, Inc., 1963), edited by Elizabeth Kerr and Ralph Aderman.

History of Language

The Miracle of Language (World Publishing Co., 1953) is a very readable and enjoyable account of the origin and development of English, as is *The Tree of Language* (World Publishing Co., 1957). Both are by Charlton Laird, the latter in collaboration with Helene Laird. Mario Pei has also written extensively on this subject, his works including *The Story of Language* (J. B. Lippincott Co., 1949) and *The Story of English* (J. B. Lippincott Co., 1952). There are many other texts on the history of language, including Otto Jespersen's *Growth and Structure of the English Language* (The Macmillan Company, 1948), which includes a section relating current grammar to its historical development.

General Semantics

In its broadest sense general semantics can include almost anything that facilitates communication. This could include a tremendous variety of material. Nevertheless, certain works have stood out as classic statements of the general semantic position. Much can be traced back to Alfred Korzybski's *Science and Sanity* (International Non-Aristotelian Library Publishing Co., 1933), a lengthy and technical volume that lays the foundation for the general semantics movement. Other important works on the subject include C. K. Ogden and I. A. Richards' *The Meaning of Meaning* (Harcourt, Brace and Co., 1923), S. I. Hayakawa's *Language in Thought and Action* (Harcourt, Brace and World, Inc., 1941), *The Tyranny of Words*, by Stuart Chase (Harcourt, Brace and Co., 1938); and *People in Quandaries*, by Wendell Johnson (Harper and Brothers, 1946). Many other volumes discuss related topics. Daniel Boorstin's *The Image, or What Happened to the American Dream.* (Atheneum, 1962) talks of the illusions that make up much of our thinking. *How to Lie With Statistics,* by Darrell Huff (W. W. Norton Co., 1954) and *The Hidden Persuaders,* by Vance Packard (David McKay Co., Inc., 1957) reveal how easily human beings can be manipulated, in the former by putting up a front of statistical validity, in the latter by appealing to our unconscious fears, desires, and anxieties. Kaiser Aluminum puts out a *Newsletter* which is devoted to a semantic approach and is available from: Public Affairs Department, Kaiser Aluminum and Chemical Corporation, Kaiser Center 866, Oakland, California. Material from *Kaiser Aluminum Newsletter* is also available from Glencoe Press, Palo Alto, California, in four paperback volumes entitled *Communications, On Motivation, You and Creativity,* and *The Children of Change,* all by Don Fabun. These publications on logical thinking are among the most stimulating I have found for school use. They delve deeply into human consciousness, pointing out that some of our most basic assumptions spring not from reality but from our individual backgrounds of experience, attitudes, values, and assumptions. A bound volume, *The Dynamics of Change,* from the *Kaiser Aluminum Newsletter,* has been published by Prentice-Hall, Inc. *A Short Unit on General Semantics* (Glencoe Press, 1969) includes five good articles with questions and suggested writing assignments and is edited by Louis E. Glorfeld.

Linguistics and Reading

In recent years linguists have made significant contributions to the teaching of reading. In 1961 Leonard Bloomfield and Clarence Barnhart published *Let's Read, A Linguistic Approach* (Wayne State University Press, 1961). This volume uses a carefully arranged series of words to teach phonic principles. By grouping together words with similar phoneme-grapheme correspondence, the book teaches the principle of phonic relationships much more effectively than the old phonics textbooks. Since publication of *Let's Read,* a number of "linguistic" readers have appeared, including the *Sullivan Programmed Reading Series* (Webster Division, McGraw-Hill Book Company), the *Merrill Linguistic Readers* (Charles E. Merrill Books, Inc., 1966), by Charles Fries *et al.* (this is a six-volume series, plus workbooks, based on linguistic grouping), the *Lippincott Reading Series,* and others. Also, books based on the *Initial Teaching Alphabet* make use of the same principle of phoneme-grapheme correspondence to make the first contact with reading simpler. The *Initial Teaching Alphabet* differs from other systems, however, in designing a different version of the alphabet to achieve a closer correspondence.

Carl Lefevre, in *Linguistics and the Teaching of Reading* (McGraw-Hill Book Company, 1964), takes another approach. Instead of detailed phonic analysis of words, he theorizes that real reading competence is based on grasping the meaning of the whole sentence, and that this can be accomplished by familiarity, both on the usage and analytical levels, with language and its forms. By stressing sentence analysis, including intonation patterns, syntax, and structural analysis of words, he prepares the reader for encounter with the written forms of language.

Linguistics and Spelling

What Leonard Bloomfield has done for reading, Paul Hanna has done for spelling. His scholarly and lengthy *Phoneme-Grapheme Correspondences as Clues to Spelling Improvement* (U.S. Office of Education, 1966) lays out a series of guidelines for the teaching of spelling.

An older, simpler, and much more concise statement of phoneme-grapheme correspondence can be found in Robert Hall's *Sound and Spelling in English* (Chilton Company, 1961).

Language and Culture

Edward Sapir's *Language* (Oxford University Press, 1921) reflects the view that language is a product of culture, and that culture is, in turn, influenced by language. Another view of language as a human and social phenomenon is Robert Hall's *Linguistics and Your Language,* a republication by Anchor Books of *Leave Your Language Alone!* (Linguistics Press, 1950).

History of Grammatical Thinking

Two books by Robert H. Robins give the reader an excellent background for the history of the study of language. His *Ancient and Mediaeval Grammatical Theory in Europe* (G. Bell and Sons, 1951) and *History of Linguistics* (Indiana University Press, 1967, 1968) cover the field very well.

Periodicals

The most important periodicals in the teaching of English are published by the National Council of Teachers of English, 508 South Sixth Street, Champaign, Illinois. *Elementary English, English Journal,* and *College English* deal with elementary, secondary, and higher education, respectively. Annual membership includes a subscription to any one of the above publications and will keep the teacher informed of not only major developments in classroom linguistics but also in the teaching of literature and other phases of language. Annual conventions and numerous workshops of NCTE and its state and local affiliates bring the teacher in contact with new developments, leaders in the field, publishers' representatives, and other teachers.

An inexpensive contact with new publications in linguistics may be obtained through the Center for Applied Linguistics, 1717 Massachusetts Avenue NW, Washington, D.C. Their monthly bulletin, *The Linguistic Reporter,* carries reviews of most of the publications in this area. *Etc* is the magazine of the general semantics movement, with many provocative and thought-provoking articles in every issue.

Linguistics in the Schools

Although public school textbooks have become more interesting in recent years, schools and teachers, particularly on the secondary level, still depend much too heavily on exclusive use of material prepared especially for schools and not enough on the many rich and valuable publications available outside the narrow confines of the textbook industry. Some of my most successful experiences in high school teaching occurred when I managed to break the textbook barrier. I was particularly pleased with the results obtained from *Language in Thought and Action, The Hidden Persuaders, How to Lie With Statistics* and Clyde Miller's *Propaganda—How and Why It Works* (see list of references). I have also used a number of other works already mentioned in this bibliography, including *Patterns of English, English Sentences,* and selections from *The Tyranny of Words* and *People in Quandaries.* Although I have not used the Laird books on the history of language as texts, I have discussed some of the material with my students and found it to be appropriate. I believe either *Miracle of Language* or *Tree of Language* would be successful in the classroom, as would parts of Sapir's *Language.* I have also played the record *A Word in Your Ear,* available from the National Association of Educational Broadcasters, Suite 1101, 1346 Connecticut Avenue NW, Washington, D.C., for elementary, high school, university, and teacher audiences, and it has never failed to entertain and to set off a stimulating discussion. Also, the record *Bert and I* is an interesting and amusing study of the New England dialect. (Available from Bert and I, 30 Nashua Street, Woburn, Massachusetts.)

Textbooks

Despite resistance, more and more public school language textbooks are showing the influence of the linguistics movement.

Even many of the "traditional" grammar texts have, in recent editions, added a section on the "new" grammar. See, for example, the *Macmillan English Series* (the Macmillan Company), *Warriner's English Grammar and Composition,* Revised Edition (Harcourt, Brace and World, Inc.), and *Building Better English,* Fourth Edition (Harper and Row, Publishers). Unfortunately, these textbooks cover the new grammar in only the most superficial manner.

Elementary Series

Elementary School English. (Addison-Wesley Publishing Company, 1967–1968.) This series deals with phonology, morphology, sentence structure, transformations, and history of language, along with considerable emphasis on composition and style. Although this program is highly linguistic, I have severe reservations about any series that greets a first grader on his first day of school with:

> I wonder if my drawing will be as good as theirs.
> I wonder if they'll like me or just be full of stares.

This crime against humanity is compounded two pages later by plunging the child into a series of yes-no correct-incorrect questions. For example, whether morning, noon, or night comes "first" is not an absolute. It depends on what time of day you begin. To condition a first grader not to examine beyond such superficialities is typical of how the schools carefully nurture the art of not thinking. Of course, it would be unfair to the makers of this series not to point out that the practices for which they are being criticized are quite common in textbook writing.

Ginn Elementary English. (Ginn and Company, 1967.) This series contains lessons on parts of speech, sentence structure, transformations, and composition.

English Is Our Language. (D. C. Heath and Company, 1966–1968.) This series blends traditional grammar with linguistic terminology. It uses short literary selections, most of which describe the *prettiness* of things. These bits of poetry epitomize a common problem in elementary textbook writing—a preoccupation with sentiment that tends to overshadow the masculine and the vigorous.

Today's Language. (Steck-Vaughn Company, 1968, 1969.) This paperback series presents structural and transformational grammars to elementary children. It retains much traditional terminology. The sixth-grade volume contains chapters on history of English and on composition.

Junior High Series

English 7, 8, 9. (Addison-Wesley Publishing Company, 1968.) This series includes studies in dialect, idiolect, grammaticality, phonology, parts of speech, sentence structure, transformation, literature, and composition.

Guide to Modern English Grades Seven and Eight. (Scott, Foresman and Company, 1968.) This series presents a blend of linguistic and traditional grammars, of prescriptive and descriptive approaches, progressing from a fairly traditional approach in grade seven to the introduction of linguistic concepts in grade eight. For example, parts of speech are described by a series of "clues" rather than by rigid definitions, although rules for avoiding "mistakes" are introduced in areas such as verb usage.

New Approaches to Language and Composition Grades Seven and Eight. (Laidlaw Brothers, 1969.) The grammar section is completely linguistic, dealing with phonology, morphology, parts of speech, sentence structure, transformations, and language variation. Prescriptive grammar is included as "The Conventions of Written English." There are also sections on historical as well as descriptive linguistics and some material on composition.

Patterns In English Grades Seven and Eight. (William H. Sadlier, Inc., 1967, 1968.) Basically a traditional text, this series introduces such concepts as intonation patterns, form and structure words, and sentence position as a determiner of part of speech.

Elementary and Junior High Series

Our Language Today. Grades one through eight. (American Book Company, 1966, 1967.) This series begins linguistic instruction in the third grade. It includes structural and transformational grammar, and phonology. An interesting section in each chapter (grades seven and eight) deals with the origins of English words.

The Roberts English Series. (Harcourt, Brace, and World, Inc., 1966–1968.) Grades one through eight plus a *Complete Course* usable in grade nine or in senior high school. In addition to a series of linguistically oriented grammar lessons, including phonology, morphology, and structural and transformational syntax, this series makes extensive use of literature—particularly poetry—in early elementary grades. The poetry is used as material for linguistic as well as literary analysis. The *Complete Course* is mainly transformational grammar, with some phonology and morphology included but not the literary material.

Secondary Series

Modern Grammar and Composition. (American Book Company, 1965–1967.) Four volumes containing a linguistic approach to sentence structure, parts of speech, phonology, and morphology. They also deal with style and composition.

English Composition and Grammar. (Ginn and Company, 1968.) Grades seven through twelve. Essentially a composition program, this series carries in each of the first four volumes a chapter on transformational grammar by coauthors Roderick Jacobs and Peter Rosenbaum. The eleventh and twelfth grade volumes contain longer sections devoted to history of language, semantics, linguistic geography and dialectology, morphology, and language as a cultural phenomenon.

Grammar I and Grammar II. (Ginn and Company, 1967.) Authors Jacobs and Rosenbaum use many of the concepts from *English Transformational Grammar* for a concise series suitable for secondary schools. Much of the material is unique and different. Heavy emphasis is placed upon deep structure of a sentence as an expression of meaning and surface structure as the syntactic expression. Transformations are viewed as the connecting key. Semantic as well as syntactic analysis is utilized. For example, the noun *truth* is analyzed on page 3 of *Grammar II*:

> truth
> [+ N]   (is a noun)
> [+ common] (is a common noun)
> [− concrete[(abstract, not concrete object)
> [− animate] (not animate)
> [− human]   (not a human being)

New Aspects of Language. (Ginn and Company, 1965–1968.) Paperback booklets on various phases of descriptive, historical, and comparative linguistics. Emphasis on language as an expression of culture.

Hayden English Language Series. (Hayden Book Company, 1965, 1968.) *Language In Society* covers language geography; *An Introduction To Modern English Grammar* discusses descriptive linguistics, including parts of speech, linguistic development in children, transformations, and an approach to writing style.

Discovering Language. (D. C. Heath and Company, 1969.) These paperback booklets are designed to awaken interest in language. They deal with history, growth and development of language, etymology, dialectology, lexicography, semantics, vocabulary development, logic, usage, and style, along with descriptive linguistics. This is one of the few series that is brought up to date with a discussion of the mass media, particularly television, and its effect on man. Quotes from Marshall McLuhan and Edward T. Hall bring language into the *now*. Unfortunately lacking in depth, these little books do supply lots of breadth, and contain many jumping-off places for greater exploration.

The Postman English Series. (Holt, Rinehart and Winston, Inc., 1963–1967.) Neil Postman and company make a gallant effort to bring out a discovery-oriented language series. Its success, in my observation, depends largely upon the teacher and his ability to select material suited to the sophistication level of the class and to get the pupils "turned on" to discovering language data. Although the material is simple and limited, this is one of the few language series that approaches the study of English as a *search* rather than a series of neat little formulas.

Single Volumes Usable in Secondary Classrooms

These listings range from comprehensive treatments of language and composition to short booklets designed for reference or supplementary use.

Garrison, Webb B. *Why You Say It*. New York: Abingdon Press, 1947–1955.

Interesting little biographies of English words. It is an excellent publication to keep on a teacher's desk for reading to class during a break of a few minutes—or even a few seconds.

Pei, Mario (editor and chief contributor). *Language Today*. New York: Funk and Wagnalls, 1967.

A collection of writings by Mario Pei, William Marquardt, Katherine Le Mee, and Don L. F. Nilsen, including a debate between two of the authors on the old prescription-description question and a summary of the history of linguistics. Particularly noteworthy, however, are two chapters. Chapter 3 gives some interesting and specific examples of semantic problems. Chapter 4 deals with phases of communication not usually considered in linguistic study, including gestures, kinesics (body movements and their attendant meanings), and proxemics (the way we use the space around us to indicate or facilitate a mood or emotion).

Funk, Wilfred. *Word Origins and Their Romantic Stories*. New York: Funk and Wagnalls, 1950. Paperback, 1968.

More interesting, often amusing etymological accounts of hundreds of English words.

Shanker, Sidney. *Semantics: The Magic of Words*. Boston: Ginn and Company. 1965.

This interesting paperback treatise on etymology and word structure is intended for vocabulary development.

Laird, Charlton. *A Writer's Handbook*. New York: Ginn and Company, 1964.

Laird applies the findings of linguistics to the problem of teaching composition. Essentially prescriptive, this volume shows the student which English forms are preferred (in the linguistic sense of being common, not in the traditional meaning of being correct). The reader is asked to examine the language of competent writers, then to use his own judgment in writing.

Lodwig, Richard R. and Eugene F. Barrett. *The Dictionary and the Language*. New York: Hayden Book Company, Inc., 1967.

This little book on the history and composition of dictionaries orients the student in the development of language and the operations of a lexicographer. It also includes material on the history and development of the English language.

Lefevre, Helen E. and Carl A. Lefevre. *Writing By Patterns*. New York: Alfred A. Knopf. 1965.

An exercise book covering the skills discussed in Lefevre's *Linguistics and the Teaching of Reading*. Deals with sentence patterns, transformations, inflection and structure words, as well as syntactic problems, including agreement, expansion, phrase and clause structure, substitution, compounding, subordination, punctuation, capitalization, and style.

Brown, Marshall L. and Elmer G. White. *A Grammar for English Sentences*. Columbus: Charles E. Merrill Publishing Co., 1968.

This two-volume workbook series in descriptive linguistics places heavy emphasis on transformational grammar. It is a concentrated program with considerable depth but little to inspire a student to want to learn.

McCormack, Jo Ann. *The Story of our Language*. Columbus: Charles E. Merrill Books Inc., 1967.

A brief and interesting paperback dealing with the history of English from Indo-European to the present.

Francis, W. Nelson. *The English Language—An Introduction*. New York: W. W. Norton & Company, Inc., 1965.

A completely linguistic approach, this volume deals with historic and comparative aspects of language as well as descriptive. It does not include transformational grammar, but discusses constituents, parts of speech, phonology, morphology, phrase and sentence structure, history of English, and usage. The section on usage attempts to view language as it exists—with regional variations and social and situational differences. It stimulates the student to consider problems of style, but does not prescribe "right" and "wrong." The chapter on history is available from the publisher as a separate pamphlet, *The History of English*.

Brown, Dona Worrall, Wallace C. Brown, and Dudley Bailey. *Form in Modern English*. New York : Oxford University Press, 1958.

Comprehensive treatment of inflection of nouns, verbs, adjectives, adverbs, and pronouns, with a discussion of sentence patterns and grammatical constructions within sentences. A short history of English is followed by problems of usage. Usage difficulties are described as being either of a "social" nature—no communication problem, but involving a linguistic form not ordinarily considered socially acceptable among educated people, or of a "communication" nature—"that mislead the reader or destroy linguistic communication altogether" (p. 203). Considerable emphasis on usage problems with prescriptive orientation. Most of the prescriptions, however, deal with genuine communication or stylistic problems, such as misplaced modifiers, parallelism, and punctuation.

Potter, Simeon. *Our Language*. Baltimore : Penguin Books, 1950–1968.

Deals with historical background, phonology and its relationship to spelling, language development, etymology, dialectology, and related topics.

index

a

Abstraction ladder, 247–53, 256
Accent, 88
  Dionysus Thrax, 13
  Donatus, 17
Accretion, 206
Acoustic phonetics, 70
Active voice
  Priscian, 18
  Varro, 15
Addition of morphemes, 115
Adjective, 133, 135, 140–41, 143, 158,
    172, 187–88, 209, 241
  Dionysus Thrax, 13
  Fries, Charles, 35
  Jespersen, Otto, 126
  Priestly, Joseph, 126
  Sweet, Henry, 31
Adjective suffix, 112
Adjective transformation, 191, 194
Adverb, 134, 135, 139–42, 143, 158–59,
    187
  of degree, 173, 174
  of time, 172–77, 181–82
  of place, 141, 172–77, 181–82

of manner 172–77, 181–82
  of frequency, 172–77, 181–82
  Fries, Charles, 35
  Priscian, 18
  Sweet, Henry, 31
  transformational grammar, 172–77,
    187–88
  Varro, 15
Adverbials, 172; *see also* Adverbs
Adverb transformation, 175–76, 177
Aelfric, Abbot of Eynsham, 19, 22
Affix morphemes, 104, 105–16, 122, 127,
    163
Affix transformation, 163, 165, 166, 177
Affricates, 78
Afghan language, 218
Afrikaans language, 218
Agglutinative languages, 47, 211, 227
Agreement, 157
Ainu language, 219
Albanian language, 217
Alfred, King of England, 222
Allomorphs, 100, 101, 104, 105; *see also*
    Morphemic system
Allophones, 85, 94, 101
Altaic languages, 220
Alveolar phonemes, 72

b

c

d

e

f

g

h

q

r

s

W

Y

Z